The Legacy of Ron Gonnella

THE LEGACY OF
Ron Gonnella
SCOTTISH FIDDLER
1930–1994

Jane Blair MacMorran

THE CHARLES K. WOLFE MUSIC SERIES
TED OLSON, SERIES EDITOR

THE UNIVERSITY OF TENNESSEE PRESS
Knoxville

FIRST EDITION.

This book was published with the support of Linda Natiello Friedland, in memory of her mother, Isabella Hislop Tait Hunter (1911–1971), born and raised in Edinburgh, and her ancestors—McLeod, Fraser, Ritchie, Trench, Orr, and Bow.

Library of Congress Cataloging-in-Publication Data

Names: MacMorran, Jane Blair, author.
Title: The legacy of Ron Gonnella : Scottish fiddler, 1930–1994 / Jane Blair MacMorran.
Description: First edition. | Knoxville : The University of Tennessee Press, 2025. | Series: Charles K. Wolfe music series | Includes bibliographical references and index. | Summary: "This biography of Ron Gonnella includes a discography of his extensive recordings and provides an in-depth analysis of his contributions to Scottish fiddling, along with an analysis of his role in reviving interest in and establishing performance standards for the instrument in the United States. Rather than presenting a typical musicological analysis of Gonnella's performances or musical scores, MacMorran examines Gonnella's body of work in the cultural context of the 1960s, 70s, and 80s in a career that paralleled yet was far removed from the folk music revival and other shifts in popular music. In doing so, MacMorran seeks to recover the work of a noted fiddler who has been overlooked in the larger pantheon of music history"— Provided by publisher.
Identifiers: LCCN 2025001847 (print) | LCCN 2025001848 (ebook) | ISBN 9781621909804 (paperback) | ISBN 9781621909828 (adobe pdf) | ISBN 9781621909811 (kindle edition)
Subjects: LCSH: Gonnella, Ronald. | Fiddlers—Scotland—Biography. | Folk music—Scotland—History and criticism. | Fiddle tunes—Scotland—History and criticism. | Dance music—Scotland—History and criticism. | Composers—Scotland—Discography.
Classification: LCC ML418.G67 M33 2025 (print) | LCC ML418.G67 (ebook) | DDC 787.2092 [B]—dc23/eng/20250124
LC record available at https://lccn.loc.gov/2025001847
LC ebook record available at https://lccn.loc.gov/2025001848

Contents

Illustrations

Foreword

Ron Gonnella (1930–1994) was a master musician and a musical ambassador; he was respected across the world among the comparatively small coterie of fiddlers and fans who know and love Scotland's fiddle heritage. Gonnella, though, is not widely known beyond that tightknit circle. Artistic mastery always merits broader recognition—within the region or nation in which that artist resides, of course, but also worldwide, since humanity perpetually yearns for inspiration from the gifted few who brilliantly embody a cultural tradition. If they're fortunate, master musicians receive recognition within their immediate communities, but rarely is international attention bestowed upon a musician who embodies a regional or national artistic tradition (there are obvious exceptions, such as India's Ravi Shankar and Jamaica's Bob Marley). More commonly, tradition-bearers tend to fall into obscurity despite the significance of their contributions (take, for instance, the case of early-twentieth-century Trinidadian bandleader George Robertson Lovelace "Lovey" Baillie, who has yet to be widely recognized for first recording and popularizing calypso). Gonnella possessed a broad repertoire, he performed with an exquisite tone, and he was committed to teaching others the tradition he graced with his artistry; for all his contributions to the Scottish fiddle tradition, Gonnella was a legend, and his story deserves to be more widely known. *The Legacy of Ron Gonnella: Scottish Fiddler, 1930-1994* is the perfect vehicle for making that happen.

In an interview conducted for this foreword, the author of this book, Jane Blair MacMorran, assessed Gonnella's importance: "In her seminal book *Scottish Fiddlers and Their Music*, Mary Anne Alburger states, 'What will never change about Scottish fiddling is its essentially amateur nature. No one, not even Niel Gow, has ever made his entire lifetime's living out of only playing Scottish fiddle music' (1983, 209). And this was true of Ron Gonnella, a fiddler who worked as a clerk in his early adult years and later as a teacher. While we are less likely to describe Gonnella's skilled playing, persona, and notoriety as amateur in today's terms, in the old sense of the word, Scottish fiddle music was a natural and essential part of his life."

MacMorran, a native of Johnson City, Tennessee, is one of the privileged few to have studied with Gonnella. A conservatory trained teacher of the Western violin repertoire and an experienced orchestral performer, MacMorran became fascinated by Scotland's fiddle tradition several decades ago, as explained in the aforementioned interview: "Some of my most enjoyable and memorable musical experiences have involved playing Scottish fiddle music. My enchantment with Scottish fiddling spans decades and continents. It takes the form of sessions with friends and strangers, formal performances, competitions, workshops, classroom teaching, individual lessons, intense academic study, symposia, and, best of all, the sharing of tunes with my son Will MacMorran at home and on stage."

MacMorran's reputation as a champion of the Scottish fiddle tradition—and as a Scottish fiddle champion—has spread on both sides of the Atlantic. According to MacMorran, "During a recent visit to the East Tennessee State University campus, Scottish fiddler Alistair Fraser remarked he was glad to see I was still 'flying the flag,' noting my sustained commitment to the tradition. And I do feel that I am part of the Scottish fiddle tradition—one that welcomed me and invited my participation in its intertwining traditions of orality and text within a shared cultural space. I experienced the power and beauty of the music full force at a time when I was experiencing 'burn out' as a symphony concertmaster and Suzuki violin teacher. In 1986, when friend Carole Sease suggested we attend John Turner's Jink & Diddle School of Scottish Fiddling in Valle Crucis, North Carolina, I felt it was the last thing I wanted to do. But I relented, spending an intensive week playing Scottish fiddle music in the Blue Ridge Mountains. Corny as it might sound, I fell in love with the violin again. I happily experienced the music's ceilidh spirit far from formal stages and expectations of perfection. Years later, I would return to Jink & Diddle as an instructor, each time rekindling my love for the instrument and finding inspiration for my personal style in the music."

Through the years, MacMorran has developed an international reputation as a leading teacher of that tradition, practiced through freelance instruction and in the role as a professor at East Tennessee State University.

"My work at ETSU led to the creation of an undergraduate minor as well as a major concentration in Scottish and Irish traditional music within the Bachelor of Arts degree offered in the Bluegrass, Old-Time, and Roots Music Studies program. While individual instruction and band classes advance students' musical skills and performance capabilities, the study-abroad experiences and the specialized courses we offer deepen students' contextual understanding of the music they love to play."

Motivation for researching and writing *The Legacy of Ron Gonnella* grew out of MacMorran's longtime commitment to the Scottish fiddle tradition: "With this book, I am in essence advocating for the inclusion of this notable fiddler in the broader pantheon of Scottish traditional music. Like many others, I was inspired by Ron Gonnella's albums, learning most of the tunes he recorded. Through my lessons with Gonnella, I joined the "carrying stream" of tradition (to borrow Hamish Henderson's phrase). My PhD thesis—and thus this book—grew out of my commitment to the Scottish fiddling tradition and my appreciation for my experiences, especially the time I spent with Ron Gonnella. I have sought to enrich readers' understanding of the Scottish fiddle tradition by placing Gonnella's body of work in the social context of the 1960s, the '70s, and the '80s through an examination of the perceptions of three primary musical communities with whom Gonnella interacted, thus revealing his contributions to the Scottish fiddle tradition."

The Legacy of Ron Gonnella will appeal to readers who are specifically interested in the Scottish fiddle repertoire as well as those who participate in fiddle competitions held in Scotland, elsewhere in the UK, and in the United States and Canada; the book will also appeal more generally to readers curious to learn about the traditional music of Scotland and about folk music revivals. Because of this book, Ron Gonnella will hereafter be a significant figure in all those lines of discussion.

TED OLSON
East Tennessee State University

Preface

CRIEFF, SCOTLAND

A small brass plaque bearing the name "Barga" greeted me as I stepped, fiddle case in tow, onto the porch of the modest single-story residence at 27 Boyd Avenue, Crieff, for another lesson with Ron Gonnella, a Scottish fiddler who was legendary among Scottish traditional music aficionados in the United States. It was June 1988. The Scottish referendum defeat of 1979 had receded into the past, but that summer I watched as a new initiative fueled by Thatcherism and the poll tax gained momentum. Scotland was feeling the long-term effects of a depressed economy, but a strong dollar helped defray my expenses and it would still be six months before the Lockerbie bombing made transatlantic travel to Scotland less a carefree holiday and more a leap of faith for an American who wanted to study with a master fiddler. I had first met Gonnella three years earlier at the Potomac Valley Scottish Fiddling competition in Alexandria, Virginia, where he was serving as adjudicator. It was my first regional competition and one in which I claimed first place, along with an invitation to enter the national competition the following day. While my attempt was not successful, Gonnella's encouragement and judging comments motivated me to learn more about Scottish fiddling and inspired future bids. The stocky man who opened the front door of "Barga" was in his late fifties with a shock of thick silver hair brushed to the side, much as I remembered him, minus the kilt and tweed wool jacket, too warm for Virginia's late July heat. As I walked in, I couldn't help but notice his golf clubs propped against the entryway wall, perhaps in readiness for a quick escape at lesson's end?

FIGURE 0.1. Author with Ron Gonnella at his home in Crieff, 1987.

As I and all of Gonnella's peers attest, his polish and technical ability indicate that his early teacher, F. Routledge Bell, adopted a pedagogical approach focused on technique and mastery of the violin classics. Bell must also have encouraged the young musician to have fun playing the traditional Scottish fiddle canon, but with the finesse of a classical background, resulting in his distinctive style and an intercultural understanding between classical and traditional music. I aspired to such an understanding and the ability to move between repertoire and style. While my lessons included work on several types of tunes, my main interest was getting the "feel" of jigs from a fiddler who was well known for his inimitable jig playing. The two-hour lesson passed quickly, and I left with recordings to listen to, a list of tunes to learn, and the promise of more lessons. I left, too, with a feeling that Gonnella "got it" (as Gary West says)—that he approached the music "with a deep understanding of the roots of the tradition" (2012: 85). By taking me as his student, Gonnella "form[ed] a bridge to tradition" (2012: 60) that I did not yet possess. It was high summer and as I walked down the hill, I thought he could easily complete a round of golf before ten o'clock twilight.

This reflexive study examines the cultural environment in which Gonnella developed and articulated his musical skills and his role in perpetuating and influencing the Scots fiddling tradition. To state that this work is *reflexive* reveals an awareness that the researcher's voice is entangled in the biographical "story" or cultural portrait. As I said, my personal dialogue with Gonnella began in the late 1980s when he adjudicated my performances at various Scottish fiddling competitions in the United States and continued as I studied with him in Scotland until his death in 1994. The dialogue has continued through my role as former United States National Scottish Fiddling Champion, adjudicator for Scottish fiddling competitions, teacher, and performer of Scots fiddle music. To begin with, I am an American who resides in the northeast corner of the state of Tennessee—commonly identified as the Appalachian Highlands region. While my family has resided in the southeastern United States for several generations, my parents instilled an awareness of our Scots and Scots-Irish heritage from an early age. This knowledge would later stimulate my interest and affinity for Scottish fiddling. Secondly, I am a "formally trained" classical violinist. Years of classical training appear to share some similarities with Ron Gonnella and several interview respondents, though during this period of intense classical training I only dabbled in Scottish fiddle music. After a career as a professional musician, I completed my PhD in cultural studies at the University of the Highlands and Islands (awarded by the University of Aberdeen) and joined the faculty of the Appalachian Studies department at East Tennessee State University where I direct the Appalachian, Scottish, and Irish Studies Program.

My "guided" study of Scottish fiddling began with John Turner at the Jink and Diddle School of Scottish Fiddling in North Carolina and led to my participation in numerous Scots fiddling competitions in the late 1980s and early 1990s, including the United States National Scottish Fiddling Championship, which I won in 1992. I first met Gonnella more than twenty years after he began his active association with Royal Scottish Country Dance Society branches in New England and his five-month stay in Toronto, and nine years after Gonnella first judged the United States National competition; hence, intercultural connections had been building for decades and were established long before he judged his first US competition. The community of American competitive fiddlers, of which I was a part, saw Gonnella as "the real thing," an authoritative source of Scottish fiddling history, interpretation, and performance practice. Gonnella would have felt at home with this community, which shared a common repertory, and for most, a similar background that included, at least some classical training. As an official adjudicator for the organization that sanctions American Scottish fiddling competitions, Scottish Fiddling Revival or F.I.R.E., I have judged US National Scottish Fiddling Championships as well as regional competitions and am "at home" with the repertoire and performance of Scots fiddle music.

While definitions of insider research vary, Chou Chenier defines the term as "researchers who are themselves already experienced musicians within the tradition that they subsequently choose to investigate ethnomusicologically" (2002: 458). This is the situation in which this researcher finds herself; one, I contend, that benefits from both experience in the musical tradition and reflective narration. The literary process of reflective narration will be particularly apparent in the chapter biography of Ron Gonnella, in which my personal recollections provide the frame story that organizes the events of Gonnella's life; and in the stories told by the interviewees, the use of which flavors the portrait of Gonnella far more effectively than an objective observation. As a former competitor and official F.I.R.E. judge, my perspective is that of an insider. My insider role continues as Scottish fiddle teacher and active performer of Scots fiddle music. In Scotland, my status as a former student of Ron Gonnella, a fellow Scottish fiddler, and a member of the academic community positions me as an insider. I find Kirin Narayan's description of "shifting identifications amid a field of interpenetrating communities and power relations" apropos (1993: 671) and subscribe to her notion of the field as a "flexible concept" (1993: 673). The fact that I do not live in Scotland affects my access to fiddlers and regular participation in the Scottish fiddle scene, and in this respect, I am an outsider. However, I have found that once a musical community is established lines of communication remain open. The insider position facilitated data collection and enriched this project through my own personal experience and interaction with both the subject and those interviewed. While I knew the majority of the interviewees, those who I did not know readily agreed to participate in interviews, perhaps in part because I was seen as an insider, or at the least, I *knew* insiders who led me to new respondents—both in Scotland and North America. My various perspectives seem to support Dwyer and Buckle's challenge to the restrictive notion of insider *versus* outsider status, instead embracing the notion that a researcher can be both insider *and* outsider (2009: 60). This is not to argue in any way that I have occupied "a privileged vantage point from which all was clear . . . ," to use Jonathan Stock's phrase (2010: 339), but find myself, instead, in the midst of Narayan's "shifting identities."

In order to appreciate Gonnella's contribution to Scottish traditional music, it is important to understand the ways in which he read, constructed, and thus interpreted, musical texts, engaging Stanley Fish's notion that the reader is a writer engaged in a dialogue between text and context. Unexpectedly, my fieldwork revealed that different communities of listeners held varying views of Gonnella's playing, and thus, his contributions to Scottish fiddling. As a member of a musical community that holds Gonnella in high esteem, this very much surprised me and set me on a course to understand why. These surprising findings led me to consider different musical communities, each with their own way of interpreting Gonnella's playing and contributions. While it will suffice for now to adopt Kay Shelemay's notion of a musical community simply as a "social entity, an outcome of a combination of social and musical processes rendering those who participate in making or listening to music aware of a connection among themselves' (2011: 14); a deeper dive into the study led me to call upon the notion of musical communities as "*interpretive* communities." Thus, I have identified three primary communities of listeners/players with whom Gonnella interacted and influenced in the United States and Scotland. An examination of their perceptions of Gonnella's legacy provides the social context and the structural framework for this study.

Acknowledgments

I am very grateful to the people who graciously consented to participate in interviews and conversations whether in person, via zoom, email, or phone calls: Dr. Stuart Eydmann, Dr. Gary West, Mr. Douglas Lawrence, Mr. James Alexander, Mr. Alistair McCulloch, Mr. Ronnie Gibson, Mr. Hebbie Gray, Dr. Matt Sillar, Dr. Peter Cooke, Mr. Charles Gore, Mr. Robbie Shepherd, Dr. John Turner, Ms. Bonnie Rideout, Ms. Evelyn Murray, Mr. Ian Rattray, Ms. Liz Maxwell, Dr. Jo Miller, Ms. Christine Martin, and Mr. Alastair Savage. I also appreciate the kind assistance of Ms. Carolyn Dingwall at Morrison's Academy in Crieff, Scotland, along with Ms. Mollie MacCallum and Ms. Alison Hunter, former Morrison's Academy teaching colleagues of Ron Gonnella, as well as Ms. Jayne Allan, registrar for the City of Dundee, Scotland, David Arbuthnott, Dunkeld Cathedral Archives, and David Chipping, archivist at BBC Written Archives Centre. Very special thanks to Professor Donna Heddle at Orkney College UHI and to Lu Livingston. And finally, Magnus—for his companionship and unique critical perspective.

Introduction

The Legacy of Ron Gonnella is drawn from a range of sources including oral histories of musicians who knew, studied, worked, or performed with Gonnella, as well as those who were informed by his work. It is a dialogue between differing musical styles and artistic points of view; it is a dialogue between several historical periods and the musical fashions associated with each—a polyphonic dialogue that begins in Barga, Italy, with distinctive dialects and accents, spends several generations in Scotland, before emigrating to North America for more discussion, only to return again to Scotland to engage in political, popular, and academic debate.

The scarcity of academic or even popular culture evidence on Gonnella's body of work is problematic for the researcher and necessitates the use of a more subjective methodology that employs personal interviews and anecdotal evidence that are characteristically the province of oral historians. While these oral sources may be conditional, historian Lynn Abrams argues, they nonetheless are valid and useful if appraised differently from orthodox academic documentary materials (2010, 6). This different perspective for judging a resource involves acknowledgment that while at face value the oral history narrative provides useful descriptive and factual evidence, its primary implications lie in the fact that it is a respondent's recollection of the past filtered through the lens of the present. Recollections, then, of Ron Gonnella and his work have had twenty-five years and more to be tempered by the passage of time and the narrator's own experience. Thus, avenues of research were significantly limited by the passage of time and resulted in the use of evidence that is both informal and anecdotal. The lack of conventional resources necessitated alternative ways of considering and assessing Gonnella's musical contributions.

As stated in the preface, my fieldwork revealed that different communities of listeners held varying views of Gonnella's playing and his contributions to Scottish fiddling, leading me to consider and call on Stanley Fish's notion of interpretive communities. In its most basic form, an interpretive community is a group with an established tradition of interpretation. Each community's interpretation is based on socially shared meanings and can change with context (1980, 312). Likewise, each of Gonnella's interpretive musical communities developed its own expectations, experiences, and knowledge, making it uniquely qualified to participate in the dialogue of determining his contributions to the Scottish fiddling tradition (Fish 1980).

MUSICAL "TEXTS" AND INTERPRETATION

The interpretation of the Scottish fiddling repertoire, the canon that includes Niel Gow, William Marshall, and James Scott Skinner's published compositions, follows the form the interpretive community's tradition prescribes. Jeff Todd Titon agrees, stating, "right" interpretations of texts are right only within particular contexts; there is no universal or foundational or eternally correct interpretation of a text" (Titon 2003, 71). This study of Gonnella's contributions interprets "text" to mean not only words, but also notes on a printed page, public performance, recorded or broadcast music, and the body of work by a single performer—an expression of content from a particular point of view in a specific situation. If we adopt the assumption that text equals a unity of a performer's work, text can be considered a musical expression ranging from a single musician playing a simple tune to an orchestra performing a symphony. Thus, music becomes a concrete expression of content, always permeated with values, delivered and received from particular points of view. And the interpretation of music (text) is sanctioned by a community of like-minded individuals of which that musician (reader) is a member. Regardless of context, the interpretive variability of that text is governed by the interpretive community, not necessarily, as Gonnella humorously indicates in his comical judging soliloquy (see appendix E), a tune played "exactly as Niel Gow played it in 1785" (Gonnella n.d.).

Wider social forces inform Gonnella's work and these forces ensure the predominance of context over text. For example, this is exactly the result when Gonnella plays "Miss Hannah's Jig" by William Marshall. Without explicit instructions from the composer, the tune becomes an artistic reworking that incorporates not only the socio-ideological position of the composer, but also that of a performer with a classical background. In spite of the fact that Gonnella spent years researching the eighteenth and nineteenth-century fiddle masters to academically inform his interpretations, the particular "meaning" of "Miss Hannah's Jig," when Gonnella performs it, becomes context over text in the sense that his interpretation of the tune is shaped by a social process within what Simon McKerrell refers to as "a community of practice" (2016, 4). As another example, well before the end of the "A" section of Gonnella's recording of Niel Gow's "Lament for James Moray of Abercairney," a listener from Gonnella's "community of practice" realizes that this rendition is executed by a fiddler of excellent technical ability, evident in the tonal quality of his playing, accurate intonation, the expressive use of vibrato, and rhythmic control—all qualities valued by *that* community. In Gonnella's case, the mingling of classical training, historical research, international performance experience as a solo fiddler, dance band member, and composer of traditional tunes led to Gonnella's particular perspective. Gonnella acknowledges a single performance contains elements of both the classical tradition, in which Gonnella was firmly rooted, and of his appreciation of the traditional nature of the tune itself; as such it becomes a dialogue between perspectives. For Gonnella, the task of interpreting traditional fiddle tunes surpassed socially shared meaning, relying not only on the original manuscripts, but also on his professional "artistic knowledge" developed over years of experience and scholarship. As Jonathan Stephens explains,

> Artistic knowledge includes the dimensions of perception, opinion and belief: it is propositional, experiential, theoretical and procedural. A musical performance that is deemed *appropriate* represents one perception or interpretation of an unwritten musical tradition or of a notated musical score (2013, 80).

While interpretation and understanding develop within the "historical context of traditions," interpretive communities remain fluid, each building on earlier interpretations and knowledge (2013, 83). Interpretation is the product of the merger of the collective agreement of a community with the personal perspective of the performer. By applying his artistic/professional knowledge, Gonnella was able to reconstruct approximate contextual meanings and develop a dialogue with Gow, Marshall, Skinner, and others.

GONNELLA'S INTERPRETIVE MUSICAL COMMUNITIES

Since the 1980s, Gonnella's interpretive communities have followed a pattern of growth and decline, shift and slippage, as individuals move from one camp to another, as his interpretations of traditional tunes become the indisputable authority during one decade with one interpretive community and then gradually fall out of favor with another. If boundaries between communities are continually being redrawn, and if interpretive communities are no more than sets of practices, it seems obvious that the character of a performance changes in response to events and that past performance, social, and historical factors play a large part in shaping a performance. Christopher Small seems to agree, arguing the meaning of music texts can only be considered in the totality of the performance. Coining the term "musicking," he proposes "the act of musicking establishes in the place where it is happening a set of relationships, and it is in those relationships that the meaning of the act lies" (1998, 13). Small also suggests there is a reciprocal relationship between performers and listeners, especially between those with whom we have a positive relationship, which affects our response to a performance and often bonds us together as interpretive communities (1998, 210). For Gonnella, "musicking" represented a dialogue with the fiddlers who preceded him, as well as the opportunity to influence the fiddling tradition through his own interpretations of tunes. Through the juxtaposition of multiple voices, some contradictory and some mutually supplemental, communities of like-minded participants in the conversation can be identified and the interpretive strategies can be revealed.

I have identified three primary communities of listeners/players with whom Gonnella interacted and influenced in the United States and Scotland; and their perceptions of Gonnella's legacy provide the social context in which to examine Gonnella's contributions. Gonnella's endorsement by and association with BBC Scotland and its listeners, the first interpretive community, played a large role in Gonnella becoming one of Scotland's first commercially successful fiddlers and the reinvigoration of Scottish fiddle repertoire. The Music Department of British Broadcasting Company in Scotland made the collective decision to endorse Ron Gonnella's interpretation of traditional Scottish fiddle tunes by offering him broadcast opportunities. His labeling as a "refined" player put him on the solo performance pathway, later also serving as introducer, presenter, and host of various programs. In its role of gatekeeper of cultural standards, BBC Scotland effectively put its seal of approval on not only his interpretation of Scottish fiddle tunes, but on the entire Gonnella "package" and became his most influential public advocate, broadcasting his interviews, performances, and persona to an interpretive community of listeners across its broadcast area.

By examining representatives of two of Gonnella's interpretive musical communities in Scotland: classically trained fiddlers and revivalist fiddlers, we can explore the notion of Ron Gonnella as an authority figure. Viewing Gonnella's body of work in the cultural context of the 1960s, 70s and 80s, we see a career that parallels, but was far removed from, the folk music revivals of the period. Though Gonnella's performance, recording, and adjudicating career unfolded concurrently with the mid-twentieth-century Scottish music revival, Gonnella was not emulated by most revivalist musicians, in part, because he was classically trained, commercially successful, and was seen as "establishment." However, in one important respect Gonnella was an active agent in the effort to restore fiddle repertoire and performance practice so revered by revivalist musicians, for the scholarship he conducted into the unpublished manuscripts of the eighteenth-century masters resulted in bringing into the fiddle repertoire neglected tunes of these masters. Gonnella's research led to the selective performance and recording of eighteenth-century fiddle tunes, many of which were adopted by revivalist fiddlers as part of their repertoire. While the communities of classically trained and revivalist fiddlers may appear to be quite distinct, they share a common repertory of traditional tunes and the view of Gonnella as an authority figure. As revivalist fiddler and Scots fiddle scholar Stuart Eydmann states, "an important part of the fiddle revival was the rediscovery and exploration of important seams of repertory which was either overlooked or awaiting exploitation" (Eydmann 2014). Gonnella's performance and recording of these tunes provided "new" material for the revivalist fiddlers that was previously unknown, thus he was active in "reinterpreting, modifying, and forging new histories" as Bithell and Hill suggest. And these new histories were assimilated into the received history of the revivalist musicians and survive in the post-revival fiddle canon (2014, 13). The revivalist community endorsed Gonnella by listening to his broadcasts, attending his concerts, and purchasing his recordings. In contrast, when questioned about their participation in the instrumental revival in the early 1970s, numerous fiddlers in Scotland replied that from their perspective the music did not need reviving because it was never dead. Similarly, Gonnella did not see the need to revive the music he had been playing for more than three decades. In response, Eydmann observed that this was an "insider" view, contending there was a well-established, pre-existing, and self-contained school of competitions, concerts, and violin playing to which Ron Gonnella, Hector MacAndrew, Angus Fitchet, James Alexander, Douglas Lawrence, and others from northeast Scotland belonged, and which existed prior to the instrumental revival of the late 1960s onward (Eydmann 2014).

Through his recordings, printed collections of fiddle tunes, concert performances, and competition adjudication, Gonnella played a role in establishing interpretation, repertoire, style, and performance standards for Scottish fiddling in the United States. In the case of performance and competition of traditional Scottish fiddle tunes in America, the highly prescriptive "shared ways of seeing" endorsed by Scottish Fiddling Revival (F.I.R.E.), by its judges, and by its competitors became the accepted institutional practices and established an interpretive community of fiddlers in the US. Established in the mid-1970s, F.I.R.E. is the only organization in America that certifies Scottish fiddling judges and sanctions competitions. This organization single-handedly established performance standards and learning opportunities for North American fiddlers unfamiliar with the Scottish fiddling tradition and unaware of its leading musicians. It was into this relative wilderness of the United States Scottish fiddle scene in 1980 that Gonnella strode, already well established in Scotland and one of the first recognized masters of the Scottish fiddle to adjudicate an American competition. Barely five years after competitions commenced, Gonnella, with his formal Highland attire and his polished style of playing traditional tunes, arrived to the applause of a community of aspiring American fiddlers. As an early and frequent adjudicator for competitions sanctioned by F.I.R.E. Gonnella helped establish performance practice for this group, still strong forty years after his tenure as adjudicator. Scottish F.I.R.E. offered a singular community for North American musicians interested in Scottish fiddling, gradually developing into a full-fledged interpretive musical community with its own set of practices.

By exploring the perceptions of each musical community, a picture of Gonnella's legacy emerges and shows that Gonnella participated in a lifelong dialogue between musical text and social context, and that his contributions influenced the character of what is considered traditional Scottish fiddling today. The social dialogue is important because the meaning of Gonnella's texts varies depending on which socio-ideological language is spoken. For example, the "meaning" of his interpretation of traditional tunes was selected by institutional BBC Scotland to represent the norm and presented to the listening public in its characteristic socio-ideological language; by virtue of BBC Scotland's endorsement, it became the accepted norm for traditional Scottish fiddling for many listeners. However, Gonnella's interpretation of traditional Scottish fiddling can mean something entirely different in the socio-ideological language of revivalist fiddlers in which his blend of traditional tunes performed with classical finesse is considered by some to be inauthentic. Although there are dissenters within each audience, there is by and large agreement within each particular group of listeners—there is tacit agreement upon the meaning of Gonnella's texts that is characteristic, as we shall see, of an "interpretive community."

A study of Gonnella's legacy illustrates that the social nature of the dialogue between the three communities continues. It is this free incorporation of socio-ideological languages in Gonnella's texts that makes them social constructions; their meanings vary depending not only on the performance context, but also on which socio-ideological language is spoken. The interpretation of the Scottish fiddling repertoire, the canon that includes master-fiddlers Gow, Marshall, and Skinner's published compositions, follows the form the musical community's tradition prescribes; and regardless of context, the interpretive variability of that text is governed by the interpretive community. Soliciting perceptions of Gonnella's contributions to the Scottish fiddling tradition from each musical community builds a picture of Gonnella's legacy and shows that he participated in a lifelong dialogue between musical text and social context, and that his contributions influenced the character of what is considered traditional Scottish fiddling today.

CHAPTER ONE

Historical Overview of Scottish Fiddling

The fiddle, in some form, has been part of Scottish life for more than five hundred years. As early as 1450 there have been references to fiddling in Scottish documents, such as the infamous fiddle serenade Mary Queen of Scots heard for several nights in the summer of 1561. Prior to the violin's arrival in the latter half of the seventeenth century, musicians played native music on such instruments as the fydel, rebec, croud, and viol. Viols were widely played by the French, Italian, and German court musicians and a substantial repertoire of music was composed for these instruments of the court and refined society. Glimpses of early fiddling in Scotland, as seen in works of art, oral narrative, and poetry, for example, feature the fiddler in a range of roles from itinerant "scraper" to courtly musician, though providing accompaniment for dancing was the fiddle's primary historical function. Thus, the instrument and the fiddler became part of the social fabric—a participant in Scottish society and culture. While we have no crystal-clear picture of what fiddling was like in Scotland prior to the arrival of the modern violin, music scholar David Johnson suggests it is possible ". . . to estimate what 17th-century fiddle music was like simply by taking the 19th-century repertory and deducting all its contemporary features. Short dance pieces—jigs and reels—seem to be the answer, along with a few slow airs," states Johnson (4).

Though impossible to pinpoint, it has been generally accepted that the first of the perfected "modern" Italian violins, along with written music collections, reached Scotland by 1670, if not earlier. However, as Frances Collinson points out in his seminal work *The Traditional and National Music of Scotland*, the Amati family had been making and selling their Italian violins since the sixteenth century so the modern violin may have reached Scotland earlier than 1670. And Aaron MacGregor, based on his analysis of the earliest music *manuscripts*, argues the modern violin, the instrument as we know it today, was likely played in Scotland as much as one hundred years earlier (http://hms.scot). Numerous scholars, including Mary Anne Alburger in *Scottish Fiddlers and Their Music*, do concur that the earliest Scottish manuscript written specifically for the violin was "Lessones for ye Violin," printed in Newbattle Abbey near Edinburgh about 1680 (1997, 3). But it was likely the case that some fiddlers, collectors, and promoters transcribed tunes they played and heard prior to their inclusion in printed collections. Reliance only on written sources to date the violin in Scotland largely overlooks the presence and importance of aural transmission. As we shall see, study of the development of Scottish fiddle/violin music during the eighteenth and nineteenth centuries reveals parallel and intertwining oral and written traditions.

By the closing decade of the seventeenth century the highly restrictive stances toward secular music and dance were just beginning to relax when a collection of Scottish melodies for violin, *A Collection of Original Scotch-Tunes (Full of the Highland Humours)*, was printed in London by English music publisher Henry Playford. The highly popular collection included reels and Scotch measures (twosome dances). As Alburger points out, though the collection did not include composers' names, and the strathspey form was yet to appear, we see "many of the roots of Scottish fiddle music." "When these are added," continues Alburger, "fiddle music reaches its zenith, and the final connections are made between the creators of the music, the players who interpret it and the individuals who dance to it or appreciate it from the audience" (27). Reflecting the repressive power of the Scottish Kirk, the establishment of public dancing assemblies in Scotland lagged far behind those in England. While early manuscripts featured instructions and music, the dances were primarily country dances accompanied by reels, rather than minuets popular in England. Numerous collections printed in London, such as Playford's *Dancing Master*, featured music and instructions for hundreds of dances. Other collections featured dance sets, made up of three to four Scottish tunes in related keys or one tune with variations, often reflecting the influence of the bagpipe with its nine-note modal scale. Despite the availability of the printed music, it is likely that musicians played the tunes from memory. Early in the century fiddlers also played bagpipe transcriptions with little alteration. This imitative style included elements such as the use of open strings as drones, birls (three repeated notes bowed very quickly), grace notes, and the limited nine-note bagpipe scale. Composers later experimented with writing pibroch expressly for the fiddle in imitation of ceol mor, the highly ornamented classical music of the bagpipe.

In Scotland, music publishing finally began in 1726 with the printing of several works in Edinburgh. As Alburger observes, "Taken as a whole, they present not only the expanding interests of the era, but foreshadow the directions music would take in the country for the remainder of the century" (40). These early publications, printed on Scottish soil, inspired and encouraged musicians to publish their own arrangements and in some cases, their own compositions. While fiddle music played in the first two decades of the eighteenth century primarily featured slow airs, hornpipes, reels, jigs, and pibrochs common to native music and largely free of European influence, music played after 1720 clearly evidenced European influences.

Between 1720 and 1745, Edinburgh saw the development of what David Johnson termed the "Scots drawing room" style by a group of composers including Adam Craig, Alexander Stuart, Alexander Munro, James Oswald, Francesco Barsanti, Charles McLean, and William McGibbon. With the exception of Barsanti, all were Scots, and all had extensive knowledge of European music. Existing Scottish melodies were harmonized in a modern classical, or so-called art music style, often with extensive variations, while variation sonatas such as James Oswald's "Pentland Hills" or William McGibbon's "Leith Wynd," along with fiddle pibrochs, minuets, and long variation sets, were built on newly-composed melodies. Fiddles, or violins, were most often accompanied by cello and harpsichord, with composers notating a simple keyboard accompaniment and a bass line. Sonatas by Oswald, McGibbon, Mackintosh, and the Earl of Kelly required a certain degree of advanced technique for both players and composers, while the duration of the long variation sets challenged the attention spans of listeners. The variation sonata incorporated the most European elements while the fiddle pibroch imitated Scottish bagpipe music. The long variation set incorporated a range of European art music techniques such as scordatura (re-tuning), slurs, higher positions, doublestops, arpeggios, and the use of the lower range of the instrument. While variations were notated, performers also improvised their own variations. As the popularity of dancing the minuet increased, Scottish composers published their own minuets to accompany the dance. Many minuets were dedicated to patrons and as a result, composers enjoyed financial and social benefits. Best known is the patronage of three Dukes of Atholl in support of the legendary fiddler/fiddle composer Niel Gow. Some Scottish composers also tried their hand at writing violin sonatas, though their performance, along with that of the variation sonata, was limited and their popularity short-lived.

Johnson contends this newly embraced eighteenth-century style was an "artistic movement which was both aggressively nationalistic and aggressively fashionable"—one that can be traced to the Act of Union of 1707 and the dissolution of Scotland's parliament and the country's loss of self-esteem (34). The last two decades of the eighteenth century saw the rise of Romanticism in art, literature, and politics, inspiring nationalism and the elevation of folk traditions. The forms that remained popular and became part of a fiddler's typical repertoire were the shorter dance forms such as strathspeys, slow airs, reels, hornpipes, and jigs—forms easily transmitted aurally—rather than the long variation sets, fiddle pibrochs, minuets, and sonatas that would have been more dependent on the printed page. While some contend these art music-inspired compositions would have been more likely heard in the Lowlands or in urban regions rather than rural settings such as the western Highlands, it may not be so unlikely for a rural fiddler to be asked for a minuet to accompany a dance. And it follows that some fiddlers may well have incorporated some of the art music techniques into their performance of traditional Scottish fiddle tunes.

BECOMING "TRADITIONAL" SCOTTISH FIDDLING

Today we think of Scottish fiddling as a *traditional* art form, but as Johnson contends, Scots fiddle music of the eighteenth century, considered the heyday of Scottish fiddling, was caught between European art music and native Scottish musical traditions, what Gibson refers to as the "folk-art split," and perhaps, can be better described as *progressive* (Johnson 1997, 2). While it is true that much of the music of the time was tied to a local culture and maintained a strong sense of national identity, the Scottishness of the music developed and changed over the course of the eighteenth century, according to Johnson, primarily because of the influences of European art music (Johnson 1997). However, ethnomusicologist Peter Cooke (1985) criticizes Johnson's emphasis on the importance of eighteenth-century publications on the fiddle tradition and the portrayal that the majority of Scots fiddlers belonged to a literate tradition. Cooke goes on to say, "The probable truth (though we have little contemporary data for supporting either view) is that outside the homes of the Scottish aristocracy and the middle-class households of Edinburgh New Town there was very little literacy" (1985, 274). Instead, Cooke asserts,

> What is more likely is that experiments in 'developing' the popular fiddle repertory of the day never became widely known outside the milieu of the urban upper classes, since they depended on two conditions that did not exist: firstly, there were few musically literate fiddlers, and secondly there was no established concert going tradition where a listening repertory rather than a dance music repertory could find an audience (1985, 275).

The fact that we know who composed the majority of eighteenth-century fiddle tunes and actually know quite a bit about composers' lives is another challenge to the old definition of what constitutes "traditional." Written music collections accompanied the arrival of the modern violin in the latter half of the seventeenth century, so some fiddlers learned tunes from written manuscripts rather than by ear through oral transmission, disputing another hallmark of the oral tradition, though the tunes would have been performed by memory. Johnson goes so far as to suggest that, "It follows that mainstream Scots-fiddle playing and mainstream European-violin playing cannot have differed from each other in the 18th century nearly as much as 'folk fiddle' and 'classical violin' playing do today" (Johnson 1997: 5).

Music scholar Ronnie Gibson suggests another concept that is fundamental to the study of the Scots fiddle tradition: the passage of time. In the case of Scottish fiddling, Gibson contends, "it was not until the mid-nineteenth century that fiddle players could be said to conceive of their practice in the context of a tradition. Only at this time was the significance of the past fully recognized, and its influence in shaping the music the [then] present felt" (Gibson 2014). While the eighteenth century was undoubtedly the heyday of composition and performance by charismatic fiddlers and fiddle composers, the process of selection and repetition was not recognized until it could be seen in retrospect. Gibson argues the mid-nineteenth century acceptance and establishment of a Scottish fiddling tradition happened for two main reasons: the publication of definitive texts and the identification of performance style (Gibson 2014). Further, performance style was usually associated with a geographical region—a region with a key charismatic fiddler or composer where fiddling was mostly continuous and well-preserved, such as in the Northeast or Shetland.

The last quarter of the eighteenth century was a prolific period of composition for the fiddle with the publication of collections of the great masters: Niel Gow, Nathaniel Gow, William Marshall, and Captain Simon Fraser, along with those of many "lesser lights," to use Alburger's words. Gow, Marshall, and Skinner, the focus of much of Gonnella's work, will be the primary fiddlers and fiddle composers highlighted here. Niel Gow was born in 1727 near Dunkeld in Perthshire to parents who worked as weavers. Gow was largely a self-taught fiddler, though he studied briefly with a fiddler named James Cameron who was employed by Sir George Stewart of Grandtully. *The Scots Magazine and Edinburgh Literary Miscellany* published "A brief biographical account of Neil Gow" in January 1809, which included an account of Niel's participation in what was likely his first fiddle contest in which the blind umpire awarded him first prize ". . . in the justice of which the other competitors cheerfully acquiesced. On this occasion, giving his decision, the judge said, that he could distinguish the stroke of Neil's Bow among a hundred players" (3). Continuing the glowing description of Gow's playing the author stated:

> There is perhaps no species whatever of music executed on the violin, in which the characteristic expression depends more on the power of the bow, particularly in what is called the upward or returning stroke, than the Highland reel. Here accordingly was Gow's forte. His bow-hand, as a suitable instrument of his genius, was uncommonly powerful; and when the note produced by the up-bow was often feeble and indistinct in other hands, it was struck, in his playing, with a strength and certainty, which never failed to surprize and delight the skilful hearer. We may add the effect of the sudden shout, with which he frequently accompanied his playing in the quick tunes, and which seemed instantly to electrify the dancers; inspiring them with new life and energy, and rousing the spirits of the most inanimate (3).

The above description captures something of Gow's style and charisma, highlighting what may have been the most singular aspect of his playing—his bowing—or what we now refer to as the "up-driven-bow." As described in Christine Martin's guide to *Traditional Scottish Fiddling,* this technique "consists of a quick down bow followed by three up bows played individually within the straight up bow slur," adding a distinctive lift and drive (128). While Gow enjoyed the patronage and encouragement of the Dukes of Atholl, whose support undoubtedly contributed to his national celebrity status and his ability to make a living as a musician, he played for dances and entertainments in and around Perthshire for more than four decades, famously carrying his fiddle in its green baize bag. Descriptions such as the one included in *The Scots Magazine*: "the violin, in his hands, sounded like the harp of Ossian, or the lyre of Orpheus; and gave reality to the poetic fictions which describe the astonishing effects of their performance" (3), elevated Gow's legendary status, while the abundance of folksy "tales" of Gow's adventures further embedded his name and deeds in popular consciousness (3). Gow enjoyed many notable meetings and occasions, including one he shared with Robert Burns in 1778. Meeting in the inn at Inver, Gow charmed Burns with his playing and the two shared a dram. Much like Burns, Gow is said to have had the ability to engage honestly and directly with people from different stations in life, endearing him to all classes of society. Burns must have agreed, describing Gow as "A short, stout-built Highland figure, with his greyish hair shed on his honest social brow—an interesting face, marking strong sense, kind open heartedness mixed with unmistrusting simplicity" (1828, 158).

Gow has been credited with the composition of between seventy to eighty tunes, though the number is hard to pinpoint due to re-use of tunes to honor various patrons along with claims of plagiarism, claims that have now largely been quelled. While his collections were sometimes criticized for including tunes without attribution, Gow was often lax in claiming authorship of many of his own tunes, perhaps due to modesty or humility. Gow's legacy continued through his four musician sons, especially Nathaniel, Gow's second youngest (1763-1831). Nathaniel studied cello and violin in Edinburgh and lived his life there as a busy skilled professional musician. He offered invaluable assistance in the publication of his father's first works, contributing many of his own compositions to the collections, as did sons William, John, and Andrew. According to Alastair Hardie, Gow's publications included *A Collection of Strathspey Reels* (in several parts) by "Niel Gow at Dunkeld," while *The Complete Repository of Original Slow Strathspeys and Dances* (in several parts) were by "Niel Gow and Sons." By the end of the century, Nathaniel had become a lauded musician, composer, and publisher in his own right, though never as well-known as his father. But without Nathaniel's expertise and dedication to publishing the Gow collections, it is doubtful his father's music would have survived.

William Marshall (1748–1833), born two decades after Niel Gow, was another shining light of the eighteenth century. Marshall grew up in Fochabers in North East Scotland where at the age of twelve he became assistant to the house steward at Gordon Castle, later butler to the fourth Duke of Gordon, and finally, estate factor to the fifth Duke. Unlike Gow, Marshall did not make his living as a musician and may be seen today as something of a "Renaissance man" with his wide-ranging interests, study and knowledge of clock-making, architecture, surveying, and astronomy. He was a skilled dancer, fiddler, and composer who Robert Burns (himself a fiddler) admired and honored with the well-known accolade of "the first composer of strathspeys of the age." Burns dined with the Duke of Gordon at Gordon Castle during his Highland tour of 1787; and whether or not he met Marshall at that time, Burns was familiar with Marshall's music, having written words for Marshall's "Miss Admiral Gordon's Strathspey" (renamed as "Of a' the Airts the Wind Can Blaw"). While many of Marshall's tunes carry titles that pay tribute to Gordon family members and castle guests, he frequently changed the names of tunes to suit his purpose. A prolific composer of more than two-hundred-fifty tunes, he truly excelled at the writing of expressive slow airs and buoyant strathspeys.

Marshall was seen as an innovator whose music made technical demands on fiddlers, though the same could be said for a handful of other composers at this time. In the *Glen Collection of Scottish Dance Music* (1891), John Glen notes the criticism of Marshall's melodies by other fiddlers due to "wide intervals or other transitions" and "their compass being more extensive than that to which they were accustomed" (71). Marshall's well-known response to these complaints was, "I don't write music for bunglers!" (Cowrie 1999, 59). Marshall made use of a wide range of keys, doublestops, leaps from low to high strings, and shifting up the neck of the instrument into higher positions. Glen's brief biographical sketch of Marshall sheds a bit of light on the quality and level of Marshall's own playing:

> In the estimation of his contemporaries, he held very high rank as a performer on the violin. It is said he possessed a very correct ear, and had considerable command over his instrument, which was greatly enhanced

> by the skilful management of his bow. His style was excellent, he avoided trickery of all sorts, and excelled in breath of intonation along with precision and splendid expression (69).

By 1781, Marshall had published two volumes of his *Collection of Strathspey Reels,* though these tunes appear to have been widely played even prior to printing, perhaps learned from hand-written manuscripts passed among fiddlers or through oral transmission. Marshall was not known to have played publicly at dances or concerts; and posthumously, he is remembered in quite a different way than his fellow fiddler/fiddle composer. Where Gow is hailed and romanticized as a folk fiddler, Marshall is praised for, what Gibson refers to as, "classical credentials." Interestingly, as Gibson points out, the famous Henry Raeburn portrait of Gow in his tartan trews, and the depiction of Gow in David Allan's folksy dance scene (*A Highland Wedding*), are quite a contrast to John Moir's erudite portrait of Marshall, illuminating differences in the ways the two fiddlers were perceived during their lifetimes, and to some extent, are remembered today (Gibson 2019, 89). This contrast, again, highlights the intertwining of folk and art music and the difficulty of compartmentalizing Scottish fiddle music (87).

FIDDLING IN THE NINETEENTH CENTURY

The deaths of Gow in 1831 and Marshall in 1833 left Scottish fiddling without a figurehead for more than a generation, breaking the long tradition of renowned fiddlers. This absence of charismatic fiddlers, along with attempts by the church to quell music and dance, and effects of the potato famine, resulted in an overall decline of fiddle music in Scotland through the 1840s. But in the middle of the century, there was a revival of interest in Scottish fiddle music, especially in the Northeast. Scholarship reflects conflicting opinions on reasons for the revival of interest in Scottish fiddling in the mid-nineteenth century, making it hard to pinpoint. Alburger suggests the popularity of "Balmorality" and the stimulus of visiting royalty may have awakened interest in the music (170). Some credit the prominence and popularity of fiddler/fiddle composer Scott Skinner and his status of figurehead as another catalyst. Gibson, however, also points out the development of "new performance platforms," including the changing status of violin performance toward a public setting, increased access to instruments and printed sheet music, all of which promoted the marketing of fiddle music as recreation and entertainment (n.p.). And new performance venues such as strathspey and reel societies, dance halls, and fiddle competitions led the music away from its historical function as traditional dance accompaniment. Publications of tunes by individual composers were eclipsed by large definitive collections such as the *Glen, Kerr, Athole* and *Skye* collections, which emphasized the canon of eighteenth-century tunes (Gibson 2014). Niel Gow (1727–1807) was a key figure in defining performance style, especially in regard to strathspey playing using his up-driven-bow technique. Gow's death further advanced the idea of the Gow school of playing, tying his performance style to historical roots and increasing stylistic awareness among fiddlers. Gibson argues, "The very identification of an historical perspective had a significant impact, and enhanced the move away from dance and towards an appreciation of the music for its own sake" (Gibson 2014).

Further recognition of a Scottish fiddling tradition came with the publication of William C. Honeyman's tutor, *The Strathspey, Reel and Hornpipe Tutor* (1898) and James Scott Skinner's *A Scottish Violinist* and *A Guide to Bowing,* published around 1900. *A Guide to Bowing,* in particular, offered guidance on *how* to play strathspeys and reels. Skinner (1843–1927), a professional dance master and violinist, was performing extensively by the 1870s, often featuring his original compositions alongside virtuoso solos of violin music. While Skinner's formal music education was extensive, studying both cello and violin, he also played for dances and won notable fiddling competitions, another example of the "folk-art split." A concert review from *The Highlander* newspaper in April of 1879 included the comment: "Mr. Skinner really does the instrument justice." After complimenting Skinner's performance of music by Mozart, De Beriot, and Paganini, the review raved, "And when he turned to the Strathspeys and Reels, oh, what spirit and what finish" (Hardie 1992, xvv). Skinner was a prolific composer of more than six-hundred printed pieces and one of the very first Scottish fiddlers to record. Unfortunately, even with the re-issue of Skinner's recordings, it is difficult to know how he sounded due to the crude rudimentary recording techniques, especially in regard to tonal quality, pitch, and speed.

Following much success in Scotland Skinner made the decision to join an ill-fated tour of the United States in 1893 with piper and dancer Willie MacLennan, who died mid-tour. Though the tour was a disaster, northern American audiences were exposed to Skinner's playing and repertoire. It was upon his return to Scotland that Skinner adopted the title and persona of "The Strathspey King," described by Peter Cooper as "the very embodiment of the romantic Victorian version of traditional Highland culture" (Box and Fiddle Archive). Though he had "classical credentials," Skinner enjoyed his greatest success when he played Scottish music and fully embraced the Scottish idiom, including his wearing of the kilt and Highland regalia. We get a glimpse of his nature and the influence of his training from *A Guide to Bowing* in which he states:

> Of course there were natural geniuses, such as the immortals: Knockie (Captain Simon Fraser), who *sang Gaelic* on the Fiddle; Neil Gow, who electrified a Ballroom; Marshall, with his sweet Ingleside 'Woodnotes wild' . . . All these men did good work, but would have soared even higher had they received a good sound training in manual equipment, and still remembered to render their country's music by the light of nature, maintaining its ruggedness and character; and not making it insipid and genteel (28).

Skinner (1843–1927) would effectively replace Neil Gow as figurehead by the end of the century. He was certainly the best-known fiddler of the time, with extensive compositions, a public persona, and the earliest Scottish fiddle recordings. Gavin Grieg, in his introduction to *The Harp and Claymore* collection of tunes, describes Skinner's contributions, painting him in the role of revivalist:

> [Scott Skinner] has founded a school of composition and playing that challenges effective comparison with the best achievements of the past. He has not broken with the past—no true artist ever does; but, conserving its best traditions, he has enlarged the scope and message of the strathspey, impressing on it his own strong individuality, and infusing into it a style and finish unknown before (1904: 9).

The decades following Skinner's death saw a dearth of charismatic fiddlers and fiddle composers; two world wars would disrupt the continuity of the fiddling tradition. As Skinner's wax cylinder recordings gave way to new technology, including radio and television, new listening audiences were being created and new performers were becoming stars. Change was afoot and the impact of technological advances cannot be overestimated. As Alburger states, while "the most obvious influence of recorded music is on the repertoire . . . ," "a more subtle but perhaps longer-lasting effect of recordings is on style" (199). Being able to *hear* the music, rather than just *see* it as a transcription on paper, must have made quite an impression on both those who had the ability to read music and those who learned by ear.

The BBC was founded in October 1922, launching the first radio broadcasts in Scotland in March of 1923. Early BBC programming production was centralized in London and faced criticism for a lack of Scottish material. When broadcasts did feature fiddle tunes, they were performed by classical ensembles, reflecting the BBC attitude toward the quality and merit of Scottish culture, as will be discussed more fully in a later chapter. Following World War II Scottish country dancing became very popular and radio programs included Scottish country dance music that featured the versatile accordion or "box" in a leading role rather than the fiddle, with Jimmy Shand as its most famous proponent. The Royal Scottish Country Dance Society (RSCDS) established an ongoing relationship with BBC, with a range of programming that played a major role in preserving and perpetuating the popularity of Scottish country dancing and dance music. While the Society's musical requirements encouraged the adherence to strict unwavering tempos, garnering criticism from some, these requirements influenced the way the music developed and the way it is played to this day. It was common for even the most widely-known recorded "solo" fiddlers to also have been recorded playing country dance music. Though the box overshadowed the fiddle, dance bands continued to include fiddlers. Angus Fitchet served as Shand's longtime fiddler while "Pibroch" MacKenzie played with Bobby MacLeod's band; and several prominent fiddlers, including Adam Rennie and Ian Powrie, formed their own bands and published books of original accordion and fiddle tunes. BBC continued to regard classical music as superior and performers of non-classical music, fiddlers in particular, were held to the highest standards—standards collectively agreed upon by the interpretive community that was the BBC Music Department. While programs in the 1940s began to feature solo performers, including Hector MacAndrew, Ron Gonnella, Bill Hardie, Angus Fitchet, Adam Rennie, Hebbie Gray, Jim Cameron, and Adam Rennie, they declined throughout the 1950s, instead featuring singers and Scottish dance bands (Duesenberry 2000, 88).

This overview of fiddling in Scotland has brought us to the second half of the twentieth century—a time when the old collections of fiddle tunes were now largely out of print. The 78 RPM records of Mackenzie Murdoch, David MacCallum, and Alex Sim would give way to extended play albums, and BBC Scotland would gradually begin broadcasts of solo fiddlers. Thus, we begin an examination of Ron Gonnella's participation in and influence on Scottish fiddling. The following chapters continue our historical journey utilizing various lenses, as in Chapter Two—a biographical sketch of Gonnella's life, which reveals the influences that informed his work and sheds light on Gonnella's experiences in the United States where he inspired and contributed to the concept and growing popularity of Scottish fiddling. Further, we will consider Gonnella's body of work and reception, and thus, the art of Scottish fiddling, in the changing cultural contexts of time and place.

CHAPTER TWO

Biography

Exceptional performers are not only a product of their cultures, they also impact that culture, Virginia Danielson writes. "One wants to grasp not only the life behind the myth, . . . but the myth at the heart of the life. Examining these myths offers a way of understanding what is shared between stars and their audiences" (1997, 15). In order to gain a deeper understanding of Ron Gonnella's body of work, work shared between this under-acknowledged but exceptional performer and his audiences, it is helpful to know something about the man and the influences that informed that work. This speculative biographical sketch gathers information from many disparate sources to uncover those influences and incorporates an awareness of the historical time in which Gonnella made his greatest contributions.

BARGA TO DUNDEE

"Barga" was not an arbitrary choice of names for Gonnella's home. While most literature of the Scottish migrant experience focuses on the Highland clearances and the emigration of people from Scotland to Australia, New Zealand, Ulster, and North America, another dynamic of population movement was at work in the late nineteenth century: the northern Italian diaspora and emigration of people into Scotland. The greatest phase of

FIGURE 2.1. The single-story J. Gonnella & Co. Fine Art Saloon at 81 Nethergate. Photo by Alexander Wilson.

Italian emigration was from the 1880s to the 1920s, a period when many young men left their homes in Barga, Tuscany to find work in Scotland. One of these young men, a farmer by the name of Antonio Gonnella, along with his wife and three sons, were among the families from Barga seeking relief from poverty and a new life in Scotland, and they found their way to Dundee, near Scotland's east coast (Dundee City Archives, Registrar of Births, Deaths and Marriages 2016). Turn of the century Dundee, the country's fourth largest city, was a lively town situated on one of the major ports in Scotland. Shipping companies and warehouses occupied the wharfs alongside the Firth of Tay, and the town boasted a hospital and offered educational opportunities for the children. Very soon it would offer cultural experiences through the Lochee Strathspey and Reel Society and the La Scala Cinema, its name a reflection of the Italian influence in Dundee. The 1878-9 *Scottish Post Office Directory* advertisement for J. Gonnella & Co. Fine Art Saloon touts the work of Italian sculptors from "the most celebrated studios in Italy," and lists Francesco Gonnella, the grandfather of Ronald Gonnella, as the owner (*Post Office Directory* 1878–79). Many Italian emigrants began their employment in Scotland as peddlers of plaster religious figurines, turning later to ice cream street vendors.

Hence, the extended Gonnella family would have been a bi-lingual, informed and interactive community at home with native Scots families of Dundee that participated fully in the heteroglot dialogue that would become Ron Gonnella's legacy. In the prosperous city of Dundee this trade provided a livelihood such that in 1928, at the age of 33, Alberto married Lizzie Dewar Duncan, a 29-year-old Dundee woman with family ties to Perthshire, her grandfather a fiddler himself (Dundee City Archives 2016). Two years into her marriage into the large and successful extended Gonnella family still rooted in Dundee, Lizzie Duncan Gonnella gave birth to Ronald Duncan Gonnella on 24 October 1930. Neither the Gonnella's Italian heritage nor the Duncan influence on her young son can be overestimated in making the man Ronald Gonnella was to become. Being an only child in an extended Italian family was an anomaly reserved for young Ronald and may account for his parents' indulgence in nurturing his artistic talents. Scottish country dance band leader Ian Powrie recalls visiting Gonnella's aunt and uncle in Dundee in the late 1940s and meeting "this slip of a lad. We played together, and quite clearly, I remember his solo rendition of 'Coilsfield House.' At that time I knew we had another unique sound about to burst forth" (Box and Fiddle 2016). Scottish country dancing was very popular in Dundee during the late 1950s and sources from the Dundee Strathspey and Reel Society report that Gonnella played at gatherings and participated with his mother in the group's forerunner, the Lochee Strathspey and Reel Society (Rattray 2015). It was Gonnella's mother, Lizzie, who introduced Ronald at an early age to Jimmy Shand (MBE), the popular dance band leader. As a young student Gonnella sat in with Jimmy Shand's dance band when they played at St. Patrick's Hall on Maitland Street in Dundee. While a secondary student at Harris Academy, Gonnella played in the school orchestra and studied violin with F. Routledge Bell. Shand recalled that Gonnella and his school pal Marcel Crow formed the Tayside Band and recorded three records of Scottish dance music for Beltona Records and later joined Jimmy Scott's Blue Bonnets Scottish Country Dance Band and participated in the group's early broadcasts for BBC Scotland (Box and Fiddle 2016). By the time Gonnella graduated from Harris Academy around 1948, his musical career was on a sure footing.

COMPETITION SHORT-CIRCUIT

Only scant information is available on Gonnella's competition experience. The *Dundee Courier* of October 15, 1953 reports that Gonnella competed before standing-room-only crowds in Alyth, the first contest held there since 1911. Judged by Ronald Calder of BBC Scotland and Jean Rennie of the Scottish National Orchestra, the twenty-three-year-old fiddler was among twenty-four entrants and finished in fifth place (*Dundee Courier* 1953). Many years later Gonnella competed in the first BBC National Fiddle Competition held in 1969 in Perth. The contest was judged by the celebrated classical violinist Yehudi Menuhin, the famous Scottish fiddler Hector MacAndrew, Watson Forbes, Head of Music for BBC Scotland, and BBC Scotland producer James Hunter. Out of the one hundred and sixteen entries received from all over the United Kingdom, Shetland fiddler Arthur Scott Robertson won the contest while Gonnella did not make the final cut. To my knowledge, Gonnella abandoned the contest circuit as a competitor after the Perth contest, but would later be invited to adjudicate those competitions, a job he performed in both Scotland and North America. Former US National Champion John Turner suggests Gonnella's decision to forgo competition was a business decision by which Gonnella limited the risk of damaging his reputation in the event he did not place first. Perhaps, though, this comment is less inimical than it is factual. As James Hunter notes, "The rich rewards of recordings, TV and other commercial opportunities together with the rise of ceilidh style playing have made the top players wary of risking their reputation—as they see it" (2009, n.p.).

Not relying on his music as sole support, young Gonnella pursued a career as clerk in the Export and Shipping Department of Briggs of Dundee, one he referred to as "pen-pushing." As early as 1960, Gonnella was an active performer in Scottish country dance bands in Dundee including the Cameron Kerr Band with performances in the northwest of Scotland and numerous Home Service broadcasts (*Dundee Courier* 1960). It was during this tenure that he established himself as a performer and recording artist.

Hunter, writing in the capacity of producer of Scottish dance music programs for BBC Scotland, remembered Gonnella even in the mid-1960s as "a very popular fiddler and a jovial personality" (Box and Fiddle Archive). In 1966 Gonnella recorded his first "solo" album, *Scottish Violin Music,* on the Scotdisc label.

The decade spanning 1964 to 1974 was one of intense study for Gonnella of the music of Niel Gow, William Marshall and James Scott Skinner, as evidenced by his 1973 recording of *Scottish Violin Music from the Gow Collection* on the Scottish Records label. It was during this period of time, as well, that Gonnella established a working relationship with the Duke of Atholl at Blair Castle in Perthshire that would prove to benefit not only Gonnella's career, but also would help assure that the less frequently played tunes—especially the jigs—of Gow, Marshall and Skinner became enshrined in the Scottish fiddle canon and were adopted by the revivalist fiddlers of the period. A concert at Blair Castle, and the subsequent album titled *Ron Gonnella Plays the Fiddles of Gow, Marshall and Skinner*, features Gonnella playing the fiddles of Marshall and Gow, as well as Scott Skinner's Stroh fiddle. In a tribute to Gonnella on BBC Scotland's *Take the Floor* program in February 1994, host Robbie Shepherd, Scottish National Orchestra flautist George MacIlwham, and former BBC producer James Hunter discussed Gonnella's performance on the Stroh, an ungainly instrument popular in the early decades of the twentieth century with a metal, trumpet bell-shaped resonator instead of a wooden body. Their conversation gives insight into the Gonnella his close associates knew. Shepherd: "Well, I've seen Ron playing the Stroh fiddle, and so have you many a time. It's a very difficult instrument to handle, let alone record." To which Hunter replies: "Oh, my goodness, you think you ought to pour whiskey into the top of it and drink it, rather than play it, but Ron would never waste good whiskey" (*Take the Floor* 1994). Gonnella owned several violins, among them one made for him in 1980 by Duncan MacDonald of Tullibardine aptly named "The Ron Gonnella." Two years later MacDonald made a violin for Gonnella's mother, Lizzie Duncan (Box and Fiddle). The instrument Gonnella used most often for performance was a 1722 Italian violin made by Carlo Antonio Tanegia. In a tribute to Gonnella, Perthshire musician Nigel Gatherer commented: "I have been told that after his death there were a number of fiddlers desperate to try it to achieve the same wonderful tone that Gonnella produced. In the end it turned out to be a mediocre fiddle; it was the musician who was special, not the instrument" (Gatherer 2013).

Gonnella's musical career as a whole follows what looks to be a well thought out arc, evidence of his keen business acumen rather than of a managing agent. Beginning as a youngster in the late 1940s and early 1950s he learned his craft and played in local dance bands. His groups recorded and distributed their records, and Gonnella was learning to be a professional musician, all the while working as a clerk. He auditioned for a position with BBC Scotland on 22 November 1948 and was gently denied. However, Gonnella was encouraged to re-apply and passed his second audition on 6 December 1950 and was accepted into BBC Scotland's fold. His persistence is evident in the letters he wrote to BBC Scotland representatives in 1953, 1955, and 1956 to request additional broadcast opportunities (BBC Archives). Nonetheless, between 1958 and 1964 Gonnella made nineteen appearances on the Scottish BBC Home Service radio (BBC Genome Project), substantiating fiddler James Alexander's comment that "everyone knew who Ron Gonnella was" (Alexander 2014). Although it was not until 1950 that Gonnella was accepted into BBC Scotland's elite group of solo violin performers, people took notice of him, and he actively promoted himself. The early 1960s were spent performing and making contacts in Scotland and it is easy to imagine that these supporters encouraged Gonnella to travel to North America and supplied introductions for him with their friends in Cape Breton and the Boston area. It is easy, too, to imagine Gonnella's entrepreneurial mind calculating the business opportunities that lay across the sea.

Gonnella continued his in-depth research of fiddlers and fiddle music throughout this period and can be illustrated by his meeting with Mary Ogilvie in October 1964. A recorded interview and accompanying notes included in the Smith Collection in the Archives of Appalachia detail Gonnella's visit to Ogilvie, the daughter of Jimmie Shearer, a prize-winning fiddler of the 1890-1920 era and a "bosom friend of Scott Skinner, who composed a tune in his name" and played for Queen Victoria on occasion. Gonnella tries repeatedly to lead Mrs. Ogilvie into conversation about Skinner, asking in particular about Skinner's tempos and favorite tunes, while she preferred to be recorded playing the piano and the violin with such a well-known musician as Gonnella (Smith Collection WGS-41bD1). This tenuous, brittle link to James Scott Skinner did not dissuade Gonnella from future research; instead, it may have stimulated his interest in the wealth of rarely performed musical material archived in Scotland's libraries and provided the impetus for research he would pursue a decade later to bring the work of the Gows, Marshall, Skinner and others to revivalist and classically trained fiddlers alike.

NORTH AMERICAN CONNECTIONS

After spending the early 1960s establishing a performance reputation in Scotland, Gonnella began traveling to North America in 1965 at the invitation of Scottish music devotee Herbie MacLeod to play, record, and later to adjudicate competitions—an indication that he was a recognized authority on Scottish fiddling to the Cape Breton and New England musicians. This first 1965 tour was a busy one, with concerts in Cape Breton, a concert for

FIGURE 2.2. Gonnella with Stan Hamilton on piano.

the Cape Breton Gaelic Club of Boston followed by a welcome ceilidh at MacLeod's home in Arlington, Massachusetts featuring Gonnella, Angus Chisholm (fiddle), Doug MacPhee (piano), and others, as well as ceilidhs at the home of Herbie McLeod (Smith Collection WGS-35aD1). Album notes from *Scottish Dance Masters Volume 4* indicate that it was in Philadelphia on this first trip to North America that Gonnella heard Ayr (Scotland) native Stan Hamilton and his Scottish dance band, the Flying Scotsmen, with whom Gonnella recorded and played on subsequent trips abroad. Cape Breton pianist Doug MacPhee recalls that in late fall 1968 Gonnella rented a room near his own in Toronto and that Gonnella lived there for a period of four or five months (mustrad.org). One tour in 1967 reunited Gonnella with fiddler Angus Chisholm, guitarist John Allan Cameron, and pianist-fiddler Doug MacPhee at a gathering in Boston with Cape Breton Scots, a concert at Boston's John Hancock Hall sponsored by the Boston Caledonian Club, and an interview with Canadian Broadcast Company (Smith Collection WGS 14-15). We can only speculate that during this period of time, Gonnella had given up his job as clerk to pursue life as a professional musician. Evelyn Murray, collaborator with Gonnella on the album *The New Atholl Collection*, arranged two tours in Canada and New England for him in late 1969-70, functioning as much like an agent as Gonnella would ever have. Murray remembers two concerts with Stan Hamilton, one at the Highlander restaurant in New Hampshire and, by way of contrast, another in the historic Paine Hall on the campus of Harvard University. Fiddler Douglas Lawrence remarked on Gonnella's success in Canada and the United States and his "hobnobbing" with senators such as Senator Robert Byrd of West Virginia, suggesting "It was maybe the first case of commercialism, going to the States, naming tunes after senators" (Lawrence 2014).

The 1969-1970 tour to North America included a stop in Virginia to record a track for an album produced by Colonial Williamsburg Foundation titled *The Music Teacher of Williamsburg* (1970). Liner notes to this eclectic album of period music note that Gonnella selected the music he performed because it was representative of the music Scottish immigrants to the American colonies during the eighteenth century would be familiar with. An article in the *Aberdeen Press and Journal* in November 1975 featured a photo of Gonnella "in eighteenth-century garb for his temporary job as a music assistant in Williamsburg, the living museum of colonial America situated in Virginia" (1975, n.p.). Accounts vary regarding the years between 1970 and the 1980s when Gonnella returned to North America, but most sources agree that it was primarily to adjudicate the United States National Scottish Fiddling Championship in New Hampshire. Gonnella's participation in informal house parties (house concerts) in North America during the 1970s and 1980s is documented in the *Muise Family Collection of Cape Breton and Irish Music* at John J. Burns Library's Irish Music Archives at Boston College and in the Smith Collection at Archives of Appalachia, East Tennessee State University. Janine Muise Randall, daughter of Mary and Johnny Muise, remembers one evening when Gonnella played "a tasteful rendition of 'O Sole Mio'" at their home in Boston (Randall 2015). Summers of 1982 and 1985 Gonnella was a member of the house dance band for Scottish country dance weeks at Pinewoods Camp in Plymouth, Massachusetts. He would return to the United States, again to adjudicate the national competition, in 1983, 1984 and 1985.

THE GONNELLA PERSONA

Despite his acceptance into BBC Scotland's select group of solo violin performers, it would be many years before Gonnella earned representation as a corporate standard for Scottish fiddling and commenced his dialogue with BBC Scotland. Mid-life, Gonnella decided to pursue a teaching career at Dundee Training College, and as Mollie MacCallum, former Head of Primary at Morrison's Academy noted, Gonnella "trained to become one of the increasingly rare breed, a male Primary teacher" (MacCallum 1985). Diploma in hand, he assumed his first (and only) teaching position as a primary teacher at Morrison's Academy in Crieff in September 1973 where he taught until his retirement in 1985. While at Morrison's, Gonnella served as a resident house tutor, ran drama and record clubs, and led school groups on holiday trips to France and Austria. Gonnella's relationship with Morrison's Academy is significant because traditional music was not routinely included in the curriculum for secondary schools until much later. As James Alexander remembered, during his early tenure at Milne High School in Fochabers he was allowed to teach only western classical music to his students (Alexander 2014). A progressive school, with respect to traditional Scottish arts, Morrison's Academy exposed students to Scottish traditional music while providing Gonnella opportunities to teach, perform and share his love for Scottish traditional music. According to MacCallum, Gonnella enriched the musical life of Morrison's Academy by working with recorder groups, the ceilidh band, and school orchestra, teaching music classes and

FIGURE 2.3A. Her Majesty, The Queen's Visit to Morrison's Academy. Photograph by Eunice Gavin. *The New Atholl Collection.*

playing at morning assemblies (MacCallum 2014) (Gonnella 1986,5). School photographs document members of Morrison's traditional dance troupe greeting Queen Elizabeth on her visit to the Academy on 2 July 1985, an occasion for which Gonnella composed "The Queen's Visit to Morrison's Academy" (Gonnella 1986, 5).

FIGURE 2.3B. Gonnella's music for the Queen's visit.

The period of 1973 when Gonnella began his tenure with Morrison's Academy until his retirement in 1985 was one of rising unemployment in Scotland under the governments of Ted Heath and then Margaret Thatcher. Gonnella and I never discussed politics during my lessons, but I sensed that his persuasion was decidedly nationalist. I recall that even in hot Virginia

FIGURE 2.4. Morrison's Academy, Crieff.

summer workshops he mopped sweat from his brow, but he always adjudicated competitions in woolen Highland attire. His message to US Scottish fiddlers was in his dress, it is true, but it was more in his music. The music is my country, he seemed to be saying, and I am proud of it.

During the years at Morrison's, Gonnella entered into the most productive musical period of his life, recording twelve albums between 1975 and 1985. Musically, this period of time coincides with the height of the Scottish instrumental revival (1960–1985) and is concurrent with Gonnella's study and recording of the Scottish fiddle masters, which continued during the latter third of his life. BBC Scotland's national competition in Perth in 1969 was not the last time Gonnella would professionally encounter Yehudi Menuhin. Stuart Eydmann recalls a concert at Queens Hall during the 1985 Edinburgh International Festival that paired his own traditional group, the Whistlebinkies, with Menuhin and a range of Scottish fiddlers, Ron Gonnella (and his "suavely beautiful tone"), Aly Bain (and his "fierce Norse-Shetland virtuosity") and Douglas Lawrence among them (Eydmann 2014).

FIGURE 2.5. "Mr. Menuhin's Delight" concert, Queens Hall, Edinburgh. Gonnella seated row two, center. Menuhin far right row one, standing. Photograph by Antonia Reeve (Eydmann).

The concert was dubbed 'Mr. Menuhin's Delight' for the finale number, a new slow air and reel written for Menuhin by Whistlebinkies' flautist, Eddie MacGuire. Eydmann recalls that the performers were united by a "common fear of disaster" after problems with technology and Menuhin's "fluff" on the first note of the evening. Menuhin recovered, of course, apologized and charged ahead (Eydmann 2014).

CRIEFF

Without much of a reputation as a fiddler to risk, I continued to compete and study with Gonnella over the next four years, winning the United States national competition in 1992. The following summer was spent at home in the States but plans were made to see Gonnella in early spring 1994. My family made its annual pilgrimage to Crieff, now a given destination on our itinerary. The hotel staff knew the attraction for me in Crieff was Gonnella, and they reported that he had died just two weeks before our arrival—on

17 February 1994. Few of his associates were even aware that he was ill. Ron Gonnella was an artist working amidst a society engaged in social and musical change, and I think he would be pleased that he made an enduring contribution. Gonnella managed his own career and made friends of associates on two continents. He was well-known abroad and in Scotland's streets. He was well respected by his peers, but even at the height of his career, he never achieved the near mythical proportions enjoyed by some of his contemporaries. Gonnella loved to play golf and was a middling player, continually challenged by the game, but oh so keen. He was an average tipper who rarely bought rounds or joined in sessions in pubs. He married late in life and had no children to whom he could leave his name or his and Lizzie Duncan's fiddles. Gonnella was a working musician—not an easy vocation, and not a path one rationally takes without a deep conviction that the work he loves has meaning and will endure. Gonnella probably realized that the standards he established for Scottish fiddling would set the bar for competitions in North America and that his extensive work unearthing and recording tunes of eighteenth- and nineteenth-century Scottish composers would find their way not only into the private studios of classically trained fiddlers, but also onto the festival stages of revivalist fiddlers, into pub sessions, and into community ceilidhs. He certainly never imagined that his work would be appropriated for the soundtrack of comedian Mike Myers's axe-murder film, but I think he would have been amused (1993). *The Stage and Television Today* newspaper death notice credits Gonnella with being a "prolific recording artist in radio and recording studios . . . one of Scotland's best-known and busiest concert and broadcasting fiddlers . . . an authority on the history of Scottish music [who] put long-lost Scottish violin tunes into circulation" (Irving 1994).

CHAPTER THREE

Collective Works

While claims to Gonnella's contributions to the Scottish fiddling tradition may be difficult to defend in the absence of a body of corroborating secondary source literature, texts (as we are coming to see them) abound in his recorded work and printed tune collections. We can consider Gonnella's body of work through an examination of his recordings and tune collections; through a comparison with samples of his peers' work during the same time period; reception of Gonnella's work by interview respondents; and through selected case studies of Gonnella's work. Further textual evidence of Gonnella's work is found in appendixes, including: an indicative discography of recordings; tables of tunes according to tune type and composer; contents of tune collections; BBC Scotland broadcasts; and Various ephemera.

To put Gonnella's early work into the context of recorded traditional fiddling, it is helpful to look briefly at recordings by the influential fiddlers of the 1950s and 1960s. Gonnella was preceded, and no doubt influenced, by Scottish fiddlers of the 78 RPM era including Mackenzie Murdoch, David MacCallum and Alec Sim, as well as one of the early extended play albums of solo Scottish fiddle music, Bill Hardie's (1916–1995) *Scottish Country Fiddle* (Hardie 1956). In the late 1950s and early 1960s Ian Powrie (1923–2011) recorded twelve singles, and well-known fiddler Hector MacAndrew

(1903–1980) was featured on a small number of recordings (though his playing is preserved on the 1951 archival recordings of Alan Lomax). Also recording in the 1960s was Shetland fiddler Tom Anderson. The Scots fiddle albums of the late 1950s and 1960s predominately featured airs, strathspeys, reels and hornpipes. During this period MacAndrew included only one jig; Anderson included two originals, while Hardie's recording did not feature any jigs. Marches were ignored on these early recordings and jigs only slightly less. When considered along with the reluctance of BBC Scotland to broadcast solo fiddling, these few recordings, probably difficult to obtain in many locales, formed the very limited foundation from which fiddlers could build their repertoires.

Gonnella's first recording experience came in 1964 when he and pianist Robert Campbell recorded two tracks on a compilation album titled *An Edinburgh Fancy*. Tunes selected for Gonnella's first solo-type fiddle album, *Scottish Violin Music*, were drawn primarily from eighteenth and early nineteenth-century collections, as well as from James Scott Skinner (1843–1927). The album was released in 1966, the year of one of Gonnella's successful United States concert tours, and most likely would have been available to American audiences during the course of his tour performances, as well as in Scotland. As early as 1966, Gonnella was recording tunes that were difficult to access, due to the fact that the earliest collections were out of print. As Gonnella explained,

> The selections on this record cover many facets of Scots fiddle music culled mainly from the great collections of Scott Skinner and the Gow family. Scott Skinner was rightly known as the "Strathspey King", but his genius found perhaps its finest expression in his lyrical slow airs, several of which are included in this record. So, too, are some the of the best slow airs from the extensive collections compiled by the Gows, that majestic air by Crockat "The Braes of Auchtertyre" and two selections from the Simon Fraser collection with its associations with Bonnie Prince Charlie (Gonnella 1966).

Possibly due to renewed interest in the traditional fiddle canon by revivalist fiddlers, recordings by solo fiddlers began to flourish during the 1970s, not only those by Gonnella, but also by his peers. However, jigs continued to be overlooked in comparison with other tune types. Notable solo fiddle recordings of the decade include those featuring the playing of Arthur Scott Robertson, as well as a compilation that included the playing of Robertson, Willie MacPherson, Angus Cameron, and Florence Burns—all competitors

FIGURE 3.1. *Scottish Violin Music* (1966).

at the 1969 Perth national competition. Bill Hardie's 1975 album, *The Music of Scott Skinner*, featured the playing of Hardie, as well as reproductions of Skinner's early recordings on cylinder and very early vinyl discs (Hardie 1975). The 1950s historical recordings of James F. Dickie were issued in 1976 as *James F. Dickie's Delights: Scottish Fiddling in the Style of Scott Skinner.* Aonghas Grant and Yla Steven recorded fiddle albums in the late 1970s, and Steven was also featured on *The National Fiddle Championship* recording (1977) along with Douglas Lawrence, Ian Laing, Donald Montgomerie and Angus Cameron.

While these recordings illustrate the growing revival of interest in Scottish fiddling, the recording of jigs were still sparse in comparison to the

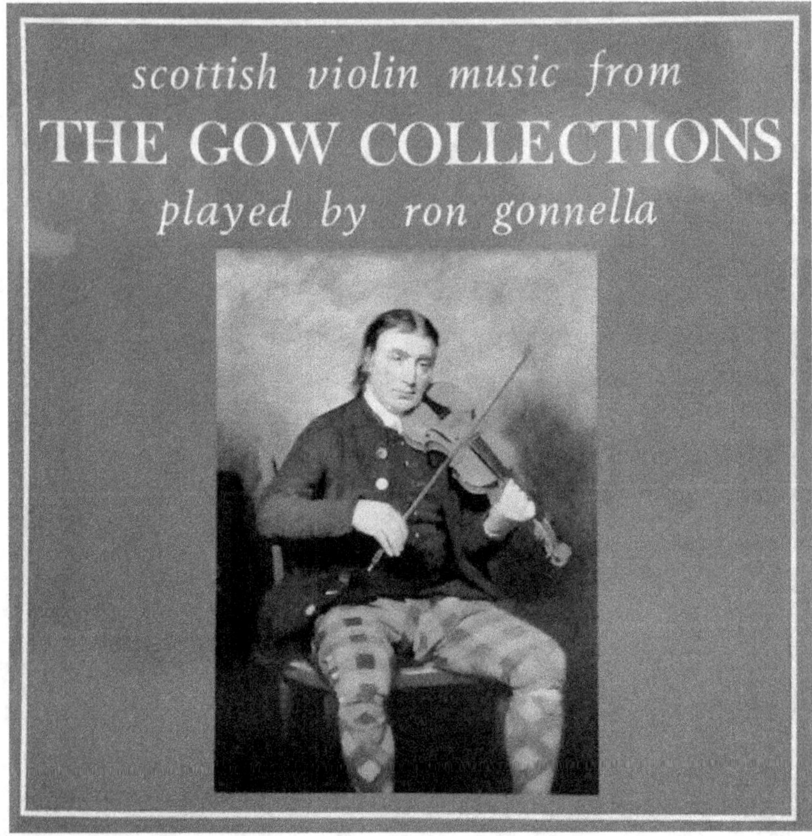

FIGURE 3.2. *Scottish Violin Music from the Gow Collections* (1973).

more popular tune types and to the number of jigs included on Gonnella's recordings. Gonnella's dedication to promoting underrepresented traditional composers continued with his second solo album, *Scottish Violin Music From the Gow Collections*, which was also released in the early 1970s (Gonnella 1973). The album, whose cover features the well-known Sir Henry Raeburn portrait of Niel Gow and used by permission of the National Galleries of Scotland, includes airs, strathspeys, hornpipes and jigs by Niel Gow and sons Nathaniel and William, as well as others.

Two years later Gonnella released *Fiddler's Fancy* (1975), his third fiddle album, beginning his long association with Lismor Recording. The album features the music of William Marshall and James Scott Skinner and in-

FIGURE 3.3. *Burns Night* (1977).

cludes many of today's best-known Skinner and Marshall airs, strathspeys, reels, and jigs. The album was reviewed in the article, "More Scots Folk Music Going Around," in *The Press and Journal* on 26 March 1975. In this rare appraisal, the reviewer noted the increasing popularity of Scottish music and labeled *Fiddler's Fancy* as the "best" of the Lismor recordings (1975). Gonnella continued to record lesser-known tunes throughout the decade including his 1976 recording, *Fiddle Gems*. This album featured music from the second collection of Captain Simon Fraser. Gonnella's liner notes underscore the scarcity of available fiddle manuscripts during the 1970s: "Wonder at the strange fate of Fraser's second collection which was lost for nearly a hundred years, found in a second-hand bookshop in 1952 by Professor Sydney Newman of Edinburgh University and now generously made available by their Keeper of Manuscripts" (Gonnella 1976).

Gonnella's comments illustrate his commitment to historical research and illuminate his role in increasing access to eighteenth and nineteenth-century collections through his solo fiddle recordings. Gonnella also recorded many of the melodies we associate with Robert Burns' lyrics on his fourth Scots fiddle recording of the 1970s, *Ron Gonnella's Burns Night,* such as "The Bonnie Wee Thing," "Corn Riggs," "Auld Lang Syne," "John Anderson My Jo," and "Ay Waukin O" to name a few (Gonnella 1977).

During the decade of the 1980s, his most productive recording period, Gonnella recorded fourteen albums—seven solo fiddle albums and seven dance band albums. As Gonnella's discography grew, so too did his commitment to making the compositions of Gow, Marshall and Skinner accessible to his listeners and filling the void left by out-of-print tune collections. Gonnella's most unique, and perhaps best-known album, was *Ron Gonnella Plays the Fiddles of Gow, Marshall and Skinner* (Ross Records 1982). The back cover of the album features the best-known portraits of Gow, Marshall and Skinner, all used by permission (Duke of Atholl, Scottish National Portrait Gallery, Dundee Museum and Art Gallery)—showing the respect accorded to Gonnella's playing, but illustrated even more so in the use of three fiddles once played by Neil Gow, William Marshall, and James Scott Skinner (Gonnella 1982). This album represents the first time the Gow and Marshall instruments have been recorded, and the first use of the Stroh fiddle since Skinner himself used it to record commercially. The use of the fiddles of Gow, Marshall and Skinner created great interest in the repertoire at a time when availability of the tunes from recordings would have been limited. I contend that Gonnella's tracks of the jigs "Miss Gordon of Park" and "Miss Hannah's Jig," in particular, led to the increased popularity of these tunes and established a level of jig playing that many fiddlers aspired to. Even today, among the generations of fiddlers who remember his playing, Gonnella is associated with these jigs.

Alongside his recordings, Gonnella encouraged and oversaw the restoration of Niel Gow's fiddle, which is displayed in Blair Castle. An unusual addition to the music on the album *Ron Gonnella Plays the Fiddles of Gow, Marshall and Skinner* is the spoken Introduction by His Grace, The Duke of Atholl, in which he speaks briefly about the restoration of the fiddle after one hundred years of rest, and Gonnella's "great skill" at playing it. In his tribute to Gonnella, John Mason, former director of the Strings of

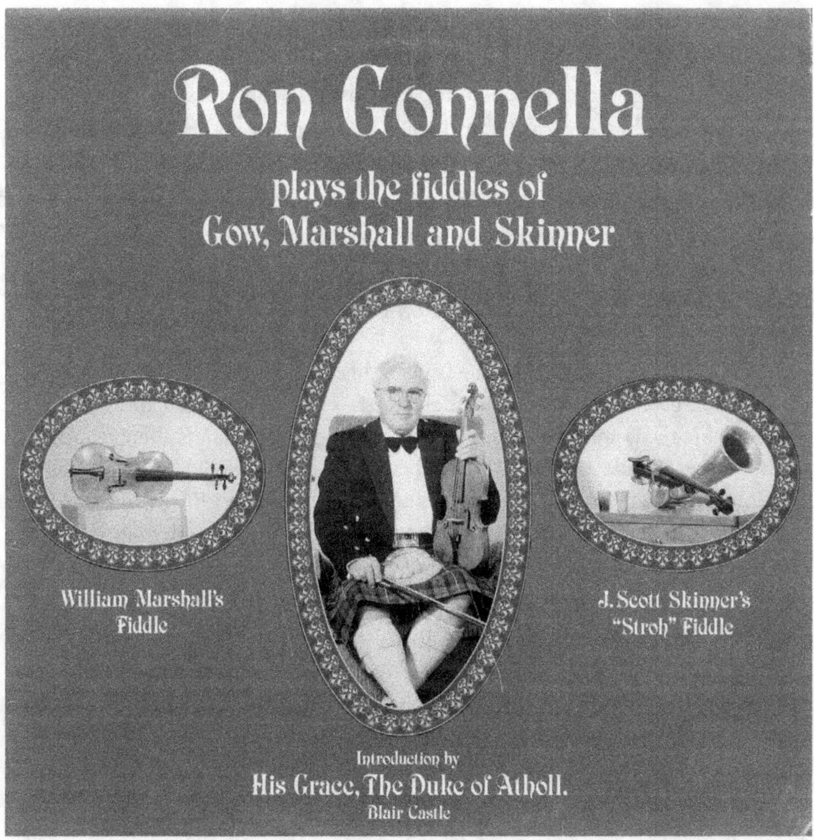

FIGURE 3.4. *Ron Gonnella plays the fiddles of Gow, Marshall, and Skinner* (1982).

Scotland, recalls Gonnella's role as "guiding light" in establishing the Niel Gow Memorial Trust, an organization formed to promote Gow's music and the restoration of Gow's gravestone at Little Dunkeld Cemetery. Mason notes the Fiddle Rally in Perth Town Hall, the culmination of Gonnella's fundraising efforts and James Hunter's assistance in televising the show on BBC Scotland (*Box and Fiddle* 2016).

SCOTTISH FIRESIDE FIDDLE CHATS: CASE STUDY

Gonnella again plays and records the fiddles of Gow and Marshall on his *Fireside Fiddle Chats* series, yet another example of his commitment to the reinvigoration of fiddle music of the eighteenth and nineteenth centuries—in this case, the music of Burns, Skinner, Marshall, Simon Fraser, the Gows and others; and his commitment to researching the history of Scottish fiddling. Three cassette tapes comprise the Fireside Fiddle Chats series, released between 1982 and 1985. The project was self-produced on Gonnella's Barga label and was also available in the United States through Evelyn Murray's Atholl Brose label. The unique recordings, a mixture of music and narrative, provide a cultural, historical, and geographical context for the Scots fiddle repertoire. The descriptive notes to volume one, *Robert Burns and Niel Gow Presented by Ron Gonnella*, state,

> Ron Gonnella has combined the fruits of his countless broadcasts and long series of recordings of Scottish Fiddle Music with his chatty and informative radio and television style to produce fascinating musical chats about Robert Burns and the fiddle and one of the father figures of Scottish Fiddle Music, Niel Gow. Listen as Ron unfolds the intriguing story of Robert Burns' deep love for his native fiddle music and its intimate links with his life and songs (1985).

This cassette features Gonnella playing airs from the Gow collections on the Gow fiddle. "This, then," the liner notes states, "is a recording which can transcend distance and time and at the touch of a button, brings two of Scotland's legendary figures, Robert Burns and Niel Gow, right into your home as the sounds and accents of Scotland, in words and music, unfold round your own fireside" (1985).

With the second volume, *J. Scott Skinner: also "Have you the Gaelic?,"* Gonnella explores the music of the northeast of Scotland "as epitomized by James Scott Skinner" and, what Gonnella refers to as "the Gaelic fiddle music of Captain Simon Fraser." The majority of the tunes are played on Skinner's own recording fiddle known as "The Stroh," with other tracks taken from Gonnella's 1984 *Stradivarius* recording. Gonnella invites the listener to "follow the Strathspey King from his early years, through his triumphs and disappointment, and learn the stories behind many of his compositions as he wended his flamboyant way through the Scotland of yester year" (1985). Gonnella plays on "bitter-sweet memories" of Bonnie Prince Charlie and the Jacobite Rebellion to entice listeners to learn about their musical past, or as Gonnella writes, "explore the fortunate heritage of the Scot":

> Turn back the pages of history to the Jacobite Rebellion in the company of Captain Simon Fraser, of which a president of the Gaelic Society of London once said, "I have never heard anyone make the fiddle speak Gaelic as

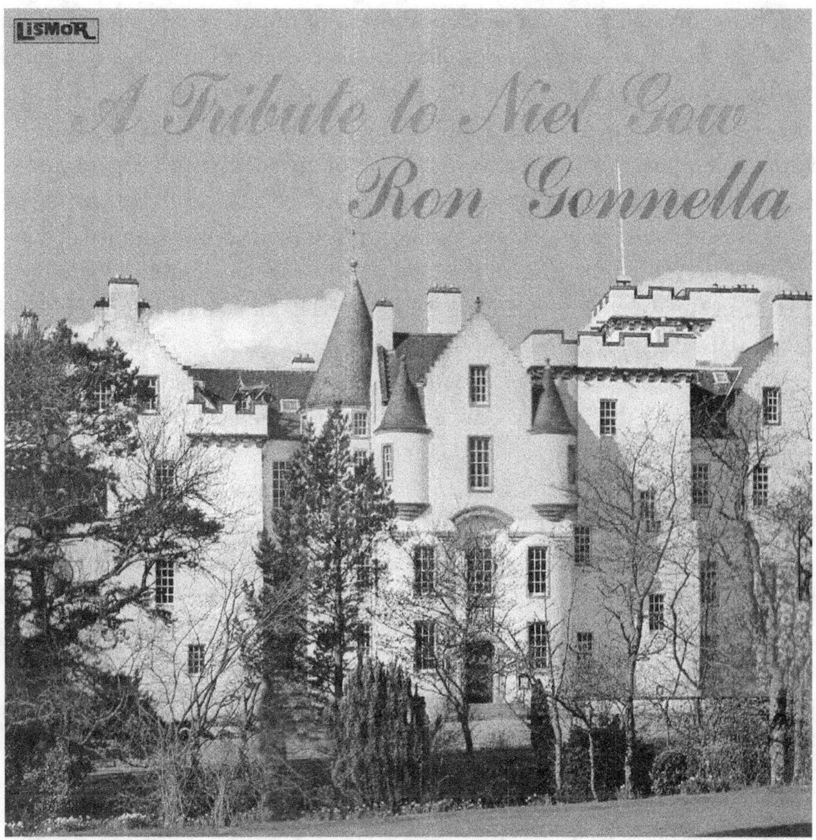

FIGURE 3.5. *A Tribute to Niel Gow* (1987).

> beautifully." Re-live the bitter-sweet memories of Bonnie Prince Charlie from a different perspective, that of the Fiddle Music of Gaeldom (1985).

A Gordon For Me and Playing Second Fiddle is the final recording in the *Fireside* series, also recorded in 1985, in which, "Gonnella moves on to consider the music of men with whom posterity has dealt a shade unfairly and who, despite exciting and original compositions, tend, at best, to remain somewhat shadowy figures in fiddle music" (1985). The title of the recording, while primarily a reference to William Marshall, also includes tunes by Robert Mackintosh, Peter Milne and the Lowe family—musicians who Gonnella describes as "steeped in the craft and lore of the fiddle" (1985). "Their real value has often gone unsung," asserts Gonnella, even though "their music stamps them as true masters of the art" (1985). It is highly doubtful that Gonnella's interest and motivation in researching, learning, and recording the cassettes was the hope of a hefty financial return. Rather, the recordings illustrate Gonnella's work to bring attention and exposure to unsung composers, highlighting the beauty of the Scottish fiddling tradition.

Another outcome of Gonnella's (and others') efforts was the formation of the annual Glenfiddich Fiddle Championship at Blair Castle. Gonnella's continued interest in the music of the Gow family was the focus of *A Tribute to Niel Gow* (Lismor 1987), featuring music by Niel, John, and Nathaniel Gow, along with tunes written by others in Niel Gow's honor (Gonnella 1987).

On behalf of the international niche market of Scottish country dancers, the Royal Scottish Country Dance Society produced a number of albums featuring Gonnella. Gonnella's dance band albums recorded in the 1980s include five albums in the *Scottish Dance Masters* series, all recorded for the RSCDS. Gonnella was featured on a large number of compilation albums—thirty-two at last count—with half the albums issued after his death. On these compilations he is most often featured playing jigs or slow airs. The jigs featured most often are "Bonnie Dundee," "The Provost of St. Vigean's," and "The Corner House," along with the slow airs "The Rowan Tree" and "Skinner's Cradle Song"; though one that may have greatly amused Gonnella, or at least amused his friends, titled *Ariel Yoga,* featured, of all things (or perhaps most fittingly), the strathspey "Niel Gow's Fiddle!" Gonnella's recording career continued into the 1990s with his last solo album, *Ron Gonnella's Fiddle Magic,* produced on his own Barga label in 1992. At the time of his death, Gonnella was at work on a new album and was just finishing a recording project for *Historic Scotland* for which he composed a set of tunes titled "The Honours of Scotland."

PUBLISHED TUNE COLLECTIONS

If recordings of eighteenth and early nineteenth-century solo fiddle music were limited in the 1960s, 70s and 80s, printed tune collections were even scarcer. Some of the main collections published in the 1970s include *Rob Gordon's Book of Scottish Music* (Gordon 1970), *Da Mirrie Dancers* (Anderson 1970), *Kerr's Thistle Collection* (1972), *Marshall's Scottish Airs, Melodies* (published in the US in 1978); *The Fiddle Music of Scotland* (Hunter 1978) and the first two Gonnella tune collections (Gonnella 1977, 1979), yet many eighteen-century collections remained out of print. *The Ron Gonnella Collection of Fiddle Music, Volume One* (1977) includes thirty-six tunes written predominately by the Gows, Marshall and Fraser. The collection includes ten airs, nine strathspeys, eight jigs and six reels, along with a single march, hornpipe and a tune that Gonnella categorizes as a quickstep. All the airs included in the collection were also available on Gonnella's recordings at that time (Gonnella 1977). Volume Two, published in 1979, features the music of Abraham and Robert Mackintosh, Robert and Joseph Lowe, Peter Milne and the Gows. It also features several of Gonnella's compositions—jigs, reels and a hornpipe. In the forward, Gonnella draws special attention to the slow airs "written by that select band of fiddle players who doubled as dancing masters, and who therefore knew intimately the subtle links between music and the dance" (Gonnella 1979). Described as "the first comprehensive instruction book for Scots fiddlers ever written" (Hunter 1988), Alastair Hardie's *The Caledonian Companion* (Hardie 1981) was published in 1981, followed by several facsimiles of late eighteenth century and early nineteenth-century collections. In Gonnella's forward to his third volume of tunes, published in 1982, he notes the recent publication of several new collections of fiddle tunes that have helped to circulate and make available many old airs. Gonnella continues, "Nevertheless, despite the increased number of tunes in print, all but a few of the airs in my third collection are now available for the first time this century" (Gonnella 1982), again illuminating Gonnella's contribution to Scottish fiddling and his role in recording and publishing tunes heretofore difficult to hear and access. The third collection includes fourteen tunes by Gonnella along with those by Joseph Lowe, Robert Mackintosh, the Gows, Marshall, and unknown authors (Gonnella 1982).

Oak Publications issued *The Gow Collection of Scottish Dance Music* in New York in 1986, the same year American publisher ScotPress published Gonnella's fourth volume of tunes, *The New Atholl Collection*. This collection was a collaboration between Gonnella and Evelyn M. E. Murray, an American RSCDS-certified dance instructor who lived in Massachusetts. *The New Atholl* Collection, created "To Commemorate the bi-centenary of Robert Burns' Highland Tour of 1787," features photographs, narrative, and six dances created by Murray that represent locations where Burns stopped during the course of his tour of the Highlands (Gonnella 1986). Gonnella explains the choice of title, stating,

THE NEW ATHOLL COLLECTION
of Scottish Fiddle Music
& Dances

by Ron Gonnella
and Evelyn M.E. Murray

Published by SCOTPRESS

FIGURE 3.6. *The New Atholl Collection* (1986).

The title, *The New Atholl Collection*, reflects the near centenary of the original *Athole Collection* (by James Stewart-Robertson, W.S. of Edradynate, Atholl and Edinburgh), which, when it appeared in 1884, was almost certainly the largest collection of Scottish dance music ever published. Finally, the title also acknowledges gratefully the sterling support of George Iain Murray, 10th Duke of Atholl, and Chief of the Murrays, who apart from

> graciously consenting to write the foreword for this present volume, unfailingly supports the fiddle music of Scotland in the same way his predecessors encouraged and helped Niel Gow (Gonnella 1986, 7).

While there were numerous tune books published, it is likely that most fiddlers had limited access to the collections. Increased availability of print collections of traditional tunes began in 1984 with the founding of The Hardie Press by Alastair and William Hardie for the purpose of promoting Scottish music. Other fiddlers such as Hector MacAndrew, Ian Powrie, Aonghas Grant and Arthur Scott Robertson joined Gonnella in publishing collections of their own original compositions. With the advent of the Internet and e-commerce, these collections were available in 1988 to Scottish fiddlers in the UK and North America. Ten years earlier, though, they were practically nonexistent. One of Gonnella's major contributions, therefore, was to publish collections of tunes from the eighteenth and nineteenth centuries, gleaned from his research on the original documents, many appearing in print for the first time in the twentieth century.

GONNELLA AND BBC SCOTLAND TELEVISION

In the 1980s, Gonnella's music and research was reaching his largest group of listeners, or interpretive community, through his BBC Scotland broadcasts of *Dancing Fiddles* and *On The Fiddle*. Gonnella served as host on eight episodes of *Dancing Fiddles* broadcast from March 1988 to July 1989. A broadcast on 31 May 1989 was billed: "Ron Gonnella introduces a lively mixture of traditional music from the Crieff Hydro Hotel, Perthshire, in the company of George McIllwham, Rhona MacKay, Angus Cameron, Walter Blair and Graham Robb" (BBC Archives). Numerous broadcasts in the *Dancing Fiddles* series featured many of the same musicians. Other BBC programs included features by Gonnella such as *Music Weekly*: "Burns and the Scottish Folk Heritage," "Songs of Praise," and "Scottish Dance Party" (BBC Genome). Gonnella was also heard on BBC broadcasts as a member of dance bands and ensembles. These projects served to reinvigorate and create interest in Scottish fiddling. One particular episode of *On The Fiddle*, filmed on-site in Gow country, gives wide exposure to the musical lives of Niel and Nathaniel Gow; and is successful in grounding the repertoire by establishing a historical, geographical and cultural context for the music. Gonnella guides the viewer to Gow's favorite spots—places where Gow was known to play the fiddle: the famous Oak Tree on the bank of the River Tay, the Hermitage folly overlooking the falls of the River Braan, and the Inver Inn. A visit to Blair Castle includes a performance by Gonnella on the Gow fiddle and a look at the Raeburn portrait of Gow. The program, broadcast, written, narrated and performed by Gonnella, may well represent the culmination of his extensive research and his authoritarian status. The production represents a substantial investment of resources by BBC Scotland and demonstrates the institution's confidence in Gonnella's authority, both as presenter and performer. The content continues to fulfill John Reith's goals for BBC programming by providing both education and entertainment to the viewing audience, two roles that Gonnella expertly assumes.

The most extensive textual body of Gonnella's work resides in his recordings and to a lesser extent, his printed tune collections and BBC Scotland broadcasts. During his lifetime Gonnella released sixteen Scots fiddle albums, six albums of dance music for the Royal Scottish Country Dance Society plus two additional dance albums, and appears on a total of thirty-two compilation albums (at last count), eighteen of which have been released since his death—more albums than any Scottish fiddler to date. Scots fiddle and dance albums boast more than 131 strathspeys, 110 jigs, 107 reels, 94 slow airs, 34 marches, as well as 24 assorted hornpipes, polkas and Scots measures. Overwhelmingly composed by the Gows, Marshall, Skinner and other eighteenth and nineteenth-century fiddle composers, until the 1980s these tunes were largely inaccessible except on recordings. In addition to recordings, Gonnella published four tune collections, three of which contain primarily eighteenth and nineteenth-century fiddle tunes.

INVIGORATING THE PLAYING OF JIGS

Interview data reveals that Gonnella's jig playing was highly regarded, primarily for its distinctive dance-like lilting quality. Several fiddlers go so far as to suggest Gonnella's recordings of jigs have played a role in the revival of interest in jig playing. Gonnella recorded a substantially greater number of jigs than his peers, jigs that were available for all fiddlers with access to his recordings. While it is difficult to determine why the jig was featured on so few recordings of the period or why the tune occupied such a small part of the fiddle performance repertoire, several factors may have contributed to the lowly status of the jig: 1) solo fiddlers were rarely featured on BBC broadcasts, thus jigs were rarely heard; 2) very limited numbers of jigs were included in available published tune collections; and 3) as earlier discussed, recordings of jigs were scarce. In their role of gatekeeper, BBC Scotland determined both performance practice and the repertoire that comprised traditional Scottish fiddle music. Exclusion of solo fiddle playing even extends to the early years of the Edinburgh International Festival. When solo fiddling was featured in the post-war years of broadcasting, it was featured in a dance context. As Peggy Duesenberry notes, "the spotlight on the dance context for fiddle tunes put the listening context, and associated performance practice, into the shadows" (2000, 295). As a result, dance medleys received more broadcast time while other genres were neglected (2000, 295). In his research on Scottish fiddle competitions, Ronnie Gibson notes that the 1969 national competition at Perth, won by Douglas Lawrence, was "important in redefining competitions," but did not yet include jigs (Gibson 2016). Gibson places the earliest inclusion of jigs at the 1977 Gathering of the Clans Championship and notes that jigs may also have been included at Accordion and Fiddle Club competitions from 1978 (Gibson 2016). In 2016, the final year of the Glenfiddich Fiddle Championship, the competition required the performance of a slow strathspey, hornpipe and jig set, as well as the option to select one or more jigs to play in a set by the year's designated composer (Maxwell 2016). Reflecting renewed interest in the performance of jigs, The Hardie Press published *A Fiddler's Book of Scottish Jigs From the 18th and 19th Century*, a collection of sixty-eight jigs selected by Charles Gore and edited by Alastair Hardie in 1998 (Gore 1998). Gonnella's distinctive style of playing jigs likely benefited from his experience of attending dances as a child and from his skill as a dance band musician. His dance band recordings feature many three-jig sets for dance accompaniment, while his solo-type fiddle recordings include single jigs played alongside strathspeys and reels, as well as the more typical three-jig sets. Gonnella's extensive recordings of jigs, many recorded for the first time, increased access to this tune form, set the bar for the performance of jigs and helped to elevate the status of the form.

AIRS, STRATHSPEYS, AND ORIGINAL COMPOSITIONS

The musicians I interviewed also accorded respect to Gonnella's playing of slow airs, commenting on his tone, intonation and interpretation. His repertoire included airs by the best-known composers of the eighteenth and nineteenth centuries, as well as some lesser-known composers of the period. In contrast to his jig playing, Gonnella's strathspey playing has been described as "safe" and lacking a bit of "the devil" in it. Perhaps his interpretation was influenced by the strict rhythmic parameters of dance band playing or simply reflects his own personal preference for a smoother strathspey style. Gonnella's own original compositions are idiomatic, following the expected traditional tune patterns in the number of bars, form, tune contour, rhythm and keys. Douglas Lawrence describes Gonnella's reels and jigs as "jaunty," perhaps not the most complimentary term, but one that captures the spirit and feeling of the tunes—tunes that have inspired both dancers and the creation of new dances; while James Alexander suggests the tunes are more in the line of dance band tunes for "a less purist audience" (2014). While I concur with both fiddlers' assessments, perhaps the real strength of Gonnella's tunes may be in their dance-ability and their potential to inspire. In the opinion of this fiddler, Gonnella's own playing embodies his tunes with a quality that can easily be overlooked on the page. Like his jigs and reels, Gonnella's strathspeys are highly danceable, with the requisite number of snaps and dotted notes, while the melodies of several of his slow airs are quite memorable with room for expression and interpretation. Gonnella's original tunes appear to be rarely played today, but were surely "read through" by the many fiddlers who owned his published collections; and a small number have been recorded on albums by other musicians.

Comparisons with the work of his peers reveal that Gonnella recorded more Scots fiddle albums than other fiddlers during the 1960s, 70s and 80s; he recorded more jigs than all his peers and began recording them earlier than other Scottish fiddlers; he included previously under-performed and unrecorded tunes by eighteenth and nineteenth-century composers, making his recordings one of very few sources for these tunes short of searching library archives for original printed collections. Because BBC Scotland featured so few solo fiddle performers, these recordings take on added significance. Gonnella's influence on the Scottish fiddling tradition up to the 1970s was limited to a relatively small niche audience of fiddlers, country dancers, and traditional music enthusiasts, however, that influence increased dramatically when Gonnella became a featured performer and host for BBC Scotland radio. His commercial success grew in the 1970s and 1980s as his discography increased and his name soon became a familiar word in thousands of households, while his interpretation of the traditional fiddle canon became an institutional standard of that tradition.

CHAPTER FOUR

BBC Scotland and Gonnella

In its role of gatekeeper of cultural standards, BBC Scotland effectively put its seal of approval on not only his interpretation of Scottish fiddle tunes, but on the entire Gonnella "package" and became his most influential public advocate, broadcasting his interviews, performances, and persona to listeners across its broadcast area. Gonnella's largest audience was the (interpretive) community of BBC Scotland listeners who enjoyed his broadcasts, internalized BBC Scotland's endorsement of Gonnella's performance style as a standard for Scottish fiddling, and made him a commercial success by purchasing his recordings. An examination of Gonnella's endorsement by and thirty-year association with BBC Scotland, perhaps Gonnella's most important interpretive community, underscores his contribution to the reinvigoration of eighteenth and nineteenth-century fiddle repertoire and to the increased understanding of the Scottish fiddling tradition.

BBC'S CULTURAL MISSION AND EARLY PROGRAMMING

In the early years of British Broadcasting Company John Reith, BBC founder and first general manager, led the institution on a cultural mission to offer programs with a social purpose that advanced the three Reithian ideals: information, education and entertainment. Reith considered a wireless program to be "concentrated essence" and placed great importance on the personality of the program "speakers," as they would be conveyed directly to listeners' (1924, 17). This Reithian ethos strongly influenced the BBC's role as an arbiter of cultural taste and dictated broadcast standards (McDowell 1992, 28–29). And it was this standard that Gonnella upheld and exemplified. Though the company attempted to reach Scottish listeners through its early programming, BBC's attitude toward the merits of Scottish culture was apparent. In a nod to Scottish culture, BBC Scotland established an ongoing relationship with RSCDS, but recitals of only Scottish fiddle tunes were rare in the early years, and when fiddle tunes were featured, they were performed by classical ensembles. In June 1936, the BBC accepted the idea of decentralization, an increased proportion of regional material, and the notion that broadcasting should be a reflection of the everyday life of a country (McDowell 1992, 37–38). This came at a time of growing national consciousness and the completion of one stage of the devolution of Scottish government affairs. Scottish Regional Director Melville Dinwiddie described the changing attitude, stating, "The Scottish Thistle was shaking in the breeze, ready to prick those who meddled with it, and the heather was alight with national fire" (1948, 14). In spite of decentralization BBC in Scotland continued to take its role as "arbiter of taste" seriously. There was nothing accidental about its message, which upheld the social tenants of BBC. Though by 1936 it had incorporated Scottish programming in its selection of Scottish dance music performed by orchestra ensembles, there was criticism of BBC Scotland programs that featured classical ensembles playing arrangements of fiddle tunes. These performances led listeners to question both the authenticity of the performance and the credibility of the source. At an organizational level BBC Scotland performed the role of cultural gatekeeper. It selected its own gatekeepers and set the policies that determined which messages could pass through the gates—content from a particular point of view in a specific situation with the potential to shape the social reality of the audience. Therefore, the messages selected for broadcast after the arduous process of gatekeeping represent the social tenants of BBC Scotland resulting in a cultural group-think—an interpretive community.

FIDDLING ON AIR

As a result of the gatekeeping standards, air-march-strathspey-reel sets—traditional tune medleys—were not heard as much as dance music.

Duesenberry's interviews with fiddlers who were listeners reveal that while not all fiddlers agreed with the standards, they continued to listen to fiddle broadcasts, primarily to learn new fiddle tunes and keep up with playing trends (2000, 37). Further, broadcasts of fiddle music led fiddlers to purchase recordings and tune books, exposed them to a variety of playing styles and techniques, and in general, inspired them to play. Following the Second World War, broadcasts began to emphasize more traditional medleys rather than stilted arrangements of fiddle tunes played by orchestral players. However, as Duesenberry notes, while "allowances were made for 'rough' performers if they represented a distinct local tradition of music-making," this exception did not apply to fiddle music where solo performers were still required to pass an official Music Department audition (2000, 86–87). The BBC Written Archive Centre contains audition reports for only three solo fiddlers: Ron Gonnella, Hebbie Gray, and Angus Cameron. Each of the teenage fiddlers was invited to play for a panel of BBC Scotland adjudicators and Cameron and Gray passed their initial audition. Gonnella was asked to play fiddle music by James Scott Skinner and art music by Frederic Chopin, but received a polite letter suggesting a second audition in eighteen months to two years (2000, 145). Gonnella passed his second audition in 1950, but received no immediate broadcast opportunities—most likely because BBC Scotland had little interest in solo fiddle performances, as well as the fact that he was in competition with older more experienced players such as Hector MacAndrew. Gonnella's audition reports from the late 1950s and early 1960s include remarks about style, authenticity, snaps, tone, phrasing, intonation, good timing, open tone and skill as a broadcaster, revealing the elements the BBC continued to find important (2000, 148).

The 1970s saw the revival of Scottish nationalism and discussion centered on whether radio should reflect the cultural diversity of the country or whether it should promote and strengthen a national identity (1992, 283). In line with the tide of growing national consciousness, BBC Scotland elected to support the latter. However, BBC Scotland continued its role as cultural gatekeeper and was still reluctant to broadcast fiddle tunes as solo performances. Clearly, BBC Scotland took its role of gatekeeper and caretaker of cultural standards regarding Scottish fiddling very seriously. Its early preference for classically trained violinists over fiddlers, its reliance on in-house ensembles for performance, and its selection of tunes to include in the "traditional" canon illustrate BBC Scotland's strict control over the performers and material allowed to be broadcast. Even after BBC succumbed to pressure from its listeners to provide more representative programming and included country dance band entertainment, it maintained its high degree of quality control by establishing a rubric for reel-playing that effectively identified the "refined" players who were accepted into the solo performance pathway and the "rough" players who occupied the dance band track. BBC's clearly stated and unchanging core values of education, information, and entertainment were conveyed in the expectation that the music it presented would be a refined sound, appropriate to the cultural level it wanted to project. In response to these expectations, BBC Scotland management accepted Ron Gonnella into its fold. Interestingly, BBC Scotland's decision to endorse Ron Gonnella as the standard bearer for Scottish fiddling was a conscious editorial decision made by cultural gatekeepers who controlled both the content and the accessibility of information to its listeners.

GONNELLA'S BROADCASTS

Gonnella's association with BBC Scotland began in earnest in the early 1980s. As a member of the BBC Scotland's community of performers, Gonnella's contributions to BBC Scotland broadcasts of fiddle music ranged from solo performer and dance band member to introducer, presenter and host. Gonnella served as host on eight episodes of *Dancing Fiddles* broadcast from March 1988 to July 1989 that featured "a lively mixture of traditional music." Other BBC programs included features by Gonnella such as *Music Weekly:* "Burns and the Scottish Folk Heritage," *Songs of Praise* and *Scottish Dance Party* (BBC Genome). Gonnella was also heard on BBC broadcasts as a member of dance bands and ensembles. He was later featured on BBC television as host of the series *On The Fiddle*. In each broadcast Gonnella interviewed well-known fiddlers, including Angus Fitchet, Tom Anderson, Douglas Lawrence, and Willie Hunter, as well as bandleader Jimmy Moir. Gonnella's choice of guests and narrative produced valuable portraits of Scottish musicians in the context of the times they lived and worked that expanded public familiarity with and knowledge of Scottish music, in particular fiddling. For musicians in the listening audience, the programs increased the availability of eighteenth and nineteenth-century repertoire and expanded knowledge of its interpretation, all the while contributing to Gonnella's image as an authoritative figure. An indicative table of Gonnella's radio and television broadcasts can be found in appendix C.

On The Fiddle

A brief semiotic case study of *On The Fiddle* reveals the specific ways in which BBC Scotland used Gonnella's skill as a presenter, his expert knowledge of Scottish fiddling, and his persona to construct a version of the Scottish fiddling tradition for a million people in its listening audience. It also underscores BBC Scotland's careful selection of program hosts—choosing only those who could successfully communicate and represent the goals of the company. However, we will find that listeners and viewers do not always interpret messages exactly the way the company intended, rather, they determine their meaning of the text based on the expectations of their own interpretive community.

While an in-depth study of semiotics and multimodality is outside the scope of this work, a consideration of the meaning-making resources that contribute to Gonnella's persona and position as an authoritarian presence on BBC Scotland can enhance our study. The focus on the "sign," the central concept of semiotics, gradually led to interest in the way in which semiotic "resources" are used, an approach known as social semiotics. Van Leeuwen defines semiotic resources as "signifiers, observable actions and objects that have been drawn into the domain of social communication and that have a theoretical semiotic potential constituted by all their past uses and all their potential uses . . ." (2005, 4). Similarly, a multimodal approach, Machin asserts, considers the way that signs are used in combination with their meaning described as "potential" instead of "fixed" rather, "the meaning of the sign is realized in context through combinations with other signs" (2007, ix). Thus, as Carey Jewitt explains, "all communicational acts are shaped by the norms and rules operating at the moment of sign making, and influenced by the motivations and interests of people in a specific social context" (2012, n.p.). This brings us back to BBC Scotland's manipulation of the "message" and Gonnella's selection as its representative. It also brings us back to the notion of interpretive communities and the ways our three identified groups interpret and react to Gonnella's BBC Scotland television broadcasts.

Recorded at "Broadcasting House" in Aberdeen in 1982, each episode of *On The Fiddle* is just under fifteen minutes in length and features music and conversation with a well-known Scottish musician. The pictures included in the analysis are photographs taken of various scenes from a copy of the broadcast recording; thus, the images reflect the age and quality of the

FIGURE 4.1. Presenter Ron Gonnella (*left*) with guest Angus Fitchet.

forty-year-old recording. My own reading position and understanding will guide this subjective analysis and interpretation of the semiotic resources on display in the program episodes, because, as van Leeuwen and Jewitt assert, "Analysis is a sociopolitical relevance, not some theoretical abstraction" (2001, 186). These semiotic resources include a range of elements from typography, poses, setting, gaze, objects, distance, to the positioning of the viewer.

Letterform, or typeface, is one element that carries meaning potential, because as Machin explains, "the basis of the transport of meaning of letters can be clearly found in simple physical and cultural associations" (2007, 83). Thus, aesthetic choices become purposeful with informational value, and as such, become a channel for communication. More specifically, the use of thicker lines communicates something solid, immovable, and, perhaps, even proud. In the case of the typeface used for Gonnella's program, it features tall bold face with capital letters. The height and mixture of straight and curved letters introduces the idea of sophistication and a slightly informal "feel." Color can also be employed to communicate meaning. Here, the

FIGURE 4.2. Gonnella with guest Tom Anderson (*right*).

use of the color white can suggest sophistication, though the color choice here may be more for its contrast to the generally dark background of the set. However, I assert the selected typeface for *On The Fiddle* goes farther than just the communication of these qualities. By featuring a font closely associated with the work of Charles Rennie Macintosh, the renowned Scottish architect, designer and artist, the typeface suggests the continuity of artistic tradition, and one could even go so far as to suggest, nationalistic pride. The typography of each participant's name expresses no particular hierarchy or importance, with all titles displayed in the same typeface, size and placement, though Gonnella's name, as presenter, is featured prior to the name of his guest.

Setting, another semiotic resource, can communicate a particular set of values and give the product the desired qualities through the objects or props. As Machin suggests, "often the presence of certain objects and their connotive powers are so taken for granted that it is hard to think of a particular context without them" (2007, 33). While this setting is certainly not the only context for fiddling or a conversation with an acquaintance,

FIGURE 4.3. Gonnella welcoming the viewer.

BBC Scotland has loaded the setting with qualities they wish to associate with Scottish fiddling and communicate to the viewer. The opening frame of each program episode features a close up of the fireplace mantel where two fiddles are placed end to end with a bronze horse statue placed in between. While the horse is given salience at the very beginning of the program and may suggest qualities such as nobility, strength or intelligence, it is part of a larger paradigm whose purpose is to produce meaning—the impression of a solid, respectable sitting room or library. The dark wood paneling and rich maroon carpet suggest luxury and masculinity; a gentle fire in the fireplace, potted plants and lamps add to the ambience of the setting (while providing a contrast to the darkness of the paneled walls). The setting of *On The Fiddle* is indexical of high culture, expertise and authority, and reveals the ideology of BBC Scotland and its own construction of reality. While this may well be the dominant reading, the interpretive community of revival fiddlers may decode the message in another way, or as Stuart Hall calls it, a "globally contrary" way (1973, 517). Whereas the community of revivalist fiddlers may welcome the opportunity to add to their repertoire and gain historical knowledge,

Gonnella's ideological and sociopolitical positions, his association with the "establishment" and his commercial success, align him with mainstream culture and society—a position the revivalist community rejects.

The physical placement of participants can serve as another semiotic resource. In each program Gonnella and his guest face each other seated in rather ornately carved straight-back wooden chairs that are placed on either side of the fireplace, the host's chair only slightly foregrounded on the left side. In the case of interviews, traditional positioning places the interviewer on the left, which, according to Machin, invites us to identify with him or her as the given or the established, while the guest is in the position of "the new" (2007, 142–43). The *absence* of microphones on the set contributes to the intimacy of the setting and, in spite of attire, the informality of sharing a tune with a friend. "The Crieff Hydro March," a fiddle tune composed by Gonnella, begins each episode. Gonnella and his guest play the tune together and it is likely that the guest would have learned the tune specifically for the program. Perhaps the choice of an original tune was a way for Gonnella to add a personal touch, share his tune with other fiddlers, or to popularize his tune with the audience (though he is not credited as composer). Whatever the reason for the choice, "The Crieff Hydro March" carries meaning potential. It features a major key signature, brisk tempo, sweeping melody, and a rhythmic "swing" to produce a tune that is bright and energetic. While the theme music may connote a slightly different thing to each person, it is a tune that likely communicates a friendly, welcoming tone for the broadcast. Attributes such as dress or hairstyle, also semiotic resources, can tell us something about the participant. A simple pose can communicate a certain kind of person, a particular way of living, or denote a set of values that a producer wants to associate with a particular product. In the programs, Gonnella and his guest sit upright but not stiffly with both feet on the floor, communicating respectability and "proper" manners. Contributing to Gonnella's authoritative demeanor is his professional, yet relaxed, attire of dress shirt, trousers, and tie, echoed in the dress of his guests. At the end of the opening fiddle tune Gonnella turns toward the camera to address the viewer, saying: "Hello, glad you could join us this Sunday evening." Gonnella smiles, his mood of address is warm, he introduces his guest to the viewer, then turns to enthusiastically welcome his guest. Gonnella's "gaze"—his direct eye contact with the viewer—is very brief, but as Machin states, "it asks something of you in an imaginary relationship" (2007, 111).

FIGURE 4.4. Guest Willie Hunter.

Along with "gaze, "angle of interaction," and "distance" are semiotic resources that help position the viewer, and have the potential to affect the way the viewer relates to and evaluates the participants (Machin 2007, 109). While the distance changes very little during the episodes, there are times when Gonnella or his guest is featured alone in a more intimate way, but the majority of the time the angle includes both participants, placing them on an equal plane and evoking conversation between friends rather than establishing a hierarchy of qualifications.

In the five episodes of *On The Fiddle,* all of Gonnella's guests are white men, and with the exception of Douglas Lawrence, are between the ages of forty-nine and seventy-two, reflecting a privileged setting. Though the number of episodes is very limited, non-representation of women or those of other ethnicities is conspicuous in today's culture. Considering non-representation in the context of the time, however, there would have been quite a small pool of fiddlers from which to draw (other than white men) and certainly none with the notoriety and public exposure of Gonnella's

FIGURE 4.5. Set piece for the *On the Fiddle* broadcast.

guests. As presenter for *On The Fiddle*, Gonnella's choice of guests and narrative produced valuable portraits of Scottish musicians in the context of the times they lived and worked, expanding public familiarity with and knowledge of Scottish music, in particular fiddling. For musicians in the listening audience, the programs increased the availability of eighteenth and nineteenth-century repertoire and expanded knowledge of its interpretation. The programs also explored the composition and performance of contemporary fiddle repertoire. Through the process of coding, I identified three themes which are present across each broadcast—each dataset: 1) learning, 2) experience, and 3) repertory. Each broadcast also contained a subset identified as "memories." Data illustrates the difference in the way fiddlers learn to play. Gonnella shows sensitivity to not only his guests, but also his viewers' learning backgrounds, welcoming everyone into the community of Scottish fiddlers of *On The Fiddle*. Conversations about "learning" lead to discussions of performance "experience" showing that though experience is a common theme, it comes in many different forms, as

Gonnella understands, while conversations about repertoire, the third theme, revealed personal preferences in both the selection of tunes, performance practice, and the creative process of composition.

Episodes of *On The Fiddle* are generally unscripted although it is apparent that Gonnella has a clear-cut direction in which he would like the conversation to go. Certainly, his guest's responses to his questions are not scripted as indicated by Angus Fitchet's spirited anecdotes of playing by the seat of his pants and being pelted by whelks, or Jimmy Moir's mirthy reminiscences of directing hundreds of fiddlers intent on their own interpretation, to the monosyllabic answers Gonnella coaxes from the somewhat dour Jimmy Shand "who's not giving anything away." Gonnella's skill as an interviewer is illustrated in the way he is able to deflect the conversation back to his guest or turn an exchange that could have ended on a negative note into an exchange that flatters the guest, a strategy seen many times in the course of these short programs. In doing so Gonnella not only reaffirms his guest's honored status as musician, but also contributes to the viewer's understanding of Gonnella's character and personality. The framing of the music and talk is essential to maintaining the intimate conversational tone of *On The Fiddle.* The dialogue between presenter and guest is often an emotional reaction to the music played, while the music can serve as something of a metaphor for the meaning of the dialogue. Tom Anderson's playing of his own composition "Da Slockit Light" with its memories of his late wife and his visit to the village where he was born illustrates this relationship between music and talk. Gonnella and Willie Hunter talk about the advantages and disadvantages of living in Shetland which leads to conversation about fiddle makers and local composers, which in turn leads to the performance of "John Pottinger's Compliments to Ronnie Cooper," a tune written by a local Shetland musician. Gonnella's knowledge of all the tunes played on each episode, frequently joining his guest's performance when invited, enhances the notion of authority and his appreciation of the significance of each guest's tune choice to both the guest personally and to Scottish fiddling generally. The relaxed interaction of host and guests provides evidence that Gonnella's presentational style is authoritative, yet at times almost self-deprecating, never self-serving and always complimentary of his guests' accomplishments, technical ability, and experience in his choice of phrases like "one of the top two fiddlers," "first class," "the greatest living exponent," and "right at the top." The overall impression of the programs is that, without having to justify it to anyone, Gonnella is the musical equal of his guests and that he and guests are having a wonderful time, a feeling that includes his viewing audience as well. These qualities—the ability to put his guests at ease and to direct the conversation, his professional knowledge of the repertoire, its performance and significance—teamed with Gonnella's warm and jovial personality and the unstated authority that came with his impressive recording career and status as a BBC Scotland representative to project a persona that, as James Alexander observed, made Ron Gonnella "a household word."

BBC Scotland was wise to form a close association with Gonnella—one that spanned more than thirty years. He established a sense of homophily with his audiences during the height of Scottish nationalism during the 1970s, and as a result, both the corporation and a large segment of the listening audience embraced him. Especially in its later televised broadcasts, Gonnella's nationalistic pride was often apparent in his choice of Highland dress and his championing of the traditional Scottish canon. Forty years after these original broadcasts, BBC Scotland's favorable response to Gonnella's contributions continues. As West states, "time tends to be the judge, the barometer of acceptability, the arbiter of taste" (West 2012: 13). As late as October 2014, a track by Ron Gonnella was featured on *Take the Floor*, a BBC Radio Scotland program hosted by the late Robbie Shepherd, which illustrates the enduring quality of Gonnella's fiddle playing (BBC Genome). The Music Department of BBC Scotland did more than endorse Gonnella's interpretation of traditional Scottish fiddle tunes and provide broadcast opportunities, though. Through its programming and performer decisions it effectively constructed, for a million people in its listening audience, a version of the Scottish fiddling tradition that drew heavily upon the repertoire and persona of its performers.

CHAPTER FIVE

Fiddlers in Scotland

Continuing to explore the notion of Ron Gonnella as an authority figure and his role in establishing interpretation, repertoire, style and performance standards for Scottish fiddling, the musical communities of revivalist fiddlers and formally trained fiddlers in Scotland join the dialogue. Each of these interpretive communities were influenced by Gonnella's research and recordings of the eighteenth-century masters, including the increased popularity of jig playing.

And while classically trained and revivalist fiddlers may appear to be quite distinct in terms of institutional norms and performance practices, they share a common repertory of traditional tunes. Although the definition of traditional varies in academic circles, both groups, or interpretive communities, of musicians will attest that no longer is a traditional tune necessarily defined by geography or ethnicity. Its origins need not be attached to a historical moment in the past or lost in antiquity, be the work of an unknown composer or a recently published tune collection. Even the requirement of aural transmission from one generation to the next is tested by transmission by digital mediation. Yet one outcome of a communal repertory of tunes remains constant. Something bigger than the music unites these two groups, and that is, as Simon McKerrell points out, "a sense of belonging to a shared culture" (2016, 3).

REVIVALIST FIDDLERS

The descriptive term *revivalist fiddler* denotes what Stuart Eydmann, himself an acknowledged revivalist fiddler, refers to as an untutored fiddler, actively performing (whether informally in sessions or more formally on stage at festivals and concerts) during the Scottish instrumental revival of the 1970s and 1980s (Eydmann 2014). Within the context of the Scottish instrumental revival, Ailie Munro argues the term *revival* is used in two primary ways: to refer to the post–World War II movement in which folk/traditional music was rediscovered and reinterpreted; or as a term that implies the music had been altered so much that it was not "the real thing" (Munro 2001, 157). In *Voicing Scotland,* always cognizant that the folk community is defined within a social context, Gary West's interpretation of revival is influenced by Hamish Henderson's vision that the central task of revivalism is to unite the subaltern folk culture with the hegemonic culture represented by the BBC (165–66). And Owe Ronstrom offers a useful definition of revival for this work, stating, "revival is only partly about 'what once was.' More importantly, it is about 'what is' and 'what is to come.'" Ronstrom continues, "Or to put it differently: in essence revival is a process of traditionalization that goes on in the present, to create symbolic ties to the past, for reasons of the future" (Ronstrom 1996, 325). Perhaps, then, as a raft of scholars assert, the only valid text for interpreting music is the context.

As periodic cultural phenomena, revivals exhibit a number of common elements, two of which are especially pertinent to this research. One element is dissatisfaction with some aspect of the present situation, the remedy of which lies in the past and may require a reinterpretation of history in an effort to find meaning and value (Bithell and Hill 2014, 12-13). Richard Blaustein points out that a strong belief exists that "forms of cultural expression embodying meaningful connections with significant others are in danger of disappearing . . . [resulting in] the selective reinvention of an idealized collective past" (567). In effect, revival activists must devise a new interpretive strategy that is a break from the present, but dependent on the past. This dependency, Fish asserts, "is reflected in the unwritten requirement that an interpretation present itself as remedying a deficiency in the interpretations that have come before it" (1980, 350). Not only must the new interpretation remedy a deficiency, it must also "claim to make the work better" (1980: 351). This presents revival activists with the problem of how to reassign the musical element from the past to the present, or as Hill and Bithell phrase it, how to "decontextualize" from the past and "recontextualize" in the present (2014, 4). This slippery process of decontextualization/ recontextualization indicates instability of the interpretation of that musical element, be it the bowing, the tempo, or the ornamentation of a traditional tune. West appears to agree, stating: "The one thing to avoid with a search for authenticity is to conceive of it as an odyssey back in time until we somehow arrive at a golden age of tradition, a time when that tradition was true or whole, perfectly formed, before time itself had eroded it down to a mere stump" (2012, 83).

Another common aspect of revivals that becomes a challenge for revival activists is how to establish themselves as the legitimate culture bearers, raising the question of the authority of their interpretation. The authority of an interpretation, like an interpretation itself, is meaningful only to those individuals who share a set of standards that makes up an interpretive strategy. The effort by revival activists to establish themselves as the legitimate culture bearers, then, proceeds from the tacit agreement of a community of believers, a legitimacy that may have little to no meaning for another community with radically different presumptions. Stability, Fish argues, lies not in the text, but in the make-up of the interpretive community, and although members may move from one community to another as their set of assumptions changes, the community and its interpretive strategies remain intact (1980, 171–72). As a result, the authority of an interpretation, for example an interpretation of what constitutes the legitimacy of a revival's culture bearers, stays in effect only as long as that community of believers continues to believe. For everyone else, that authority is irrelevant.

While the oral transmission of tradition underpins the institutional practices of revivalist fiddlers, a certain level of technique and knowledge of the folk repertoire may validate a performer more readily than formal musical training. This interpretive community presupposes that session playing and knowledge passed down from prior generations are basic experiences required for membership and validation. This community would not be disappointed with a less polished performance or with giving voice to those with tradition bearer status. They look for under-acknowledged, less visible musicians and traditions, for those that need to be salvaged and preserved, in an effort to capture music before it vanishes from the effects of modernity. Hence Gonnella, a fiddler who was considered commercially successful and "establishment," was not emulated by this group. However, Gonnella's research led to the selective performance and recording of eighteenth-century fiddle tunes, many of which were adopted by revivalist fiddlers as part of their repertoire. Bithell and Hill go even farther, adding that the mid-twentieth century Scottish music revival played a significant part in shaping and disseminating the "post-revival" (2014, 4) canon of fiddle tunes performed today and in establishing the perception of legitimacy and authenticity of its performers. That leads us to the important question, Authentic to what? (West 2012, 83). "Authenticity," Gary West asserts, "is about understanding, about empathy, about *getting* it. It is about seeing and hearing from the inside, taking the time and trouble to get in there" (83). While Gonnella may have represented hegemonic culture in the eyes of BBC Scotland that does not preclude the fact that he got it.

Crossovers between interpretive musical communities are not uncommon. Fiddler and music publisher Christine Martin, for example, considers herself a classically trained fiddler, yet plays traditional music with a variety of groups (Martin 2017). Nor is the line between revivalist and classically trained fiddler clear-cut for traditional music educator Jo Miller who identifies with the preservationist impulse of the revival, but does not necessarily recognize the two schools as different and distinct categories. Instead, she values the individual "voice" of fiddlers and opts instead for a diversity of styles (Miller 2017). Stuart Eydmann strongly identifies with the revivalist movement, performing in various venues with the band Whistlebinkies since the 1970s. Eydmann's faction sees little advantage in a classical background and, like Miller, values personal expression and interpretation without threatening the music. Eydmann characterized revivalist fiddlers, stating,

> Many of my generation of revival looked more closely to what we saw as traditional players and sought them out and their company. The setting of their playing, pubs, informal ceilidhs and festivals, etc., was much more suited to our social lives. Classical training was not seen as an immediate advantage or the best route to get to where we wished to be (2017).

Although the community of revivalist fiddlers has remained fairly stable for over forty years and the community of classically trained fiddlers spans centuries, that stability is only temporary, Fish explains: "Interpretive communities grow larger and decline, and individuals move from one to another; thus, while the alignments are not permanent, they are always there, providing just enough stability for the interpretive battles to go on, and just enough shift and slippage to assure that they will never be settled" (Fish

1980, 171–72). Of the community of classically trained fiddlers Eydmann contends, "this school of playing existed in parallel and almost separately to the folk music revival, though there would be crossovers where an individual might come and go across it" (Eydmann 2014). Eydmann asserts the members of the classically trained school of playing had an uncompromising musical identity "whereas revivals *are* a compromise full of borrowings and fusions," and notes the strong contrast between the access that fiddlers such as Gonnella had to advanced training and the "self-taught muddle-through kind of attitude" of the revivalists (Eydmann 2014).

FORMALLY TRAINED FIDDLERS

For the small community of Gonnella's peers, the classically trained fiddlers who are at home in the realms of classical and traditional music, the language of the dialogue is expressed in both an advanced level of performance execution and an in-depth knowledge of both the classical and traditional canons. Membership is evaluated on professional knowledge, technical finesse, execution, and stage presence, and its members share not one, but two cultural heritages. This was certainly the case with Gonnella, whose musical skills, performing experience, and scholarly research on the Scottish fiddling tradition gave him confidence and professional knowledge to interpret the music he played, adding another source to Gonnella's authority. While his performances reflected his own expectations, they also reflected those of the musical communities to which he belonged and represent a two-way conversation between performer and audience. Gonnella exhibited expertise that was recognized by the community of classically trained fiddlers in Scotland and North America, as well as by BBC Scotland and its listeners. Gonnella's contributions to this community include the continuation of a standard of playing, increased awareness and visibility of Scottish fiddling as BBC Scotland performer, broadcast host and adjudicator, and overall, elevating the art of Scottish fiddling. The community endorsed Gonnella by listening to his broadcasts, attending his concerts, and purchasing his recordings and printed tune collections.

The well-known Scottish fiddler and violinist Douglas Lawrence straddles the worlds of classical and traditional music, as a twenty-year member of the Scottish National Orchestra, as winner of every major Scots fiddle award, and as teacher of many of Scotland's leading young fiddlers. Lawrence recalled meeting Gonnella for the first time in 1973 at an Aberdeen fiddle competition where Gonnella served as adjudicator. As a competitor, Lawrence regarded Gonnella as a "big name" and a highly respected judge, which he suggests was reflected in the large number of competitors who participated in the Aberdeen competition. Another fiddler who participated in competitions adjudicated by Gonnella was James Alexander. When asked if there were any distinctive qualities of Gonnella's style, Alexander noted—as did other members of this interpretive musical community, his vibrato, fine sound, and excellent technique. Alexander commented on the lightness of Gonnella's sound in contrast to a powerful fiddler such as Hebbie Gray who also found much commercial work, though according to Alexander, Gonnella's tone may have been ideal for recording (Alexander 2014). Alexander also noted that Gonnella was one of the first Scottish fiddlers to experience commercial success, adding that it was unusual to record and be featured on the radio in the late 1960s and early 1970s, and as a result, Gonnella would have been a household name. Alexander claims, "Everyone in my generation knows exactly who he was. He is right up there with Angus Fitchet and Ian Powrie" (Alexander 2014). However, international recognition has not stimulated academic interest in Gonnella's career. Alexander suggests the lack of interest may reflect the school of thought that holds "if you have good technique and can play things other than Scottish music then you are an imposter" (Alexander 2014); while Peter Cooke suggests

> a lack of interest based on the fact that he played in bands (especially with accordionists) or who played regularly with accompaniments such as the piano consciously or unconsciously compromised their own individual musicality. As one fiddler said to me once, "Playing with an accordion and drums flattens your playing out like a hot iron does to a piece of clothing". I recognise that Ron had a good sound violinist technique which he applied very successfully to the Scottish repertory (Cooke, 2014).

Gonnella's position as an authoritarian or hegemonic presence in Scottish fiddling developed well before the instrumental revival of the late 1960s. For more than twenty years before the beginnings of the revival Gonnella was actively researching, performing, and recording the music that revivalist fiddlers would later play. He was of a different generation and performed the music in the context of his time, which may have contributed to the revivalists' view of Gonnella as a conservative figure. Regardless, membership in both the professional, classically trained and revivalist communities of fiddlers must be earned. "The only proof of membership," Fish observes, "is fellowship, the nod of recognition from someone in the same community" (Fish 1980, 173). Time and again Gonnella was given a nod of recognition from professional fiddlers I interviewed, from James Alexander to Douglas Lawrence. Perhaps, though, the most revealing comments come from Stuart Eydmann as they show Gonnella's true professionalism in his desire to share little-known works from the canon with all Scottish fiddlers. When asked if Gonnella should be accorded the status of tradition bearer, Eydmann suggested that tradition *barer* is a more appropriate label and urged we consider another group of people in Scotland, stating,

> They bring to our attention what is there and unlock doors for us and I think for me and probably for my generation of revivalists, Ron was one of these barers who unbared—who exposed the music that was there and told us it was there. You might not like the way he played it or want to be like him, but he's shown us this route and the direction and that is my version of a tradition *barer*. The more I think about revival, I think these people are as important or more important in setting the direction than individuals who may be carrying some little gem of something, though obviously they are both important (Eydmann 2014).

Eydmann acknowledges Gonnella's research and efforts to find great tunes and record them, saving others the time and trouble of going to the National Library to search for them. Eydmann goes on to say that "in moving traditions forward, sometimes people who go backwards—do that work for us and helps it [tradition] move on" (2014). Eydmann also asserts that many people did not associate jig playing with Scottish fiddle music prior to Gonnella's recordings. "From Ron's records," asserts Eydmann,

> I and others found tunes of great beauty that we would not have otherwise been aware of. This applied to harpists and guitarists also who recognized that much of the Gow and Marshall repertory suited their instruments brilliantly. Folk groups seeking to establish their own Scottish sound found that here was a repertory of melodies with great ensemble potential that could rival the O'Carolan material permeating from Ireland. Slow airs and slow strathspeys were very welcome but perhaps more so Ron's jig repertory which he opened our eyes and ears to. Till then we did not believe that Scotland had such a wonderful jig heritage (2017).

While revivalist fiddlers did not try to copy Gonnella's playing style, Eydmann notes that Gonnella did influence the repertoire of this interpretive community,

> And certainly with the revival groups who may have distanced themselves a bit from Ron's style. . . it was only a matter of time before all these fantastic jigs he was pulling out of the cupboard were finding their way into revival groups. They would select what they wanted to use and the repertoire was the important thing. Without a doubt he was an influence in that way (Eydmann 2014).

Eydmann suggested Gonnella carved out a niche for himself that included performances at society events and "ticked all the boxes" for BBC Scotland. He saw Gonnella "not as a lone wolf, but not necessarily going with the pack" (Eydmann 2014). Eydmann noted Gonnella's beautiful intonation and quality of his tone, and could find no fault with his jig playing. He too, suggested Gonnella's jig style might have been positively influenced by playing in dance bands as he was growing up (Eydmann 2014). While Lawrence also greatly admired Gonnella's jig playing, as previously mentioned, he did criticize Gonnella's strathspey playing as being a bit "safe," particularly "lacking a wee bit of devil in the strathspey" (Lawrence 2014).

On 16 May 2014 I am on a bold quest to meet and talk with a BBC Scotland producer at his favorite pub outside Aberdeen. I hail a taxi with a vague notion of the neighborhood I am looking for and hope the driver can help. I explain the situation and ask for his assistance. "Oh aye, I know the neighborhood," he says. We strike up a conversation about the music he is listening to as he works (it was Jimmy Shand) and I ask the driver if he remembers listening to Gonnella. "Oh aye," he says, "a fine fiddler, Gonnella. Everyone remembers Ron Gonnella." Regardless of views of his playing, Gonnella was an authority figure for both the community of revivalist fiddlers and the community of classically trained fiddlers, as evidence from Scotland and North America affirms. His authority derived from multiple sources: from the stature earned as BBC Scotland performer and program host; from professional knowledge and careful attention to his craft; from the historical responsibility that came from research and the subsequent interpretation of canonical texts; and from the tradition barer status he deserved for making his research available to all students of Scottish traditional music.

As a tribute following Gonnella's death, James Hunter devised and produced "A celebration of Scottish Music, Dance and Song to honor the memory of the fiddler Ron Gonnella" (1994). The massive concert was hosted by the Dunkeld and Birnam Arts Festival Society, in association with Bells Scotch Whisky, and took place in Dunkeld Cathedral. Included in the program are these remarks, which pay tribute to Gonnella's contribution to Scottish fiddling: "Tonight, as we perform and listen to some of the music, poetry and dances that Ron Gonnella so dearly loved, we honour his memory as a friend, fiddler, teacher and above all, as a dedicated champion of Scottish Traditional Music" (Concert Program 1994). Another tribute to Gonnella and his musical legacy comes on a 1994 episode of Robbie Shepherd's BBC Scotland program, *Take the Floor*, with guests George MacIlwham and James Hunter. These three longtime colleagues and friends of Gonnella lament his passing and pay heartfelt tribute to his contributions and to the man himself. He was "right at the top of the tree in his own brand of playing," Hunter asserted, "and as a smooth, faultless player who taught us new tunes and through research advanced our knowledge, we owe him a great debt . . . for communicating his love for the music and above all for holding to tradition and being an inspiration for those who follow on" (*Take the Floor* 1994).

CHAPTER SIX

Scottish Fiddling in the United States

With Gonnella's transatlantic connections, the dialogue became international. In the United States he continued to adjudicate fiddle competitions, establishing standards for performance and securing a supportive musical community of competitors and performers. His association with the Royal Scottish Country Dance Society in Scotland led to collaborations with the organization branches in Canada and the United States, expanding the community of dancers and musicians abroad. Arriving in North America as interest in attending Highland games and constructing Scottish identity became popular, Gonnella was endorsed by a huge community of heritage seekers eager to embrace his playing and their own "Scottishness." Throughout his lifetime, Gonnella participated in dialogue with these communities. Drawing them into the conversation at hand adds the social context for evaluating Gonnella's contribution to Scottish fiddling in the United States.

Fiddle competitions have played and continue to play a significant role in determining many aspects of the Scottish fiddle tradition both in Scotland and the United States. As Gibson explains, "Scottish violin competitions are a significant site of musical transmission. They are not a passive context for the performance of Scottish dance music in a concert setting, but rather play an active role in shaping and transmitting repertoire and performance practice" (n.p.). The dialogue between traditional Scottish fiddling text and social context acquired a broader accent in the mid-1970s with the establishment of Scottish Fiddling Revival, Ltd. (F.I.R.E.) and Scottish fiddling competitions in North America. The influence of Scottish F.I.R.E., through its sanctioned competitions is relevant to an examination of Gonnella's legacy because this organization single-handedly established performance standards and learning opportunities for North American fiddlers. Scottish F.I.R.E. exposed a generation of young fiddlers to high ideals and held them accountable for dissemination of the tradition. As these players progressed from competitions to the recording studio, to the classroom and to the stage, they became adjudicators themselves and joined an even smaller interpretive community—that of classically trained, professional fiddlers. In actuality, only a handful of American fiddlers in 1975 were familiar with the styles—let alone the repertory—of traditional Scottish fiddling, but the organizational efforts, emerging educational opportunities and the influence of well-established Scottish fiddlers resulted in a surge of interest in the United States in Scottish traditional fiddling that remains robust 40 years later. Recipients of these early efforts have gone on to performing, recording and teaching careers that perpetuate the ideals, influenced in part by Gonnella.

Working with the Virginia Scottish Games to preserve, perpetuate, standardize and ground the art of Scottish fiddling in historic tradition, Paul and Nancy Brockman of Falls Church, Virginia, avid Scottish country dancers and lovers of Scottish fiddle music, founded Scottish Fiddling Revival, Ltd. in 1976. (Donaldson 1986, 177). On a side note, I have always felt somewhat ambivalent about the inclusion of "revival" in the organization's name, with the implication of a mainstream music revival such as the American urban folk music revival of the 1950s and 60s or the Scottish instrumental revival of the 1970s. Perhaps a more apt way to consider the increased interest in Scottish fiddling in the late 1970s is as part of a larger heritage revival and Gonnella's arrival and involvement coincided with the height of the revival. American interest in ancestral and cultural ties to Scotland surged during the last three decades of the twentieth century. This was evidenced by a huge increase in St. Andrew societies, clan societies, bagpipe bands, Scottish country dance groups, Scottish Highland games, publications, interest in Scottish fiddling, and support of Scottish F.I.R.E. As anthropologist Celeste Ray states, "The search for identity became an accepted part of life in the later twentieth century, not only 'finding oneself,' but also finding a group with which to identify, as people formed communities around specific interests often to replace community life in the geographic sense" (Ray 2001, 205). Richard Blaustein adds to the conversation stating, "Traditions emerge and evolve, reflecting the desire of living people for meaningful patterns of affiliation in a constantly changing world" (Blaustein 2003, 75). For many, as Ray states, Highland games became "temporary physical expressions of an 'imagined' unity . . . an enactment of the community's guiding beliefs and the central themes of Scottish heritage" (2001, 99). The primary vehicle for promoting Scottish fiddling in the United States was the establishment of Scottish F.I.R.E. competitions, primarily as a component of these Highland games.

F.I.R.E. competition rules were based on the rules used at the Eastern Scottish Fiddling Championships held in Kinross, Scotland in 1976 (Donaldson 1986, 178). John Turner was named the first national champion in 1976 and won the competition for the next seven years. The Brockmans were surprised to find Turner, whose fiddle training included instruction from Hector MacAndrew in Scotland. Accomplished fiddler Alasdair Fraser, a Scottish-born resident of California, finished first in 1983. These two fiddlers, along with Scottish judges Ron Gonnella, Ian Powrie, Arthur Scott Robertson, Bert Murray, Charles Gore and Andy Bathgate, helped shape the early stage of Scottish fiddling in the United States. Brockman recognized the importance of having knowledgeable Scottish musicians serve as adjudicators, bringing both authority and credibility to the national competitions. The fifth national competition was held in 1980 with judge Ron Gonnella from Scotland along with two American judges. The competition was dedicated to Scottish fiddler Hector MacAndrew who died shortly before the competition (Donaldson 1986, 178). Foresight in basing F.I.R.E. rules on those of the Kinross competition and engaging recognized adjudicators provided structure for this infant endeavor and established F.I.R.E. as an extension of the interpretive community of competitions in Scotland. While the informal jam sessions that often surround competitions may do more to encourage players to play Scottish fiddle tunes, competitions aspire to reward stylistic knowledge and execution. As one of the early adjudicators of North American competitions, Gonnella was responsible for encouraging and maintaining the standards set for competitions on Scottish soil, even though American fiddlers' knowledge of traditional Scottish fiddling was limited, with few exceptions. Growing interest in Scottish fiddling led to the 1984 founding of John Turner's Jink & Diddle School of Scottish Fiddling in Valle Crucis, North Carolina, and Alasdair Fraser's Valley of the Moon

School near Santa Rosa, California. Gonnella returned to the United States to judge competitions in the late 1980s, judging the national competition a total of five times—more than any other Scottish adjudicator. Competitors, often aware of an adjudicator's background and style of playing, may try to play to the expectations of the judge. Thus, adjudicators influence performance standards and interpretation of texts, and may reward competitors who approach a playing style closest to their own.

THE F.I.R.E. COMMUNITY

Interpretation and performance of traditional music is constituted by shared ways of seeing. In the case of performance and competition of traditional Scottish fiddle tunes in America, the shared ways of seeing endorsed by the F.I.R.E. organization, by its judges, and by its competitors became the accepted institutional practices. These organizational "shared ways of seeing" define F.I.R.E. as an interpretive community in highly prescriptive terms. Participation in competitions based on expertise further delineates membership, and choice of performance material and adherence to technical standards ensure that competitors conform to a strict interpretation of tradition, one that is learned rather than intuited. Competitors and judges alike in F.I.R.E.-sanctioned competitions engage in a function of the interpretive community that Mikhail Bakhtin calls "active understanding," a set of shared meanings based upon the pre-established criteria defined by the organization (Shepherd 2001, 141). The following set of criteria is one that competitors aspire to, that judges adjudicate by, and that provides a common language for communicating meaning within this interpretive musical community. Performers are judged on the following factors: style/interpretation, execution/technique and rhythm/tempo. Style/interpretation refers to playing within the boundaries of the Scottish idiom, effective transitions between tunes and the musical coherence of the tune set; rhythm/tempo reflects the appropriateness of the tempo of each tune and execution/technique reflects the performer's command of the instrument, including tone, intonation, bowing technique, and ornamentation (F.I.R.E. 2016). F.I.R.E. competition rules state, "All performers shall be judged against pre-established and pre-published criteria which must specify the factors to be considered and the relative weight to be given to each factor" (F.I.R.E. 2016). The rules also state, "In all aspects, performance in the traditional

Scottish style will be the significant element in distinguishing otherwise technically comparable performances" (F.I.R.E. 2016).

These pre-established and pre-published criteria, formalized in F.I.R.E.'s competition rules, provide a concrete set of institutional expectations, more than any other interpretive community we have examined. If membership in the interpretive community of BBC Scotland listeners, for example, is simply a matter of pressing the radio or television "on" switch, membership in the F.I.R.E. community must be earned.

An interesting relationship emerges between the competition community and Gonnella the performer, teacher and adjudicator that makes the F.I.R.E. laundry list of performance criteria significant. Namely, that Gonnella's work (including commentary on BBC Scotland broadcasts, instruction during private lessons, and constructive comments on judging sheets) have its source in that musical community; and the performance criteria, in part developed and in whole perpetuated by Gonnella, acquire importance as an extension of his values. As an adjudicator, Gonnella helped set standards for Scottish fiddling in the United States through his written comments, ranking of competitors, education of and interaction with fellow judges, performances and demonstrations of Scottish fiddling. He influenced standards through his recordings and printed collections of Scottish fiddle tunes, which in turn have influenced repertoire, style, and interpretation. Gonnella's influence extended to the dance community through his dance band recordings, live performances, and publications. The ready availability of Gonnella's recordings in the United States indicates there was a market for his work. Gonnella also influenced standards through his instruction and influence on American fiddlers such as myself. As a former United States National Scottish Fiddling champion and F.I.R.E. adjudicator myself, Gonnella influenced my playing in myriad of ways: style, interpretation, rhythm, tempo, execution, and even repertoire, which in turn I have passed on to my students and audiences. As a new organization, F.I.R.E. embraced the performance standards and repertory of the early adjudicators of its competitions, judges who left an indelible imprint on the Scottish fiddling community in the United States. For five years during these early years, Gonnella served as adjudicator for F.I.R.E. sanctioned competitions, adding his own brand of tradition to the course of Scottish fiddling in America. The Scottish F.I.R.E. website describes and promotes competitions, stating ". . . Scottish Fiddling competitions are excellent opportunities to meet and play with fellow Scottish fiddlers; learn from judges who are recognized experts in the field through workshops and written personalized competition comments; and a chance to perform in friendly, relaxed environments." Gonnella playfully describes the complexity of the competition setting from an adjudicator's perspective in his own very tongue-in-cheek—and frankly, scathing—soliloquy, "Festivals Are Fun." I found his "soliloquy" in an audio file buried deep in the William and Gowan Smith Collection in the Archives of Appalachia. Gonnella humorously describes his personal judging experience, but acknowledges what would certainly be his own experience if he was a competitor in a "golfing festival!" (See appendix E.)

While competitions remain a major focus of F.I.R.E., with Highland games as the primary setting, the organization recently established a tune-writing competition. Original compositions in the form of reels were submitted for the competition in 2022 and jigs in 2023 with prize money for first, second, and third place. Through its website, the organization provides competition rules, judges' bios, US fiddle clubs and societies, a list of commonly played session tunes, as well as the results of F.I.R.E. competitions. In addition to F.I.R.E., there are numerous strathspey and reel societies, fiddle orchestras, music clubs, camps, and workshops scattered across the United States, providing instruction, a range of informal and formal playing opportunities, and generally perpetuating the art of Scottish fiddling.

In conclusion, evidence from the United States reveals and corroborates that Gonnella was an authority figure for the community of classically trained and competitive fiddlers, as well as for the community of revivalist fiddlers in Scotland, and for a huge community of BBC Scotland listeners and viewers. Competitive Scottish fiddlers in the United States find a common language in the institutional practices of Scottish F.I.R.E. in much the same way that professional fiddlers locate that common language in professional knowledge and performance practice, and revivalist fiddlers enrich their vocabularies with the traditional tunes Gonnella bared. For the community of classically trained fiddlers, his authority derived from professional knowledge and careful attention to his craft, while competitive fiddlers deferred to his status as adjudicator. For revivalist fiddlers his authority was earned from historical responsibility, research and dissemination of canonical texts. For the BBC Scotland audience, his authority came from the stature earned as BBC Scotland performer and program host.

CHAPTER SEVEN

Concluding Thoughts

My intent has been to provide a missing stanza, namely, recognition of Ron Gonnella's contribution to traditional Scottish fiddling. An examination of Gonnella's contributions solicited responses from several camps or communities. With the help of multiple speakers, I have produced a biography of Ron Gonnella that was previously uncollected; constructed an indicative discography of his recorded work and Gonnella's contributions to BBC Scotland's historical broadcasts; and revealed Gonnella's reinvigoration of jigs and the canon of eighteenth and nineteenth-century Scottish fiddle music.

The oral history methodology employed to reconstruct the meaningful musical events in Gonnella's life relies on decades-old memory texts of former colleagues becoming more challenging to locate as the years pass. To happen upon an Aberdeen taxi driver who remembered Gonnella is less an indicator of Gonnella's enduring popularity with listening audiences than it is merely a stroke of good luck; similarly, to meet a woman in Cape Breton who recalled Gonnella playing "O Sole Mio" in her mother's parlor in Boston is less serendipitous an occurrence than is discovering tapes featuring Gonnella among the papers of a Scottish expatriate living in Arizona in the Archives of Appalachia in Johnson City, Tennessee! Material culture sources have provided time and place-dependent perspectives of Gonnella's life. Century-old Dundee public records and vintage photographs of places long ago razed by urban renewal and liner notes from album covers increasingly difficult to obtain illustrate texts with social and historical significance. Due in part to Gonnella's own efforts it is possible to view and even play Niel Gow's violin at Blair Castle and to read the inscription on Gow's headstone in Little Dunkeld churchyard, both monuments that were important to him.

It was also my intent to study his listeners' interpretation of Gonnella's contributions, and as such I found it helpful to call upon the notion of interpretive communities. Three primary groups are recognized: classically trained fiddlers and the organization Scottish F.I.R.E. that adopted in large part Gonnella's performance preferences as requirements; the editorial staff and listeners of BBC Scotland who endorsed Gonnella's style and repertoire as representative of traditional Scottish fiddling; and revivalist fiddlers who welcomed his unearthing of Scots fiddle repertoire. I found that a variety of practices, some more institutionalized than others, define membership and distinguish one musical community from another. As an organization, Scottish F.I.R.E. maintains strict rules for not only performance, but also for sanctioning judges, competitions and venues. Published criteria for each aspect of performance assure that competitors are well-versed in the art of Scottish fiddling, upholding the ideals of the organization. BBC Scotland's core corporate values of education, information, and entertainment have been in place since John Reith envisioned the network and provide guidance for programming for the entire organization. These standards are interpreted in the daily operation of the broadcast network in editorial criteria, including the requirement for auditions of performers before acceptance. Revivalist fiddlers, on the other hand, can be self-proclaimed, self-taught, and self-supporting, validated by performance informally in sessions or formally on festival stages during the Scottish instrumental revival of the 1970s and 1980s and continuing today. These intrepid performers are adjudicated by a jury of their peers.

I also found that a musical community shares expectations, experience and knowledge that distinguish it from other communities. The expectations of the F.I.R.E. organization are that competitors display knowledge of the fiddle literature by performing selections from a canon of traditional tunes in the style of fiddlers such as Ron Gonnella, Douglas Lawrence, and Hector MacAndrew, and while it is not a requirement, with very few exceptions competitors wear Highland attire. Similarly, BBC Scotland maintained stringent quality control both of the performers it selected to broadcast and of the content of its programming. Auditions resulted in "rough" performers who were steered into the dance band track and "refined" performers who might be granted solo performances. A wide array of experience and knowledge characterizes the interpretive community of revivalist fiddlers, but the overarching presupposition of this group is that the repertoire is most often learned through oral transmission. While some individual members are still literalists when it comes to the meaning of "oral transmission," other members acknowledge that transmission now includes electronic techniques, as well.

Lastly, I asked what contributions Gonnella made to each community. The overarching contribution, regardless of musical community, is that of the reinvigoration of eighteenth and nineteenth-century fiddle repertoire. Gonnella's contributions are evidenced by his recording of well over five hundred fiddle tunes, many found by researching out-of-print collections and many recorded for the first time. Additionally, his printed tune collections made the canon available to a wide audience. His research and recording of jigs brought attention to this under-performed type of tune.

As shown, the Scottish F.I.R.E. community is relevant to an examination of Gonnella's legacy because this organization single-handedly established performance standards and learning opportunities for North American fiddlers unfamiliar with the Scottish fiddling tradition and unaware of its leading musicians. Gonnella began traveling to North America to perform and record during the 1960s, leading to his recognition as an authority on Scottish fiddling and invitations to adjudicate competitions in the United States. His involvement and influence extended to North American dance communities through RSCDS collaborations, dance band recordings, performances, and publications. In the early years of the organization, F.I.R.E. embraced Gonnella's repertory and his own brand of performance style, which in turn impacted the development of performance criteria that would evolve into expectations and institutional practices of the F.I.R.E. organization. Gonnella's influence on this community was felt through his interaction with fellow adjudicators, written comments to competitors, demonstrations and performances of Scots fiddling, published tune collections and recordings; and as the first and most frequent native Scots adjudicator, Gonnella, now, nearly 40 years later, still serves as an example of performance practice.

The clearly stated core values held by BBC Scotland and the expectations of its audience distinguish it from other musical communities. Gonnella's playing embodied the cultural level BBC Scotland wanted to project, while his persona and years of training, research and experience inspired the confidence of both management and audiences. Along with a handful of other outstanding fiddlers, Gonnella's interpretations, repertoire, and persona became synonymous with a Scottish fiddling tradition. His performances of the tunes from the Scottish fiddling canon brought the music into the homes of thousands of listeners, including the homes of fellow musicians eager to learn the tunes he played. As host of *On the Fiddle*, his interviews with important fiddlers illuminated the breadth and beauty of the Scottish fiddling tradition, while his feature on the life and music of Niel Gow celebrated the eighteenth-century master. Gonnella's endorsement by and association with BBC Scotland played a large role in Gonnella becoming one of Scotland's first commercially successful fiddlers and the reinvigoration of Scottish fiddle repertoire.

Though Gonnella's commercial success may be disconcerting to some, his work with RSCDS, BBC Scotland and the Niel Gow Memorial Trust perpetuated Scottish fiddling to the benefit of all. For the community of revivalist fiddlers, those who see little value in classical training or commercial success, Gonnella's research, recordings, and broadcasts have expanded the canon to previously unfamiliar tunes. By performing the music of lesser-known composers he supported the goals of the revivalist fiddlers, salvaging and preserving less visible traditions, including the playing of jigs. While Gonnella's playing style was not emulated, revivalist fiddlers acknowledged his authority based on his extensive research and dissemination of canonical texts.

Another contribution Gonnella made to the Scottish fiddling tradition comes from an interpretive community of one and can only be made retrospectively, intuitively, and without formal documentation, as it comes from observations during the years I listened to his recordings, learned tunes from his collections, performed for him at competitions, and studied with him in private lessons. This contribution is a sense of historical continuity with the heyday of Scottish fiddling. His frequent choice of formal Highland attire, his self-confident stage presence, his choice of repertory and venue, and his execution left no doubt that Gonnella was a professional. His performances evoked the ambience of eighteenth-century drawing rooms rather than festival stages, providing a contrarian alternative to the bohemian flair of the popular instrumental revivalists. Even by the early 1990s his persona was becoming outdated to one demographic though his elegant interpretations of traditional fiddle tunes remained a gold standard for generations of fiddlers.

My work subscribes to Narayan's notions of the field as a "flexible concept" and the "shifting identities" of insider and outsider (1993) and places an emphasis on reflexive scholarship. My research position and biases have been clearly stated, in particular my advocacy of Gonnella's contributions and legacy. I have drawn on my professional knowledge, experience and dual perspective as a researcher to interpret the collected data. It will be interesting to see how discourse surrounding Scottish fiddling has changed after a period of five, ten or more years; and the direction the conversation has taken. How are players interpreting and depicting the Scottish fiddling tradition? Of primary interest will be questions regarding the notion of "traditional" and the way it is interpreted in an increasingly accessible world. While it is likely that the composition of the traditional Scottish fiddling canon will continue to expand, what it will include and the technicalities of oral transmission will still be highly debatable topics. Gatekeepers of tradition may change, as well as an acknowledgment of wider standards of performance. Likewise, it will be interesting to see if fiddling competitions remain the bastion of "do it this way," or if they become more tolerant of alternative performance practices, all topics for future research.

With the proliferation of technology, too, Scottish fiddling has acquired global participants, and that raises questions about the nature of "style." Perhaps the most interesting questions for future research concern new (interpretive) musical communities that will no doubt arise. While traditional Scottish fiddling is alive and well with both classically trained and self-taught musicians on both sides of the Atlantic, change is afoot that challenges both BBC Scotland's role as arbiter of cultural taste and the authority that has historically been the provenance of the competition circuit. This change can be seen, for example, in the revised curriculum for the traditional music pathway at the Royal Conservatoire of Scotland (RCS) and represents a shift to "the mainstream." The RCS's interpretive strategy incorporates elements of jazz and orchestral music, ethnic and folk music so that the concept of traditional music congeals "more around performance practice . . . and less around the cultural, historical and ethnological context that so underpinned the revivalist generation's view" (RCS 2016). This additional meaning of traditional is increasingly international and deterritorialized, less authoritative, far more innovative and more interested in the individual performer's interpretation of the text than strict adherence to it.

With this interpretive strategy will come its practitioners, those who agree to an interpretation by virtue of similar training, similar views and similar tastes. From Fish we learn that an interpretive community is a group with an established tradition of interpretation. From Hobsbawm and Ranger we learn that a group's traditions are just as valid when they are invented as when they are perpetuated, as long as they are meaningful to the community (1983). In its most basic form, an interpretive musical community is a group establishing a tradition. A new musical community will come into being with its own traditions; due to its newness, by necessity many of these traditions will be invented. As Sims and Stephens assert, "For something to be considered a tradition it must contain the features *the group identifies as essential* in defining tradition. At the same time, to remain relevant, a tradition *must continually adapt* as groups develop and change" [emphasis in original] (Sims and Stephens 2011, 81). We can be assured, though, that whatever forms new interpretive musical communities take, their heritage comes from both the revivalist tradition and the classical, from the Stuart Eydmanns and the Ron Gonnellas.

GONNELLA'S LEGACY

Gonnella was a musician worthy of confidence based on his years of training, experience, and research. Certainly, the community of classically trained fiddlers recognizes that his performance practices demonstrate a high degree of expertise so that his performance of a traditional reel—let alone a slow air—takes on qualities of the classical. Revivalist fiddlers, too, appreciate his scholarship in bringing tunes from dusty eighteenth-century collections into the popular canon, evidenced by tune types and composers selected for his extensive discography. Confidence in Gonnella's work, too, resides in the influence and knowledge of recognized fiddlers who preceded him and with whom he played. He brought to each performance a tradition begun by eighteenth-century fiddlers and composers of Scottish fiddle tunes; and in this respect, Gonnella actively contributed to the narrative of the Scottish fiddling tradition.

"There is a burgeoning degree of cultural confidence in Scotland these days," Gary West asserts (2012, 15), to which I add that Gonnella's contributions are one aspect of that cultural confidence. Gonnella's brand of traditional Scottish fiddling has inspired both his own and future generations of fiddlers. His work has endured, moving from vinyl record albums to digital music files, from wireless radio broadcasts to YouTube videos. He was able to take traditional tunes of the public square, enhance the way his audiences hear them, and endow the tunes with a depth of both historical and social significance they lack in everyday discourse. Gonnella's legacy is his extensive body of work and his role in providing access to and invigoration of eighteenth and nineteenth-century fiddle repertoire.

APPENDIX A

Recorded Tunes by Tune Type and Composer

GONNELLA'S SOLO AND DANCE ALBUMS

Jigs

TITLE	COMPOSER	RECORDING
Wishaw's Delight	Traditional	*Music From the Gow Collections*
The Earl of Morton's Jig	William Gow	*Music From the Gow Collections* *Fiddle Magic*
Miss Grace Hay's Delight	Traditional	*Music From the Gow Collections*
Miss Sally Hunter of Thurston	Nathaniel Gow	*Music From the Gow Collections* *Scottish Dance Masters, Vol. 2*
Dumfries House	Traditional	*Music From the Gow Collections* *The Lad of Kyle*
Miss Johnston of Hilton's Fancy	Nathaniel Gow	*Music From the Gow Collections* *Scottish Dance Masters, Vol. 2*
The Duke of Atholl's Reel (Jig)	Niel Gow	*Plays the Fiddles of Gow, Marshall and Skinner*

TITLE	COMPOSER	RECORDING
Sir Walter Scott	Niel Gow, Jr.	*Plays the Fiddles of Gow, Marshall and Skinner* *The Countess of Dalhousie*
Pennycuik House	Niel Gow, Jr.	*Plays the Fiddles of Gow, Marshall and Skinner* *The Countess of Dalhousie*
Miss Gordon of Park	William Marshall	*Plays the Fiddles of Gow, Marshall and Skinner* *Fiddler's Fancy* *The Countess of Dalhousie*
Miss Hannah's Jig—Elgin	William Marshall	*Plays the Fiddles of Gow, Marshall and Skinner* *Fiddler's Fancy* *The Countess of Dalhousie*
The Marchioness of Huntley's Jig	William Marshall	*Plays the Fiddles of Gow, Marshall and Skinner*
Craigellachie Lasses	William Marshall	*Plays the Fiddles of Gow, Marshall and Skinner*
The Favourite Dram	Traditional	*Fiddle Gems*
The Stranger in Place of the Worthies of Yore	Traditional	*Fiddle Gems*
The Inauspicious Wedding Day	Traditional	*Fiddle Gems*
The General Gathering, 1745	Traditional	*Fiddle Gems*
The Shepherdess	Traditional	*Fiddle Gems*
Come Lads, Now Be Ready	Traditional	*Fiddle Gems*
Death and Dr. Hornbrook	James Scott Skinner	*Fiddler's Fancy*

TITLE	COMPOSER	RECORDING
Mr. Morison of Bognie	William Marshall	*Fiddler's Fancy*
Miss Stewart's Jig, of Bombay	William Marshall	*Fiddler's Fancy*
Prince Charlie's Quickstep	Traditional	*A Tribute to Niel Gow*
Lady Charlotte Bruce's Favourite	Nathaniel Gow	*A Tribute to Niel Gow* *Live From the Crieff Hydro*
Miss Margaret Brown's Favourite	Nathaniel Gow	*A Tribute to Niel Gow*
Miss Rae of Eskgrove	Nathaniel Gow	*A Tribute to Niel Gow*
Lady Charlotte Murray's Favourite	Niel Gow	*A Tribute to Niel Gow*
Miss Sophia Campbell of Saddell's	Robert Mackintosh	*Scottish Fiddle Master*
The Prince of Wales	Joseph Lowe	*Scottish Fiddle Master*
Sauteuse	Joseph Lowe	*Scottish Fiddle Master*
Jamie Gow, Crathie Bellman	Joseph Lowe	*Scottish Fiddle Master*
The Fife and Forfar Hunt's Favourite	Robert Mackintosh	*Scottish Fiddle Master*
Green Shades of Gask	Traditional	*Live From the Crieff Hydro*
The Laird of Cockpen	Traditional	*Live From the Crieff Hydro*
Mr. Duncan's Delight	Robert Mackintosh	*Live From the Crieff Hydro*
Miss Rattray	Traditional	*Live From the Crieff Hydro*
The Braes of Glenturrote	Traditional	*Live From the Crieff Hydro*
Wi' a Hundred Pipers	Traditional	*Live From the Crieff Hydro*
The Road and the Miles to Dundee	Traditional	*Live From the Crieff Hydro*
Campbell's Road	Dan R. MacDonald	*International Friendship of the Fiddle*
The High Bridge Jig	Dan R. MacDonald	*International Friendship of the Fiddle*

TITLE	COMPOSER	RECORDING
The Provost of St. Vigean's	Lindsay Ross	*International Friendship of the Fiddle*
The Corner House Jig	Andrew Rankine	*International Friendship of the Fiddle*
Sir Torquil Munro	Adam Rennie	*International Friendship of the Fiddle*
Elizabeth Donald, Moss-side	Adam Rennie	*International Friendship of the Fiddle*
Donna's Wedding March (Jig)	Ron Gonnella	*International Friendship of the Fiddle*
Bert Gonnella's Jig	Ron Gonnella	*Ron Gonnella Playing a Stradivarius*
Lizzie Duncan's Jig	Ron Gonnella	*Ron Gonnella Playing a Stradivarius*
Alex and Hazel Barbour of Bonskeid	Ron Gonnella	*Ron Gonnella Playing a Stradivarius*
Happy May the Pair Be	Ron Gonnella	*Ron Gonnella Playing a Stradivarius* *Live From the Crieff Hydro*
Rev. Archibald Minto's Farewell to St. Andrews	Ron Gonnella	*Ron Gonnella Playing a Stradivarius*
Peggy's Wedding Music	Traditional	*Fiddle Magic*
Newcastle Bridge	Abraham Mackintosh	*Fiddle Magic*
Jackson's Bottle of Claret	Traditional	*Fiddle Magic*
The Academy Jig	J. Rule	*Fiddle Magic* *Music for Eight Scottish Country Dances*
Drumdelgie	Nathaniel Gow	*Fiddle Magic*
Merrily Danced the Quaker's Wife	Traditional	*Fiddle Magic*
The Auld Inn	Traditional	*Fiddle Magic*
Kinloch of Kinloch	Traditional	*Fiddle Magic*
Bonnie Strathmore	Traditional	*Fiddle Magic*

TITLE	COMPOSER	RECORDING
Todlen Hame	James Aird	*Scottish Dance Masters, Vol. 2*
The Island of Mull	Earl of Eglinton	*Scottish Dance Masters, Vol. 2*
The Rakish Highwayman	Traditional	*Scottish Dance Masters, Vol. 2*
Pibroch of Bonnie Strathearn	Traditional	*Scottish Dance Masters, Vol. 2* *Live From the Crieff Hydro*
Cavehill	Traditional	*Scottish Dance Masters, Vol. 2* *Platinum—70 Years of Dancing in St. Andrews*
The Shaggie Burn	Ian MacPhail	*Scottish Dance Masters, Vol. 2*
The Deil's Awa' Wi' the Excise Man	Traditional	*Scottish Dance Masters, Vol. 3*
Here's to Ane I lo'e Dear	Traditional	*Scottish Dance Masters, Vol. 3*
No Churchman Am I	Traditional	*Scottish Dance Masters, Vol. 3*
Craigieburn Wood	Traditional	*Scottish Dance Masters, Vol. 3*
Aw' Wi' Your Witchcraft o' Beauty's Alarms	Traditional	*Scottish Dance Masters, Vol. 3*
Duncan MacDonald's Fiddle	Ron Gonnella	*Scottish Dance Masters, Vol. 3* *Live From the Crieff Hydro*
Edith Raitt's Jig	Ron Gonnella	*Scottish Dance Masters, Vol. 3* *Live From the Crieff Hydro*
Captain Whiteside's	John Hall	*Scottish Dance Masters, Vol. 4*

TITLE	COMPOSER	RECORDING
A Coggie o' Ale and a Pickle Airmeal	Traditional	*Scottish Dance Masters, Vol. 4*
Jean Mullen's Jig	Ron Gonnella	*Scottish Dance Masters, Vol. 4*
Taymouth Heritage	Traditional	*Scottish Dance Masters, Vol. 4*
The Hundred Pipers	Lady Nairne (Caroline Oliphant)	*Scottish Dance Masters, Vol. 5* *Live From the Crieff Hydro*
I Ha'ed Laid a Herring in Salt	Traditional	*Scottish Dance Masters, Vol. 5*
Janie Duncan's 92nd Birthday	Ron Gonnella	*Scottish Dance Masters, Vol. 2*
Waterman's Jig	Alexander McGlashan	*Scottish Dance Masters, Vol. 5*
The Queen's Fancy	Alexander McGlashan	*Scottish Dance Masters, Vol. 5*
James Morrison	Ron Gonnella	*Scottish Dance Masters, Vol. 5*
Wha'll Be King But Charlie	Traditional	*Scottish Dance Masters, Vol. 5* *Live From the Crieff Hydro*
The Inverary Wedding	Traditional	*Scottish Dance Masters, Vol. 5*
Ye Banks and Braes	Traditional	*Scottish Dance Masters, Vol. 5*
Come Under My Plaidie	Traditional	*Scottish Dance Masters, Vol. 5*
I Lo'ed Naie a Laddie But Ane	Traditional	*The Lad of Kyle*
My Wife's a Winsome Wee Thing	Traditional	*The Lad of Kyle*
O Kenmure's On an Awa' Willie	Traditional	*The Lad of Kyle*
The Duke of Atholl's Jig	Ron Gonnella	*The Lad of Kyle*

TITLE	COMPOSER	RECORDING
Captain Frank Thomson, Crieff Golf Club	Ron Gonnella	*The Lad of Kyle*
Bill Craig's Jig	Ron Gonnella	*The Lad of Kyle*
Roxburgh Castle	Traditional	*The Lad of Kyle*
Over the Hills and Far Away	Traditional	*The Lad of Kyle*
Here's to Thy Health, My Bonnie Lass	Melody of Laggan Burn	*The Lad of Kyle*
The Lassies of Melrose	Traditional	*The Lad of Kyle*
An I'll Awa' to Bonnie Tweedside	Traditional	*The Lad of Kyle*
Joe MacDiarmid's	Rob Loch	*Music for Eight Scottish Country Dances*
The Steamboat	Traditional	*Music for Eight Scottish Country Dances*
Jockey's Dance	Traditional	*Music for Eight Scottish Country Dances*
The Bobbie O	Traditional	*Music for Eight Scottish Country Dances*
Archibald Minto	Ron Gonnella	*Music for Eight Scottish Country Dances*
The West Port	Billy Anderson	*Platinum—70 Years of Dancing in St. Andrews*
Mrs. Ross	Traditional	*Platinum—70 Years of Dancing in St. Andrews*
Lord MacPherson of Drumochter	Angus Graham	*Fiddle & Pipe Favourites*

Airs

TITLE	COMPOSER	RECORDING
Hard Is My Fate	Traditional	*Scottish Violin Music*
Miss Graham of Inchbraikie	Nathaniel Gow	*Scottish Violin Music*
The Fallen Chief	James Scott Skinner	*Scottish Violin Music*
Cluny Castle	Alexander Troup	*Scottish Violin Music*
The House of Skene	James Davie	*Scottish Violin Music*

TITLE	COMPOSER	RECORDING
Niel Gow's Lament for James Moray of Abercairnie	Niel Gow/Arranged by Henderson	*Scottish Violin Music*
The Rover	James Scott Skinner	*Scottish Violin Music*
The Highland Society of Scotland	Traditional	*Scottish Violin Music*
Coilsfield House	Nathaniel Gow	*Scottish Violin Music*
The Fallen Hero	Nathaniel Gow	*Scottish Violin Music*
The "Bonnie Ann"	James Scott Skinner	*Scottish Violin Music*
General Robertson of Lawars	John Bowie	*Scottish Violin Music From the Gow Collections*
The Mill, Mill O'	Traditional	*Scottish Violin Music From the Gow Collections*
Auld Robin Gray	Traditional	*Scottish Violin Music From the Gow Collections*
Niel Gow's Farewell to Whisky	Niel Gow	*Scottish Violin Music From the Gow Collections* *International Friendship of the Fiddle*
Colonel Hamilton of Pencaitland	Nathaniel Gow	*Scottish Violin Music From the Gow Collections*
Niel Gow's Lament for the Death of His Second Wife	Niel Gow	*Scottish Violin Music From the Gow Collections* *Plays the Fiddles of Gow, Marshall and Skinner* *A Tribute to Niel Gow*
Lady Cunningham of Livingstone	Nathaniel Gow	*Scottish Violin Music From the Gow Collections*

TITLE	COMPOSER	RECORDING
Roslin Castle	Traditional	*Scottish Violin Music From the Gow Collections*
Bothwell Castle	Nathaniel Gow	*Scottish Violin Music From the Gow Collections*
Mrs. Hamilton of Pencaitland	Nathaniel Gow	*Scottish Violin Music From the Gow Collections*
The Bonniest Lass in a' the Warld	Traditional	*Scottish Violin Music From the Gow Collections*
The Caledonian Hunt's Delight	James Miller	*Scottish Violin Music From the Gow Collections*
The Caledonian Hunt	Alexander Don	*Scottish Violin Music From the Gow Collections*
Mrs. Hay of Yester's Reel	Traditional	*Scottish Violin Music From the Gow Collection*
Niel Gow's Lamentation for Abercairney	Niel Gow	*Plays the Fiddles of Gow, Marshall and Skinner* *The Countess of Dalhousie*
MacPherson's Lament	Traditional	*Plays the Fiddles of Gow, Marshall and Skinner*
Here Awa', There Awa', Wandering Willie	Traditional / Burns	*Plays the Fiddles of Gow, Marshall and Skinner* *The Countess of Dalhousie*
Bessie Bell and Mary Gray	Traditional	*Plays the Fiddles of Gow, Marshall and Skinner* *The Countess of Dalhousie*

TITLE	COMPOSER	RECORDING
The Duchess Tree	James Scott Skinner	*Plays the Fiddles of Gow, Marshall and Skinner* *The Countess of Dalhousie*
Miss Laura Andrew	James Scott Skinner	*Plays the Fiddles of Gow, Marshall and Skinner* *The Countess of Dalhousie*
Ashton Gonnella of Shreveport, Louisiana	Ron Gonnella	*Plays the Fiddles of Gow, Marshall and Skinner* *The Countess of Dalhousie*
Homage to the Gows, Marshall and Skinner	Ron Gonnella	*Plays the Fiddles of Gow, Marshall and Skinner* *The Countess of Dalhousie*
Lament for Sir Harry Niven Lumsden of Achindoir	William Marshall	*Plays the Fiddles of Gow, Marshall and Skinner* *Fiddler's Fancy* *The Countess of Dalhousie*
Niel Gow's Fiddle	Nathaniel Gow	*Plays the Fiddles of Gow, Marshall and Skinner* *The Countess of Dalhousie*
Mrs. Major L. Stewart of the Island of Java	William Marshall	*Plays the Fiddles of Gow, Marshall and Skinner* *The Countess of Dalhousie*

TITLE	COMPOSER	RECORDING
Well May My True Love Arrive	Traditional	*Fiddle Gems*
Well May Charlie Wear the Crown	Traditional	*Fiddle Gems*
Sitting in the Stern of a Boat	William McLeod	*Fiddle Gems*
Good Wife, Admit the Wanderer	Traditional	*Fiddle Gems*
The Fall of Foyers	Simon Fraser	*Fiddle Gems*
Archibald MacDonald of Keppoch	Traditional	*Fiddle Gems*
Hymn to the Saviour	Traditional	*Fiddle Gems*
Caledonia's Wail for Niel Gow	Traditional	*Fiddle Gems*
In Dispraise of Whisky	Alexander MacDonnell	*Fiddle Gems*
The Bonnie Lass of Bon Accord	James Scott Skinner	*Fiddler's Fancy* *Ron Gonnella Playing a Stradivarius*
Donald MacPherson's Lament	James Scott Skinner	*Fiddler's Fancy* *The Countess of Dalhousie*
Chapel Keithack	William Marshall	*Fiddler's Fancy*
Cradle Song	James Scott Skinner	*Fiddler's Fancy* *Ron Gonnella Playing a Stradivarius*
Corgarff Castle	James Scott Skinner	*Fiddler's Fancy*
Music of Spey	James Scott Skinner	*Fiddler's Fancy*
Lady Niven Lunsden of Achindoir	William Marshall	*Fiddler's Fancy*
Roseacre	James Scott Skinner	*Fiddler's Fancy*
Nathaniel Gow's Lament for the Death of His Brother	Nathaniel Gow	*A Tribute to Niel Gow*
Cam' Ye By Atholl?	Niel Gow, Jr.	*A Tribute to Niel Gow* *Plays the Fiddles of Gow, Marshall and Skinner* *The Countess of Dalhousie*

TITLE	COMPOSER	RECORDING
Lady Ann Hope's Favourite	Niel Gow	*A Tribute to Niel Gow*
Flora MacDonald's Lament	Niel Gow, Jr.	*A Tribute to Niel Gow*
Caller Herring	Nathaniel Gow	*A Tribute to Niel Gow* *Ron Gonnella Playing a Stradivarius*
Miss Lucy Johnston's Compliments to Niel Gow	Lucy Johnston	*A Tribute to Niel Gow*
Annie Laurie	Lady Jane Scott	*A Tribute to Niel Gow*
Miss Campbell of Saddell	Robert Mackintosh	*Scottish Fiddle Master*
Durisdeer	Lady Jane Scott	*Scottish Fiddle Master* *Ron Gonnella Playing a Stradivarius*
Bonny Aboyne	Peter Milne	*Scottish Fiddle Master*
R.G.'s Compliments to Oona and Brian Ivory	Ron Gonnella	*Live From the Crieff Hydro*
The Rowan Tree	Traditional	*Live From the Crieff Hydro*
The Auld Hoose	Traditional	*Live From the Crieff Hydro*
The Lad of the Leal	Traditional	*Live From the Crieff Hydro*
Will Ye No Come Back Again?	Melody by Niel Gow	*Live From the Crieff Hydro*
Kelvin Grove	Traditional	*International Friendship of the Fiddle*
Mrs. Jamieson's Favourite	Charles Grant	*International Friendship of the Fiddle*
Pibroch of Bonnie Strathearn	Ron Gonnella	*International Friendship of the Fiddle* *Live From the Crieff Hydro*
Fil-O-Ro	Traditional	*International Friendship of the Fiddle*

TITLE	COMPOSER	RECORDING
Ron Gonnella's Compliments to Jimmy Shand [Waltz]	Ron Gonnella	*International Friendship of the Fiddle*
The Flower of the Quern	James Scott Skinner	*International Friendship of the Fiddle*
Ye Banks and Braes	Traditional	*International Friendship of the Fiddle*
June and Harry Goldenberg's Air	Ron Gonnella	*International Friendship of the Fiddle*
Kinrara	William Marshall	*International Friendship of the Fiddle*
Ae Fond Kiss	Traditional	*Ron Gonnella Playing a Stradivarius*
Bovaglie's Plaid	James Scott Skinner	*Ron Gonnella Playing a Stradivarius*
A Faery Lullaby	Traditional	*Scottish Dance Masters, Vol.3*
Lass of Humberside	Traditional	*Scottish Dance Masters, Vol.4*
Wild Mountain Thyme (Waltz)	Francis McPeake	*Scottish Dance Masters, Vol.5*
The Queen's Visit to Morrison's Academy	Ron Gonnella	*The Lad of Kyle*
Afton Water	Traditional	*The Lad of Kyle*
Mary Morison	Traditional	*The Lad of Kyle*
O' a' the Arts the Wind Can Blaw (Miss Admiral Gordon's Strathspey)	William Marshall	*The Lad of Kyle*
Ay, Waukin' O	Traditional	*The Lad of Kyle*
The Heights of Dargai (Retreat Air)	J. Wallace	*Fiddle & Pipe Favourites*
The Battle of the Somme (Retreat Air)	Willie Lawrie	*Fiddle & Pipe Favourites*

TITLE	COMPOSER	RECORDING
Belmont (Psalm Tune)	William Gardiner	*Fiddle & Pipe Favourites*
Stracathro (Psalm Tune)	Charles Hutcheson	*Fiddle & Pipe Favourites*
Down By the Sally Gardens	Traditional [Yeats]	*Fiddle & Pipe Favourites*
I'm a' Doon for Lack o' Johnnie	Traditional	*Fiddle & Pipe Favourites*
A Waltz for Elizabeth	Ron Gonnella	*Fiddle & Pipe Favourites*

Reels

TITLE	COMPOSER	RECORDING
Jamie Shearer	James Scott Skinner	*Scottish Violin Music*
The Perth Assembly	Samson Duncan	*Scottish Violin Music* *Music forEight Scottish Country Dances*
Loch Leven Castle	Traditional	*Scottish Violin Music*
Bleaton Gardens	Traditional	*Scottish Violin Music*
The Duke of Montrose	Traditional	*Scottish Violin Music*
Pretty Peggy	Traditional	*Scottish Violin Music*
The Flowers of Edinburgh	Traditional	*Scottish Violin Music* *Ron Gonnella's Burns Night*
The High Road to Linton	Traditional	*Scottish Violin Music*
The Earl of Seafield	Duncan Grant	*Scottish Violin Music*
Kincaldrum's Reel	Traditional	*Scottish Violin Music from the Gow Collections* *Music for Eight Scottish Country Dances*
Mr. Sharp's Favourite	Traditional	*Scottish Violin Music from the Gow Collections*

TITLE	COMPOSER	RECORDING
Lord Mauchline's Reel	William McLeod	*Scottish Violin Music from the Gow Collections*
Mrs. Stirling of Keir	John Bowie	*Scottish Violin Music from the Gow Collections*
Miss Gibson	Traditional	*Scottish Violin Music from the Gow Collections*
Mrs. MacDouall Grant	Nathaniel Gow	*Plays the Fiddles of Gow, Marshall and Skinner*
The White Cockade	Traditional	*Plays the Fiddles of Gow, Marshall and Skinner* *The Countess of Dalhousie*
Mount Stewart House	Traditional	*Plays the Fiddles of Gow, Marshall and Skinner*
Bonnie Banchory	James Scott Skinner	*Plays the Fiddles of Gow, Marshall and Skinner* *The Countess of Dalhousie*
The Northern Racecourse	Traditional	*Fiddle Gems*
The Sprightly Minikin	Traditional	*Fiddle Gems*
The Merry Making	Traditional	*Fiddle Gems*
My Ain, Kind Deary	Traditional	*Fiddle Gems*
Three Sheep's Shanks	Traditional	*Fiddle Gems*
Sandy Grant o' Battangorm	James Scott Skinner	*Fiddler's Fancy*
Mr. John Smith, Alford	James Scott Skinner	*Fiddler's Fancy*
Major L. Stewart's Reel, of the Island of Java	William Marshall	*Fiddler's Fancy*
Davie Work	James Scott Skinner	*Fiddler's Fancy*
Lochrynach	Traditional	*Fiddler's Fancy*

TITLE	COMPOSER	RECORDING
Gibson's Whisky	James Scott Skinner	*Fiddler's Fancy* *Ron Gonnella Playing a Stradivarius*
Landlady of Inver Inn	Niel Gow	*A Tribute to Niel Gow*
Inver Lasses	Traditional	*A Tribute to Niel Gow*
Mrs. MacDonald of Clan Ranald	Nathaniel Gow	*A Tribute to Niel Gow*
Hon. James Ramsay's	Niel Gow	*A Tribute to Niel Gow*
Ayr Races	John Gow	*A Tribute to Niel Gow*
Lady Mary Hay's Scotch Measure	Nathaniel Gow	*A Tribute to Niel Gow*
Largo's Fairy Dance	Nathaniel Gow	*A Tribute to Niel Gow*
Miss Barstow's Reel	Robert Mackintosh	*Scottish Fiddle Master*
Sir David Davidson of Cantray	John Lowe	*Scottish Fiddle Master* *International Friendship of the Fiddle*
James Miller, Bullionfield	Traditional	*Scottish Fiddle Master*
Ron Gonnella's Compliments to Senator Robert Byrd of West Virginia	Ron Gonnella	*Scottish Fiddle Master* *Scottish Dance Masters, Vol. 4*
Hon. Mrs. Maule's Reel	Robert Mackintosh	*Scottish Fiddle Master*
Rachel Rae	John Lowe	*Scottish Fiddle Master*
Miss Sandra Webster	Ron Gonnella	*Scottish Fiddle Master* *Ron Gonnella Playing a Stradivarius*
Rut Bell's Reel	Ron Gonnella	*Scottish Fiddle Master*
The Forfar Hunt	A. Allan	*Scottish Fiddle Master*
Loch Earn	Nathaniel Gow	*Live From the Crieff Hydro*
Gillan's Reel	Peter Milne	*International Friendship of the Fiddle*
The Strathearn Herald Reel	Ron Gonnella	*International Friendship of the Fiddle*

TITLE	COMPOSER	RECORDING
Lord MacDonald's Reel	Alexander MacDonald	*International Friendship of the Fiddle*
Mrs. MacLeod	Traditional	*International Friendship of the Fiddle*
Bill Sutherland	Adam Rennie	*International Friendship of the Fiddle*
Staten Island	Traditional	*International Friendship of the Fiddle*
The Morayshire Farmers' Club	Traditional	*International Friendship of the Fiddle*
The Bonnie Wee Thing	Traditional	*Burns Night*
Black Jock of Skellatur	James Scott Skinner	*Ron Gonnella Playing a Stradivarius*
Evelyn M.E. Murray of Cambridge, Massachusetts	Ron Gonnella	*Ron Gonnella Playing a Stradivarius*
Bonnie Mally Lee	Traditional	*Ron Gonnella Playing a Stradivarius*
Miss Rattray	Traditional	*Ron Gonnella Playing a Stradivarius* *Music for Eight Scottish Country Dances* *Live From the Crieff Hydro*
Lady Harriet Hope's Reel	Robert Mackintosh	*Fiddle Magic*
The Mill Burn	James Fraser	*Fiddle Magic*
Mrs. Johnston's Reel	David Grant	*Fiddle Magic*
Hielan Brochan	Traditional	*Fiddle Magic*
The Peat Fire Flame	Marjory Kennedy-Fraser	*Fiddle Magic*
Sweet Maid of Glendaruel	Traditional	*Fiddle Magic*
Menstrie Castle	Andrew Rankine	*Fiddle Magic*

TITLE	COMPOSER	RECORDING
Dornoch Links	James MacDonald	*Fiddle Magic*
Wind That Shakes the Barley	Traditional	*Scottish Dance Masters, Vol. 2*
Willie Davis	Traditional	*Scottish Dance Masters, Vol. 2*
Dancing Feet	George S. McLennan	*Scottish Dance Masters, Vol. 2*
Merry We've Been	Traditional	*Scottish Dance Masters, Vol. 2*
The Ale Wife and Her Barrell	Traditional	*Scottish Dance Masters, Vol. 2*
The Drummer	Traditional	*Scottish Dance Masters, Vol. 2*
Babes in the Woods	Traditional	*Scottish Dance Masters, Vol. 2*
The Rose Tree	Traditional	*Scottish Dance Masters, Vol. 2*
Halloween	Alexander McGlashan	*Scottish Dance Masters, Vol. 3*
The No Name Tune	Ron Gonnella	*Scottish Dance Masters, Vol. 3*
Caber Feidh	Traditional	*Scottish Dance Masters, Vol. 3*
The Deuk's Dang Ower My Daddie O'	Traditional	*Scottish Dance Masters, Vol. 3*
Mrs. Oswald of Auchencruive's Favourite	Robert Mackintosh	*Scottish Dance Masters, Vol. 3*
Mrs. Trotter of Castlelaw's Reel	Robert Mackintosh	*Scottish Dance Masters, Vol. 3*
The Lass of Patie's Mill	Traditional	*Scottish Dance Masters, Vol. 4*
Stan and Anne Hamilton's Reel	Ron Gonnella	*Scottish Dance Masters, Vol. 4*
John Turner's Compliments to Governor Adams	John Turner	*Scottish Dance Masters, Vol. 4*
Burning of the Piper's Hut	Traditional	*Scottish Dance Masters, Vol. 4*

TITLE	COMPOSER	RECORDING
The Caves of Mieuville St. Vaast	Traditional	*Scottish Dance Masters, Vol. 4*
Caller Herrin' (played as a reel)	Nathaniel Gow	*Scottish Dance Masters, Vol. 5*
The Nut Brown Maiden	Traditional	*Scottish Dance Masters, Vol. 5*
The Boatie Rows	Traditional	*Scottish Dance Masters, Vol. 5*
The Lass o' Gowrie	Traditional	*Scottish Dance Masters, Vol. 5*
The Blank Dance	Rutherford	*Scottish Dance Masters, Vol. 5*
Hebridean Wauking Song	Traditional	*Scottish Dance Masters, Vol. 5* *Music for Eight Scottish Country Dances*
Aiken Drum	Traditional	*Scottish Dance Masters, Vol. 5*
Rumbling Brig	Ron Gonnella	*Scottish Dance Masters, Vol. 5*
Lord Saltoun	Traditional	*Scottish Dance Masters, Vol. 5*
The Bob of Fettercairn	Traditional	*Scottish Dance Masters, Vol. 5*
John Collie, Insh	Gonnella	*Scottish Dance Masters, Vol. 5*
Bonnie Charlie	Niel Gow	*Scottish Dance Masters, Vol. 5*
Dunkeld Steeple	Niel Gow	*Scottish Dance Masters, Vol. 5*
Rantin' Rovin' Robin	Traditional	*The Lad of Kyle*
Willie Brew'd a Peck o' Maut	Traditional	*The Lad of Kyle*
My Love's She But a Lassie Yet	Traditional	*The Lad of Kyle*
Lovely Polly Stewart	Traditional	*The Lad of Kyle*
Speed the Plow	Traditional	*The Lad of Kyle*

TITLE	COMPOSER	RECORDING
Loch Rynach	Traditional	*The Lad of Kyle*
Mr. Charles Stewart, Pettyvaich	William Marshall	*The Lad of Kyle*
Miss Margaret Brander	David Findlay	*Music for Eight Scottish Country Dances*
Hon. James Rasay's	Traditional	*Music for Eight Scottish Country Dances*
The Ladies of Dingwall	Morrison	*Music for Eight Scottish Country Dances*
Archie Patterson	Nan Main	*Music for Eight Scottish Country Dances*
Miss Campbell of Saddell	Robert Mackintosh	*Music for Eight Scottish Country Dances*
Willie's Gaen to Melville Castle	Traditional	*Music for Eight Scottish Country Dances*
Heather Donald of Saint Andrews	Sandy Donald	*Platinum—70 Years of Dancing in St. Andrews*
The Black Boy	Traditional	*Platinum—70 Years of Dancing in St. Andrews*
Jenny Lind	Traditional	*Platinum—70 Years of Dancing in St. Andrews*
The Pends	Billy Anderson	*Platinum—70 Years of Dancing in St. Andrews*
Far Frae Hame	Traditional	*Platinum—70 Years of Dancing in St. Andrews*
Miss Monaghan	Seamus Ennis	*Platinum—70 Years of Dancing in St. Andrews*

TITLE	COMPOSER	RECORDING
John McNeil's Reel	Peter Milne	*Platinum—70 Years of Dancing in St. Andrews*
The Square Tower	Billy Anderson	*Platinum—70 Years of Dancing in St. Andrews*
Rosemary's Reel	Ron Gonnella	*A Beginner's Guide* *Live From the Crieff Hydro*
Miss Ivory of Brewlands	Ron Gonnella	*Fiddle & Pipe Favourites*
Master Euan Ivory's Reel	Ron Gonnella	*Fiddle & Pipe Favourites*
Barbara Bane of New Deer	Lindsay Ross	*Fiddle & Pipe Favourites*
Miss Kirsty Batchelor	Lindsay Ross	*Fiddle & Pipe Favourites*
Jim MacBay's Welcome	J. Robertson	*Fiddle & Pipe Favourites*

Strathspeys

TITLE	COMPOSER	RECORDING
The Miller O' Dervil	James Barnett	*Scottish Violin Music* *Ron Gonnella Playing a Stradivarius*
Mrs. Greig's Strathspey	Traditional	*Scottish Violin Music*
Glen Rinnes	Charles Grant	*Scottish Violin Music*
J.F. Mackenzie, Stornoway	William Ross	*Scottish Violin Music*
The Duke of Montrose	Traditional	*Scottish Violin Music*
Kilwinning Archers	Traditional	*Scottish Violin Music* *Music for Eight Scottish Country Dances*
The Weavers of Newly	Traditional	*Scottish Violin Music*
Lady Madeline Sinclair	Traditional	*Scottish Violin Music*

TITLE	COMPOSER	RECORDING
Mrs. Reid of Kilcalmkill	David Grant	*Scottish Violin Music*
Colonel H.F. Campbell	Traditional	*Scottish Violin Music From the Gow Collections* *Scottish Dance Masters, Vol. 2*
Lady Charlotte Campbell	Robert Mackintosh	*Scottish Violin Music From the Gow Collections*
The Perthshire Volunteers	Traditional	*Scottish Violin Music From the Gow Collections* *Scottish Dance Masters, Vol. 3*
The Duchess of Hamilton	Traditional	*Scottish Violin Music From the Gow Collections* *Music for Eight Scottish Country Dances*
Mrs. Adye	William Logan	*Scottish Violin Music From the Gow Collections*
The Kirrie Kebbuck	James Scott Skinner	*Plays the Fiddles of Gow, Marshall and Skinner* *The Countess of Dalhousie*
The Laird of Drumblair	James Scott Skinner	*Plays the Fiddles of Gow, Marshall and Skinner*
Glenmorriston	Traditional	*Fiddle Gems* *Scottish Dance Masters, Vol. 2*
Belladrum House	Traditional	*Fiddle Gems*
The Northern Meeting	Traditional	*Fiddle Gems*
The Beauty of the North	Simon Fraser	*Fiddle Gems*

TITLE	COMPOSER	RECORDING
The North Side of the Grampians	Traditional	*Fiddle Gems*
The Expert Dancer	Traditional	*Fiddle Gems*
Huntley's Wedding Medley	Simon Fraser	*Fiddle Gems*
The Hawthorn Tree of Cawdor	Campbell	*Fiddle Gems*
Angus Fraser's Strathspey	Angus Fraser	*Fiddle Gems*
Mrs. Will	James Scott Skinner	*Fiddler's Fancy*
Mrs. James McInnes, Edinburgh	William Marshall	*Fiddler's Fancy*
Mr. Michie	Angus Fitchet	*Fiddler's Fancy*
The Earl of Fife	William Marshall	*Fiddler's Fancy*
Forbes Morrison	James Scott Skinner	*Fiddler's Fancy*
The Weeping Birches of Kilmorack	James Scott Skinner	*Fiddler's Fancy*
The Glen Cottage	James Scott Skinner	*Fiddler's Fancy*
Master Francis Sitwell	Nathaniel Gow	*A Tribute to Niel Gow*
Mrs. Chisholm of Chisholm	Niel Gow	*A Tribute to Niel Gow*
Lady MacKenzie of Coul	Traditional	*A Tribute to Niel Gow*
Mrs. MacDougall Grant	Niel Gow / Duff / Traditional	*A Tribute to Niel Gow*
Niel Gow's Compliments Returned to Mr. Marshall	Niel Gow	*A Tribute to Niel Gow*
Niel Gow's Strathspey	Duncan MacIntyre	*A Tribute to Niel Gow*
Niel Gow's Recovery	Niel Gow	*A Tribute to Niel Gow*
The Duchess of Bucchleauch's Favourite	Niel Gow	*A Tribute to Niel Gow*
Sir George Clerk of Pennycuik	Nathaniel Gow	*A Tribute to Niel Gow*
Lady Mary Ramsay	Nathaniel Gow	*A Tribute to Niel Gow* *Scottish Dance Masters, Vol. 4*
Duchess of Atholl's Slipper	Niel Gow	*A Tribute to Niel Gow* *Scottish Dance Masters, Vol. 2*
Lady Clementina Loughlan	Nathaniel Gow	*A Tribute to Niel Gow*
Dandy Dinmont	Joseph Lowe	*Scottish Fiddle Master*

TITLE	COMPOSER	RECORDING
The Morrisonian Strathspey	Ron Gonnella	*Scottish Fiddle Master*
Miss Marianne Oliphant's Strathspey (Rossie)	Robert Mackintosh	*Scottish Fiddle Master* *Scottish Dance Masters, Vol. 2*
Johnny Faa	Traditional	*Scottish Fiddle Master* *Fiddle & Pipe Favourites*
Miss Agnes Loudon	Robert Lowe	*Scottish Fiddle Master* *Scottish Dance Masters, Vol. 2*
Mr. Eager's Strathspey	Joseph Lowe	*Scottish Fiddle Master*
Willie Blair, Queen Victoria's Fiddler	Joseph Lowe	*Scottish Fiddle Master* *Scottish Dance Masters, Vol. 4*
Willie's Fair and Willie's Rare	Traditional	*Scottish Fiddle Master*
The Flowers of the Forest	Traditional	*Scottish Fiddle Master*
Miss Gray of Carse	Traditional	*Scottish Fiddle Master*
Glasgow Highlanders	Traditional	*International Friendship of the Fiddle*
The Master of Barga	Wilfred Gillies	*International Friendship of the Fiddle*
Neil and Rhona Gonnella's Silver Wedding	Ron Gonnella	*International Friendship of the Fiddle*
Brochan Lom (Orange and Blue)	Traditional	*International Friendship of the Fiddle*
Elliot's Fancy	Jimmy Shand	*International Friendship of the Fiddle*
The Duke of Gordon's Birthday	Traditional	*International Friendship of the Fiddle*
The Miller's Wedding	Robert Bremner	*Ron Gonnella's Burns Night*

TITLE	COMPOSER	RECORDING
Lennox Love to Blantyre	Traditional	*Ron Gonnella's Burns Night*
Castles in the Air	Traditional	*Ron Gonnella Playing a Stradivarius*
Miss Lyall	Traditional	*Ron Gonnella's Fiddle Magic* *Scottish Dance Masters, Vol. 2*
Gallaton	James Scott Skinner	*Ron Gonnella Playing a Stradivarius*
Milladen	James Scott Skinner	*Ron Gonnella Playing a Stradivarius*
Lady Louisa Gordon's Strathspey	Robert Mackintosh	*Ron Gonnella's Fiddle Magic*
Miss Clementina Drummond	Traditional	*Ron Gonnella's Fiddle Magic*
Cutty's Wedding	Traditional	*Ron Gonnella's Fiddle Magic*
The Banks of Clyde	Traditional	*Ron Gonnella's Fiddle Magic*
Miss Dow's Fancy	James Scott Skinner	*Ron Gonnella's Fiddle Magic*
The Standard on the Braes of Mar	Traditional	*Ron Gonnella's Fiddle Magic*
Bob Johnstone	Traditional	*Ron Gonnella's Fiddle Magic* *Platinum—70 Years of Dancing in St. Andrews*
She's Ower Young Tae Marry Yet	Traditional	*Scottish Dance Masters, Vol. 2*
Colonel Byng's Favourite	Niel Gow	*Scottish Dance Masters, Vol. 2*
Lady Graham's Strathspey	Traditional	*Scottish Dance Masters, Vol. 2*
The Braes of Tulliemet	Traditional	*Scottish Dance Masters, Vol. 3*

TITLE	COMPOSER	RECORDING
Duke of Alexander	Alexander Walker	*Scottish Dance Masters, Vol. 3*
Jessie Smith	Traditional	*Scottish Dance Masters, Vol. 3*
Mrs. Grant of Grant	Robert Mackintosh	*Scottish Dance Masters, Vol. 3*
Marquis of Huntley's Strathspey	William Marshall	*Scottish Dance Masters, Vol. 3*
Brechin Castle	Traditional	*Scottish Dance Masters, Vol. 3*
From Scotia's Shores We're Noo Awa'	Stan Hamilton	*Scottish Dance Masters, Vol. 4*
Miss Maureen Fraser's Strathspey	Ron Gonnella	*Scottish Dance Masters, Vol. 4*
Mrs. MacDonald of Clan Ranald	Nathaniel Gow	*Scottish Dance Masters, Vol. 4*
The Piper of Dundee	Traditional	*Scottish Dance Masters, Vol. 4* *Live From the Crieff Hydro*
Loudon's Bonnie Woods and Braes	Traditional	*Scottish Dance Masters, Vol. 4*
Struan Robertson's Rant	Traditional	*Scottish Dance Masters, Vol. 4*
South of the Grampians	James Scott Skinner	*Scottish Dance Masters, Vol. 4*
Captain Horne	Traditional	*Scottish Dance Masters, Vol. 4*
Bob and Anne's Strathspey	Ron Gonnella	*Scottish Dance Masters, Vol. 5* *Live From the Crieff Hydro*
Miss Jane Stewart	William Marshall	*Scottish Dance Masters, Vol. 5*
Miss Stewart's Strathspey, Pettyvaich	William Marshall	*Scottish Dance Masters, Vol. 5*

TITLE	COMPOSER	RECORDING
Duchess of Manchester	William Marshall	*Scottish Dance Masters, Vol. 5*
The Marchioness of Huntley's Strathspey	William Marshall	*The Lad of Kyle*
The Marquis of Huntley's Farewell	William Marshall	*The Lad of Kyle*
Mr. Gordon of Hallhead's Strathspey	William Marshall	*The Lad of Kyle*
Lady Ann Hope	John Pringle	*The Lad of Kyle*
Miss Barbara Stewart, West Part, Elgin	William Marshall	*The Lad of Kyle*
The Scotsman in America	Traditional	*The Lad of Kyle*
Ayrshire Lasses	Traditional	*The Lad of Kyle*
Green Grow the Rashes O	Traditional	*The Lad of Kyle*
Janet Leckie's Strathspey	Ron Gonnella	*Live From the Crieff Hydro*
The Woodbridge Strathspey	Gonnella	*Live From the Crieff Hydro*
Barbara Bruce of Upper Cairnie	Gonnella	*Live From the Crieff Hydro*
Miss Oliphant of Gask's Delight	Traditional	*Live From the Crieff Hydro*
Miss Amelia Oliphant	Traditional	*Live From the Crieff Hydro*
Our Highland Queen	James Scott Skinner	*Music for Eight Scottish Country Dances*
Arbeadie	James Scott Skinner	*Music for Eight Scottish Country Dances*
Davie Taylor	James Scott Skinner	*Music for Eight Scottish Country Dances*
Tuchan Lodge	James Scott Skinner	*Music for Eight Scottish Country Dances*

TITLE	COMPOSER	RECORDING
Hamilton's	James Scott Skinner	*Music for Eight Scottish Country Dances*
The Reel of the Royal Scots	Muriel Johnstone	*Music for Eight Scottish Country Dances*
Dunie Mains	James Stewart Robertson	*Music for Eight Scottish Country Dances*
Duncan Donald's Strathspey	Sandy Donald	*Platinum—70 Years of Dancing in St. Andrews*
Tom Dey	James Scott Skinner	*Platinum—70 Years of Dancing in St. Andrews*
Ceres Green	Traditional	*Platinum—70 Years of Dancing in St. Andrews*
Sister Thomson's Strathspey	Billy Anderson	*Platinum—70 Years of Dancing in St. Andrews*
Kinloss	J.S. Brown	*Platinum—70 Years of Dancing in St. Andrews*
Mr. Eagers	Traditional	*Platinum—70 Years of Dancing in St. Andrews*
Fiddler Play the Light Strathspey	Traditional	*Platinum—70 Years of Dancing in St. Andrews*
Charlie Todd's Strathspey	Billy Anderson	*Platinum—70 Years of Dancing in St. Andrews*
Dr. Alexander of Balmerino	Traditional	*Platinum—70 Years of Dancing in St. Andrews*
The Minister of Birse	Traditional	*Platinum—70 Years of Dancing in St. Andrews*

TITLE	COMPOSER	RECORDING
The Countess of Dalhousie	William Marshall	*The Countess of Dalhousie*
The Laird of Dumblair	James Scott Skinner	*The Countess of Dalhousie*
Dorrator Bridge	Traditional	*Fiddle & Pipe Favourites*
Irene Meldrum's Welcome to Bon Accord	William Meldrum	*Fiddle & Pipe Favourites*
Glen Caladh Castle	John MacClellan	*Fiddle & Pipe Favourites*

Marches

TITLE	COMPOSER	RECORDING
Scott Skinner's Compliments to Dr. MacDonald	James Scott Skinner	*Scottish Violin Music*
The Countess of Dalhousie	Niel Gow, Jr.	*Plays the Fiddles of Gow, Marshall and Skinner*
Louis Gonnella of Muirhead	Ron Gonnella	*Plays the Fiddles of Gow, Marshall and Skinner*
Captain Cameron's Volunteers' March—Balvenie	William Marshall	*Plays the Fiddles of Gow, Marshall and Skinner*
The March to Reform Street	Ron Gonnella	*The Lad of Kyle*
The Maid That Made the Bed to Me	Traditional	*Fiddle Gems*
My Wife is Forever Storming at Me	Traditional	*Fiddle Gems*
The Rebel War Song	Traditional	*Fiddle Gems*
Dumbarton Castle	James Scott Skinner	*Fiddler's Fancy*
Hoo Dinna Ye Play Mair?	James Scott Skinner	*Fiddler's Fancy*
Atholl Volunteers' March	Niel Gow	*A Tribute to Niel Gow*
The Dunkeld Volunteers	Niel Gow	*A Tribute to Niel Gow*
Earl of Dalhousie's Happy Return to Scotland	Niel Gow	*A Tribute to Niel Gow*

TITLE	COMPOSER	RECORDING
Lady Dorothea Stewart Murray's Wedding March	Aeneas Rose	*A Tribute to Niel Gow*
Willie Smith	Peter Milne	*Scottish Fiddle Master*
Jamie Lyall	Peter Milne	*Scottish Fiddle Master*
Murdoch McPherson's March	Ron Gonnella	*International Friendship of the Fiddle*
Professor Blackie	James Scott Skinner	*International Friendship of the Fiddle*
Morrison's Academy Anniversary March	Ron Gonnella	*Ron Gonnella Playing a Stradivarius*
Morrison's Academy Anniversary March	Ron Gonnella	*Ron Gonnella Playing a Stradivarius*
Crieff Hydro March	Ron Gonnella	*Ron Gonnella Playing a Stradivarius* *Live From the Crieff Hydro*
General Baille	James Scott Skinner	*Ron Gonnella Playing a Stradivarius*
Cape Breton March	Traditional	*Ron Gonnella Playing a Stradivarius*
The Queen's Welcome to Invercauld	James Scott Skinner	*Ron Gonnella Playing a Stradivarius*
The Cock o' the North	Traditional	*Scottish Dance Masters, Vol. 2*
Miss MacLachlan's March	Traditional	*Scottish Dance Masters, Vol. 2*
Mr. and Mrs. Victor Jamieson	Ian MacPhail	*Scottish Dance Masters, Vol. 2*
Campbell's Farewell to Redcastle	William Ross	*Scottish Dance Masters, Vol. 3*
The Barren Rocks of Aden	Traditional	*Scottish Dance Masters, Vol. 3*
Donald Mowatt's March	Ron Gonnella	*Scottish Dance Masters, Vol. 3*
Highland Laddie	Traditional	*Scottish Dance Masters, Vol. 3*

TITLE	COMPOSER	RECORDING
Auchmountain's Bonnie Glen	John Balloch	*Scottish Dance Masters, Vol. 3*
Mount Stewart House	Traditional	*The Countess of Dalhousie*
The Skye Gathering	Traditional	*Fiddle & Pipe Favourites*
The Taking of Beaumont Hamel	John MacClellan	*Fiddle & Pipe Favourites*

Hornpipes

TITLE	COMPOSER	RECORDING
Dunkeld Steeple	Gow	*Violin Music From the Gow Collections*
Admiral Nelson's Hornpipe	Gow	*Plays the Fiddles of Gow, Marshall and Skinner* *Scottish Dance Masters, Vol. 2*
Lowe's Hornpipe	Marshall	*Fiddler's Fancy*
Herbie MacLeod's Hornpipe	Gonnella	*Scottish Fiddle Master* *Ron Gonnella Playing a Stradivarius*
Miss Mary Lee's Delight	Abraham Mackintosh	*Scottish Fiddle Master*
The Beaux of Oak Hill	Traditional	*International Friendship of the Fiddle*
Aldridge's Hornpipe	Traditional	*Ron Gonnella Playing a Stradivarius* *Scottish Dance Masters, Vol. 2*
Mr. Wilson's Hornpipe	Traditional	*Fiddle Magic*
Fancy Hornpipe	Traditional	*Fiddle Magic*
Kirk's Hornpipe	Traditional	*Fiddle Magic* *Fiddle & Pipe Favourites*

TITLE	COMPOSER	RECORDING
Hey, Johnnie Cope	Traditional	*Fiddle Magic*
Miss Jessie Scales' Hornpipe	Traditional	*Scottish Dance Masters, Vol. 2*
Bonnie Charlie	Gow	*Scottish Dance Masters, Vol. 2*
The Storrers Hornpipe	Traditional	*Scottish Dance Masters, Vol. 3* *Fiddle & Pipe Favourites*
The Victoria Hornpipe	James Hand	*Fiddle & Pipe Favourites*
The Stonehaven March (Horn.)	Traditional	*Fiddle & Pipe Favourites*
Angus MacKinnon	Traditional	*Fiddle & Pipe Favourites*

Polkas

TITLE	COMPOSER	RECORDING
Laggan Burn	Traditional	*Burns Night*
Peter Alliss' Polka	[Unknown]	*Fiddle & Pipe Favourites*

Scots Measures

TITLE	COMPOSER	RECORDING
The Marchfield Brae Scots Measure	Ron Gonnella	*Ron Gonnella Playing a Stradivarius*
Lady Mary Hay's Scotch Measure	Niel Gow	*Scottish Dance Masters, Vol. 3*
The Lass O' Livingstone	Traditional	*Scottish Dance Masters, Vol. 3*
The Cairdin O't	Traditional	*Scottish Dance Masters, Vol. 3*

Compilation Albums

TITLE	COMPOSER	RECORDING	RECORDING
The Weavers of Newly	Strathspey	Traditional	*An Edinburgh Fancy*
The Flowers of Edinburgh	Reel	Traditional	*An Edinburgh Fancy*
Niel Gow's Lament for James Moray Esq. of Abercairnie	Air	Niel Gow	*An Edinburgh Fancy*
Cradle Song	Air	James Scott Skinner	*Treasures of Scotland* *Sounds of Scotland* *The Tartan Top Twenty* *Highland Magic* *A Beginner's Guide to Traditional Scottish Music*
Roseacre	Air	James Scott Skinner	*Treasures of Scotland*
Forbes Morrison	Strathspey	James Scott Skinner	*Treasures of Scotland*
Davie Work	Reel	James Scott Skinner	*Treasures of Scotland*
The Dunkeld Volunteers	March	Niel Gow	*Treasures of Scotland*
Niel Gow's Lament for the Death of His Second Wife	Air	Niel Gow	*Treasures of Scotland*
Lady MacKenzie	Strathspey	Traditional	*Treasures of Scotland*
The White Cockade	Reel	Traditional	*Scotland Forever*
Mount Stewart House	March	Traditional	*Scotland Forever*

TITLE	COMPOSER	RECORDING	RECORDING
Miss Mary Douglas	Reel	James MacDonald	*Scotland Forever*
Captain Cameron's Volunteers' March—Balvenie	March	William Marshall	*Scotland Forever*
The Marchioness of Huntley's Jig	Jig	William Marshall	*Scotland Forever*
Craigellachie Lasses	Jig	William Marshall	*Scotland Forever*
The Bonnie Lass o' Bon Accord	Air	James Scott Skinner	*Sounds of Scotland* *The Tartan Top Twenty*
A Man's a Man (Lady MacIntosh's Reel)	Reel	Traditional	*The Tartan Top Twenty*
Annie Laurie	Air	Traditional	*Scotland—The Music of a Nation*
Miss Barstow's Reel	Reel	Robert Mackintosh	*Scotland—The Music of a Nation*
Miss Robertson's Reel	Reel	Traditional	*Scotland—The Music of a Nation*
John Anderson My Jo	Air	Traditional/Burns	*The Whisky Collection*
Green Grow the Rushes, O	Strathspey	Traditional	*The Whisky Collection*
Willie Brewed a Peck o' Maut	Reel	Traditional	*The Whisky Collection*
The Provost of St. Vigeans	Jig	Lindsay Ross	*FolkMusic From Scotland* *Hawks & Eagles* *Folksongs From Scotland* *Great Folk Medleys* *Flowers of Edinburgh* *Dancing in the Kyle*

TITLE	COMPOSER	RECORDING	RECORDING
The Corner House	Jig	Andrew Rankine	*Folk Music From Scotland* *Hawks & Eagles* *Folksongs From Scotland* *Great Folk Medleys* *Flowers of Edinburgh* *Dancing in the Kyle*
Bonnie Dundee	Jig	Traditional	*Folksongs From Scotland* *Flowers of Edinburgh*
Athole and Breadalbane Gathering	March	William Ferguson	*1st National Festival*
Lady Madeline Sinclair	Strathspey	Traditional	*1st National Festival*
The High Road to Linton	Reel	Traditional	*1st National Festival*
The Rowan Tree	Air	Traditional	*A Scottish Evening*
Durisdeer	Air	Lady John Scott	*Tartan Top Twenty*
Aye Waukin O	Air	Traditional	*Tartan Top Twenty*
Caller Herring		Traditional	*Best of Accordion & Fiddle*
My Love is Like a Red, Red Rose	Air	Traditional	*Best of Accordion & Fiddle*
Haig of Bemersyde	Strathspey	Johnson / Skinner	*A Fife Fairing*
Dunie Mains	Strathspey	James Stewart Robertson	*A Fife Fairing*
Kilwinning Archers	Strathspey	Traditional	*A Fife Fairing*
The Duchess of Hamilton	Strathspey	Traditional	*A Fife Fairing*

TITLE	COMPOSER	RECORDING	RECORDING
Jockey's Dance	Jig	Traditional	*A Fife Fairing* *Music for Fifteen Dances*
Lady Charlotte Bruce's	Jig	Nathaniel Gow	*A Fife Fairing*
The Gobbie O'	Jig	Traditional	*A Fife Fairing* *Music for Fifteen Dances*
Rev. Archibald Minto's	Jig	Ron Gonnella	*A Fife Fairing* *Music for Fifteen Dances*
Joe MacDiarmid's Jig	Jig	Rob Loch	*A Fife Fairing*
The Academy	Jig	J. Rule	*A Fife Fairing*
Hot Punch	Jig	Traditional	*A Fife Fairing*
The Steamboat	Jig	Traditional	*A Fife Fairing*
Our Highland Queen	Strathspey	J. Scott Skinner	*A Fife Fairing*
Gallaton	Strathspey	J. Scott Skinner	*A Fife Fairing*
Arbeadie	Strathspey	J. Scott Skinner	*A Fife Fairing*
Davie Taylor	Strathspey	J. Scott Skinner	*A Fife Fairing*
Tulchan Lodge	Strathspey	J. Scott Skinner	*A Fife Fairing*
Hamilton's Strathspey	Strathspey	J. Scott Skinner	*A Fife Fairing*
Milladen	Strathspey	J. Scott Skinner	*A Fife Fairing*
Niel Gow's Fiddle	Strathspey	Nathaniel Gow	*Ariel Yoga*
A Waltz for Elizabeth	Waltz	Ron Gonnella	*Bill McCue Visits The Heart of Scotland*

APPENDIX B

Tune Collections

This appendix includes the foreword and contents of Gonnella's tune collections.

Foreword

We, in Scotland, are fortunate to possess a vast heritage of tuneful fiddle music which was written and collected some two hundred years ago by men like Niel Gow, William Marshall, and Robert Burns. Their music gives us a fascinating glimpse into the past and, as life today becomes increasingly impersonal, the picture of a bygone age which such music evokes for so many Scots satisfies their deep need for a sense of identity. Not surprisingly then, fiddle music is now being heard by far greater audiences than ever before and, in addition, more and more people are rediscovering the delights of personal music making. Many, however, who would like to play vintage fiddle music often find this well-nigh impossible since the great collections of the eighteenth- and nineteenth-century fiddle player-composers have been out of print for many years. My first collection of fiddle music makes available, again, the music of the Gows, William Marshall, Captain Simon Fraser, and others. All the airs have been specially selected from my current series of record albums of the fiddle music of Scotland and are written, in my own hand, as I play them. I hope you will enjoy playing these fine old fiddle tunes as much as I do!

Contents

Archibald MacDonald of Keppoch (Collected by Captain Simon Fraser)
Aw' wi' Your Witchcraft o' Beauty's (Collected by Robert Burns)

Belladrum House (Fraser)
Chapel Keithack (William Marshall)
Dunkeld Volunteers (Gow)
Earl of Fife, The (Marshall)
Expert Dancer, The (Fraser)
Favourite Dram, The (Fraser)
General Gathering, 1745, The (Fraser)
Glemorriston (Fraser)
Hon. James Ramsay's Reel, The (Niel Gow, Junior)
Lady Anne Hope's Favourite (Gow)
Lady Charlotte Bruce's Favourite (Nathaniel Gow)
Lady Niven Lumsden of Achindoir (Marshall)
Lochrynach (Marshall)
Lowe's Hornpipe (Marshall)
Merrymaking, The (Fraser)
Miss Gordon of Park (Marshall)
Miss Hannah's Jig—Elgin (Marshall)
Mrs. James McInnes, Edinburgh (Marshall)
Mrs. Macdonald of Clan Ranald (Nathaniel Gow)
Mrs. Macdouall Grant (Nathaniel Gow)
My Love is Like a Red, Red Rose [Major Graham] (Burns)
Nathaniel Gow's lament for the Death of His Brother
Niel Gow's Compliments Returned to Mr. Marshall
Niel Gow's Strathspey (Macintyre)
Northern Meeting, The (Fraser)
Northern Racecourse, The (Fraser)
O, Wert Thou in the Cauld Blast [Lenox Love to Blantyre] (Burns)
Prince Charlie's Quickstep (Coll. by Anne, Duchess of Atholl)
Rebel War Song, The (Fraser)
Sitting in the Stern of a Boat (McLeod)
Sprightly Minikin, The (Fraser)
Well May Charlie Wear the Crown (Fraser)
Well May My True Love Arrive (Fraser)

FOREWORD

Following the enthusiastic reception given to my first collection of vintage fiddle music, and in response to numerous requests from players in many parts of Scotland and overseas, I am now happy to present my second collection. Many of the features which proved so successful in Volume One have been retained. The tunes are again carefully selected from all facets of my recording and broadcasting repertoire and included specially is music by Nathaniel Gow's teacher, Robert Mackintosh, of whom John Glen said that "His compositions stamp him as a musician of the first order in Scottish Music." In addition, Volume Two contains several of my own compositions and also highlights many of the magnificent airs written by that select band of fiddle players who doubled as dancing masters, and who therefore knew intimately the subtle links between music and the dance.

Join me then and recreate for yourself some more of Scotland's finest fiddle music.

CONTENTS

The Atholl Volunteers (Niel Gow)
Bert Gonnella's Jig (Gonnella)
Earl of Dalhousie's Happy Return to Scotland, The (Niel Gow, Junior)
Fife and Forfar Hunt's Favourite, The (David and Archie Allan)
Herbie McLeod's Hornpipe (Gonnella)
James Miller, Bullionfield (Traditional)
Jamie Gow, Crathie Bellman (Robert Lowe)
Jamie Lyall (Peter Milne)
Lizzie Duncan's Fancy (Gonnella)
Miss Agnes Loudon (Lowe)
Miss Barstow's Reel (Robert Mackintosh)
Miss Campbell of Saddell (R. Mackintosh)
Miss Jessie Scales' Hornpipe (Abraham Mackintosh)
Miss Loudon (Lowe)
Miss Lucy Johnston's Compliments to Niel Gow
Miss Robertson (Mackintosh)
Miss Sandra Webster (Gonnella)
Miss Sophia Campbell (of Saddell's) Reel (R. Mackintosh)
Morrisonian Strathspey, The (Gonnella)
Mr. John Trotter's Hornpipe (R. Mackintosh)
Mrs. Trotter (of Castlelaw's) Reel (R. Mackintosh)
Prince of Wales, The (Lowe)
Rut Bell's Reel (Gonnella)
Sauteuse (Lowe)

Gonnella, R. (1982) *The Ron Gonnella Collection of Fiddle Music, Volume Three*. Crieff: Ron Gonnella.

Willie Blair [Queen Victoria's Fiddler] (Joseph Lowe)
Willie Smith (Milne)

FOREWORD

Since my first volume of vintage fiddle music was published in 1977, several other collections have also helped to circulate many airs from Scotland's heritage of fiddle music.

Nevertheless, despite the increased number of tunes in print, all but a few of the airs in my third collection are now available for the first time this century. As before, the tunes are mostly in playing sets and are presented with chord symbols equally suited for Scottish dance band work. As with Volume One and Volume Two, I have not offered any interpretative indications since most fiddle players will play the tunes their own way in any case and also because many of the qualities essential for satisfying performances—mellow fiddle tone—lilting musicianship—security of pitch and spontaneity are difficult if not impossible to convey on the printed page and are better acquired through selective listening and imitation. The fruits of my thirty years' experience in broadcasting, recording and concertising have gone in to the selection and interpretation of the 80-odd melodies in my three collections and these interpretations are available on my many record albums, the tenth of which is a unique recording of the personal fiddles of Niel Gow, William Marshall, and James Scott Skinner.

CONTENTS

Ashton Gonnella of Shreveport, Louisiana (Ron Gonnella)
Barbara Bruce of Upper Cairnie (Gonnella)
Braes of Glenturrote (Traditional)
Bob and Anne's Strathspey (Gonnella)
Countess of Dalhousie (Niel Gow, Junior)
Crieff Hydro March (Gonnella)
Dandie Dinmont (Joseph Lowe)
De'il Among the Mantua-Makers (William Marshall)
Duncan Macdonald's Fiddle (Gonnella)
Earl of Morton's Jig (Will Gow)
Edith Raitt's Jig (Gonnella)
Elizabeth Donaldson's Reel (Gonnella)
Happy May the Pair Be (Gonnella)
Hymn To The Saviour (Traditional)
In Dispraise of Whisky (Traditional)
Janet Leckie's Strathspey (Gonnella)
Landlady of Inver Inn (Niel Gow)
Louis Gonnella of Muirhead (Gonnella)
Major L. Stewart's Reel of the Island of Java (Marshall)
Miss Oliphant of Gask's Delight (Traditional)

Gonnella, R. and Murray, E.M.E. (1986) *The New Atholl Collection of Scottish Fiddle Music and Dances: Commemorating Robert Burns' 1787 Highland Tour*. Bruceton Mills, W.V.: ScotPress.

Miss Rattray (Traditional)
Mr. Duncan's Delight (Robert Mackintosh)
Ron Gonnella's Compliments to Senator Robert Byrd of West Virginia
Ron Gonnella's Homage to the Gows, Marshall and Skinner
Rosemary's Reel (Gonnella)
Sir Walter Scott (Niel Gow, Junior)
Woodbridge Strathspey (Gonnella)

"To commemorate the bicentenary of Robert Burns' Highland Tour of 1787, being a compilation of Scottish fiddle music, Scottish Country Dances, descriptive text and photographs." [Includes photographs and information about each location.] Foreword by His Grace, The Duke of Atholl. Introduction to Burns' Tour.

CONTENTS

The Queen's Visit to Morrison's Academy
Dollar
Dance: Senator Robert C. Byrd of West Virginia
Music: Senator Robert C. Byrd of West Virginia / Herbie MacLeod's (32-bar Reel)
Hornpipe / The No-Name Tune
Strathearn
Morrison's Academy Anniversary March
Dance: The Scottish Fiddler o' Crieff (32-bar Jig)
Music: Bert Gonnella's Jig / Lizzie Duncan's Fancy
Crieff Hydro March
Captain Frank Thomson, Crieff Golf Club
Rev. Archie Minto's Farewell to St. Andrew's Kirk
Atholl
Dance: The Vale of Atholl (32-bar Jig)
Music: The Duke of Atholl's Jig
Dance: Colonel Anne of Moy Hall (32-bar Reel)
Music: Miss Sandra Webster / Evelyn M.E. Murray of Cambridge, Massachusetts
Fochabers: William Marshall and Gordon Castle
Dance: Our Compliments to William Marshall (32-bar Strathspey)
Music: Bob and Anne's Strathspey
Dundee
The March to Reform Street
Dance: The Rose and the Saltire (32-bar Medley)
Music: Woodbridge Strathspey / Rosemary's Reel
Bill Craig's Jig
Dance: The Scottish Fiddle Jig (32-bar Jig)
Music: Duncan MacDonald's Fiddle

APPENDIX C

Indicative Table of Gonnella's BBC Scotland Broadcasts

BROADCAST	DATE	DESCRIPTION	MUSICIANS
BBC Home Service Scottish	Thursday 14 August 1958 18.45	Ronald Gonnella	Ronald Gonnella
BBC Home Service Scottish	Friday 3 October 1958 20.30	The Edinburgh Players	Ronald Gonnella Tryphena Nixon (contralto) John Tainsh (tenor)
BBC Home Service Scottish	Wednesday 26 March 1958	Scots Fiddle Music	Ronald D. Gonnella
BBC Home Service Scottish	Thursday 1 January 1959 21.45	"Music for a While" The Edinburgh Players	Ronald Gonnella Margaret Fraser (soprano)
BBC Home Service Scottish	Tuesday 3 March 1959 19.00	[No title]	Ronald Gonnella Thomas Pearston (bagpipes)
BBC Home Service Scottish	Sunday 26 April 1959 15.45	"Music for a While": Scots Tunes The Edinburgh Players	Ronald Gonnella Neiliann MacLeod (soprano) John Renwick (baritone)
BBC Home Service Scottish	Friday 13 November 1959 15.45	"Music for a While" The Edinburgh Players	Ronald Gonnella James Kelman Ursula Davidson

BROADCAST	DATE	DESCRIPTION	MUSICIANS
BBC Home Service Scottish	Saturday 15 April 1961 18.50	"Scots Fiddle Music"	Ronald Gonnella
BBC Home Service Scottish	Saturday 21 October 1961 18.50	"Scottish Fiddle Music"	Ronald Gonnella
BBC Home Service Scottish	Thursday 15 February 1962 21.00	The Edinburgh Players	Ronald Gonnella Dorothy Robertson
BBC Home Service Scottish	Saturday 31 August 1963 18.45	Ronald Gonnella and His Scottish Dance Quartet	Ronald Gonnella and His Scottish Dance Quartet
BBC Home Service Scottish	Saturday 19 October 1963 18.40	Ronald Gonnella and His Scottish Dance Quartet	Ronald Gonnella and His Scottish Dance Quartet
BBC Home Service Scottish	Wednesday 11 December 1963 18.35	Ronald Gonnella and His Scottish Dance Quartet	Ronald Gonnella and His Scottish Dance Quartet
BBC Home Service Scottish	Sunday 8 March 1964 13.40	Ronald Gonnella, Fiddle	Ronald Gonnella
BBC Light Programme	Wednesday 15 April 1964 7.00	[No Title]	Ronnie Pleydell and His Orchestra, Sidney Sax and His Music, The Frank Willoughby Trio. Ron Gonnella and His Scottish Dance Quartet
BBC Home Service Scottish	Saturday 20 June 1964 18.30	Ronald Gonnella and His Scottish Dance Quartet	Ronald Gonnella and His Scottish Dance Quartet
BBC Home Service Scottish	Wednesday 26 August 1964 18.35	Ronald Gonnella and His Scottish Dance Quartet	Ronald Gonnella and His Scottish Dance Quartet

BROADCAST	DATE	DESCRIPTION	MUSICIANS
BBC Home Service Scottish	Friday 27 November 1964 18.35	Ron Gonnella and His Scottish Dance Quartet	Ron Gonnella and His Scottish Dance Quartet
BBC Home Service Scottish	Saturday 26 December 1964	Ronald Gonnella Robert Wardrope (baritone) Jimmy McIntosh and His Band	Ronald Gonnella Robert Wardrope (baritone) Jimmy McIntosh and His Band
BBC Home Service Scottish	Monday 8 February 1965 18.37	Ron Gonnella and His Scottish Dance Quartet	Ronald Gonnella and His Scottish Dance Quartet
BBC Network Three	Sunday 14 March 1965 10.30	'Music in Miniature' A musical entertainment given by The Scottish Trio: Louis Carus (violin) Joan Dickson (cello) Wight Henderson (piano)	Ronald Gonnella (violin) Margaret Fraser (soprano) Bernard Sumner (harpsichord) Henry Morrison (clarinet) Julian Dawson (piano)
BBC Home Service Scottish	Wednesday 28 April 1965 12.30	Ron Gonnella and His Scottish Dance Quartet	Ron Gonnella and His Scottish Dance Quartet
BBC Home Service Scottish	Wednesday 30 June 1965 18.35	Ron Gonnella and His Scottish Dance Quartet	Ron Gonnella and His Scottish Dance Quartet
BBC Home Service Scottish	Saturday 24 July 1965 18.30	Ron Gonnella; Martin Hayes and His Band	Ron Gonnella; Martin Hayes and His Band
BBC Home Service Scottish	Wednesday 1 September 1965 18.35	Ron Gonnella and His Scottish Dance Quartet	Ron Gonnella and His Scottish Dance Quartet

BROADCAST	DATE	DESCRIPTION	MUSICIANS
BBC Home Service Scottish	Saturday 27 November 1965 18.45	Ron Gonnella and His Scottish Dance Quartet	Ron Gonnella and His Scottish Dance Quartet
BBC Home Service Scottish	Saturday 21 May 1966 18.35	The Hawthorne Accordion Band; Ron Gonnella	The Hawthorne Accordion Band; Ron Gonnella
BBC Home Service Scottish	Saturday 16 July 1966 18.30	Ron Gonnella and His Scottish Dance Quartet	Ron Gonnella and His Scottish Dance Quartet
BBC Home Service Scottish	Tuesday 11 October 1966 12.30	Ron Gonnella and His Scottish Dance Quartet	Ron Gonnella and His Scottish Dance Quartet
BBC Home Service Scottish	Saturday 19 November 1966	Ron Gonnella and His Scottish Dance Quartet	Ron Gonnella and His Scottish Dance Quartet
BBC Home Service Scottish	Tuesday 14 March 1967 12.30	Ron Gonnella (violin) The Highland Country Band	Ron Gonnella (violin) The Highland Country Band
BBC One Scotland	1982 [No dates or times available] Six Episodes	On The Fiddle Series Ron Gonnella, Presenter	Guests: Angus Fitchet, Jimmy Shand, Tom Anderson, Douglas Lawrence, Willie Hunter, Jimmy Moir, Niel Gow Episode Filmed on location in Perthshire
BBC One Scotland	Sunday 25 November 1984 10.30 (and 26 Nov.) 2.0	'Music Weekly' Burns and the Scottish Folk Heritage	Ron Gonnella

BROADCAST	DATE	DESCRIPTION	MUSICIANS
BBC Radio 2	Wednesday 27 August 1986 20.30	'Scottish Dance Party from Dunblane Hydro'	Craigowl Scottish Dance Band with Ron Gonnella
BBC Radio 2	Wednesday 2, 9, 16 March 1988 20.30	'Dancing Fiddles' Series A Programme of 'light' Scottish music as interpreted by Ron Gonnella (fiddle)	George MacIlwham (flute/piccolo) Rhona McKay (harp/clarsach) Walter Blair (piano) Graham Robb (bass)
BBC Radio 2	Wednesday 7, 14, 21, 28 June 1989	'Dancing Fiddles' Series Ron Gonnella, Presenter	[Same as above] Angus Cameron (fiddle) joined the ensemble beginning with the 14 June 1989 broadcast
BBC Radio 2	Wednesday 5 July 1989	'Dancing Fiddles' Series	George MacIlwham (flute/piccolo) Rhona McKay (harp/clarsach) Walter Blair (piano) Graham Robb (bass) Angus Cameron (fiddle)
BBC One Scotland	Sunday 26 January 1986 18.40	'Songs of Praise' from the town of Crieff. Includes a hymn written by Gonnella	'We Praise Thee, Lord,' written for primary students at Morrison's Academy, Crieff

SCOTTISH
VIOLIN
MUSIC
played by
RONALD
GONNELLA
SCOTS DISC

scottish violin music from
THE GOW COLLECTIONS
played by ron gonnella

LISMOR
Fiddler's Fancy
The Music of Scott Skinner and William Marshall
Ron Gonnella

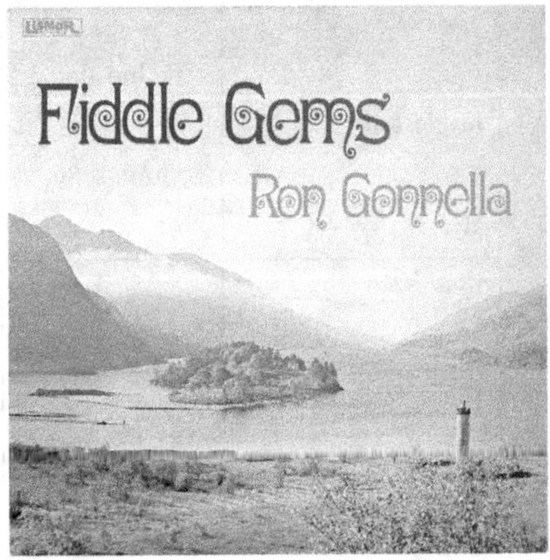
LISMOR
Fiddle Gems
Ron Gonnella

LISMOR
Ron Gonnella's
BURNS NIGHT

LISMOR
Ron Gonnella
SCOTTISH FIDDLE
MASTER

APPENDIX D

Comprehensive List of Albums

This appendix details performers and covers of each of Gonnella's recordings.

An Edinburgh Fancy (1964)
With Robert Campbell (Piano)
Scottish Violin Music (1966)
    With Robert Campbell (Piano)
My Scotland—Four Sequences of Scots Words and Music with Andrew Cruickshank (1968)
The Music Teacher of Williamsburg (1970)
    With Various Musicians from Colonial Williamsburg, Virginia
Scottish Violin Music from the Gow Collections (1973).
    With Hugh Melvin (Piano)
Lorne Scottish Dance Band: Danse Ecossaises, Vol. 2 (1973)
    With Alastair Hunter (Accordion), Jessie Cruikshank (Piano), Alasdair Cameron (Bass), Jack Stephen (Drums)
Fiddler's Fancy (1975)
Fiddle Gems (1976)
    With George Donald (Piano) and John Strachan (Bass Guitar)
Ron Gonnella's Burns Night (1977)
    With Walter Blair (Piano) and John Strachan (Bass Guitar)
Ron Gonnella: Scottish Fiddle Master (1980)
Ron Gonnella and Friends Live From the Crieff Hydro (1981)
    With Morag Murray (Vocals), Iain MacPhail (Accordion), John Gibson (Piano)
Treasures of Scotland (1981, 2007)
Scottish Dance Masters (1982)
    With Andrew Rankine (Accordion)

RON GONNELLA and friends
LIVE from CRIEFF HYDRO

The Scottish Dance Masters
Iain MacPhail - Ron Gonnella
Nine Full-length Scottish Country Dances
Volume Two
The 'Atholl Brose' 37 Blanchard Road Cambridge Mass. 02138 U.S.A

Scottish Dance Masters
Volume Three
The Ron Gonnella Strings
with George MacIlwham (flute)
Eight Full-Length
Scottish Country Dances
The Atholl Brose
37 Blanchard Road, Cambridge, Massachusetts 02138 USA

AB009D
Scottish Dance Masters
Vol. 4
Bobby Brown
Producer
Stan Hamilton
Piano
Ron Gonnella
Fiddle
Atholl Brose Recordings

Ron Gonnella
plays the fiddles of
Gow, Marshall and Skinner
William Marshall's
Fiddle
J. Scott Skinner's
"Stroh" Fiddle
Introduction by
His Grace, The Duke of Atholl.
Blair Castle

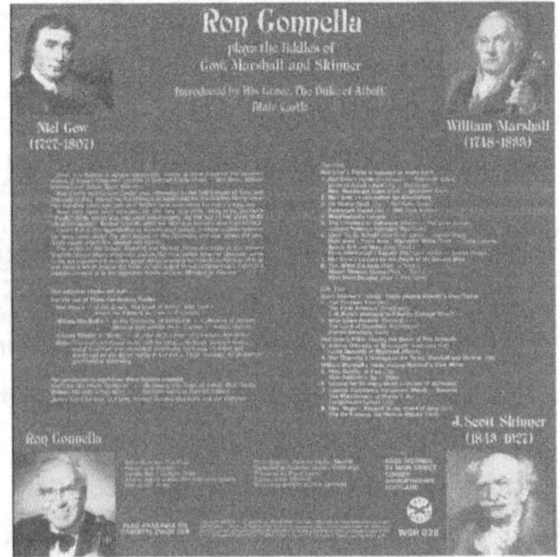
Ron Gonnella
plays the fiddles of
Gow, Marshall and Skinner
Introduced by His Grace, The Duke of Atholl
Blair Castle
Niel Gow
(1727-1807)
William Marshall
(1748-1833)
J. Scott Skinner
(1843-1927)
Ron Gonnella

Ron Gonnella Plays the Fiddles of Gow, Marshall and Skinner (1982)
With John Gibson (Piano), Graham Robb (Double Bass)
Music of the Fiddle, Vol. 5 (1982) [Same content as preceding album]
With John Gibson (Piano), Graham Robb (Double Bass)
Scottish Box and Fiddle: The Best of Accordion & Fiddle Music (1982)
Scottish Fireside Fiddle Chats
Ron Gonnella (Fiddle and Narrator]
Vol. 1: *Robert Burns and Niel Gow* (1982)
Vol. 2: *J. Scott Skinner also "Have you the Gaelic?"* (1985)
Vol. 3: *A Gordon For Me and Playing Second Fiddle* (1985)
Royal Scottish Dance Society Music for Eight Scottish Country Dances (1983)
The Ron Gonnella Quartet: Ron Gonnella (Fiddle), Iain MacPhail (Accordion), David Flockhart (Piano), Stan Saunders (Bass)
Scottish Dance Masters, Vol. 2 (1984)
With Ian MacPhail (Accordion)
Scottish Dance Masters, Vol. 3 (c. 1983)
With George MacIlwham (Flute)
The Scottish Sound of Ron Gonnella Playing a Stradivarius (1984)
With George Donald (Piano), Graham Robb (Bass)
Scotland Forever (1984, 2007)
National Scotland (1985)
Note: This recording provided radio and television producers tunes from which they could choose to accompany particular scenes or as background music.
The Lad of Kyle (1986)
With George MacIlwham (Flute), Angus Cameron (Fiddle), Bill Hendry (Piano), John Strachan (String Bass), Walter Blair (Piano)
Sounds of Scotland (1987, 2007)
A Tribute to Niel Gow (1987)
Saint Andrews Branch Golden Jubilee (1987)
With David Cunningham Trio: David Cunningham (Accordion), Graham Berry (Keyboards), Ian Adamson (Drums)
Highland Magic (1987, 2007)
Scotland—The Music of a Nation (1987)
Ron Gonnella's International Friendship of the Fiddle (1988, 2003, 2012)
With George Donald (Piano), John Strachan (String Bass)
Scottish Dance Masters, Vol. 4 (1988)
With Stan Hamilton and His Band
Music for Fifteen Dances (1990)
The Ron Gonnella Quartet (members not specified)

The Scottish Sound
of
Ron Gonnella
playing
a
Stradivarius

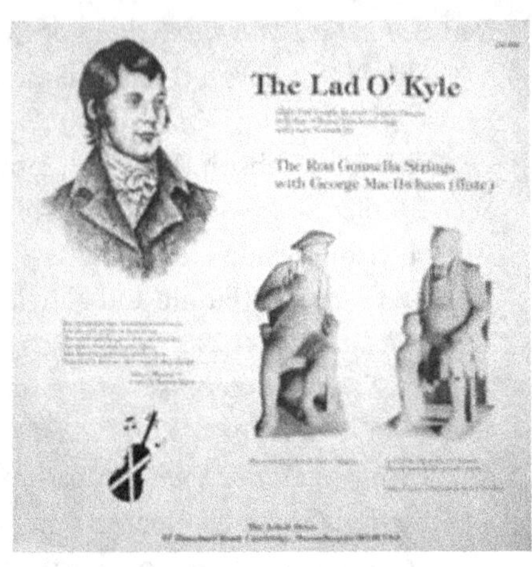
The Lad O' Kyle
The Ron Gonnella Strings
with George MacIlwham (flute)

LISMOR
A Tribute to Niel Gow
Ron Gonnella

A Tribute to Niel Gow
Ron Gonnella
250 YEARS OF FIDDLE MUSIC
SIDE ONE
SIDE TWO
LISMOR

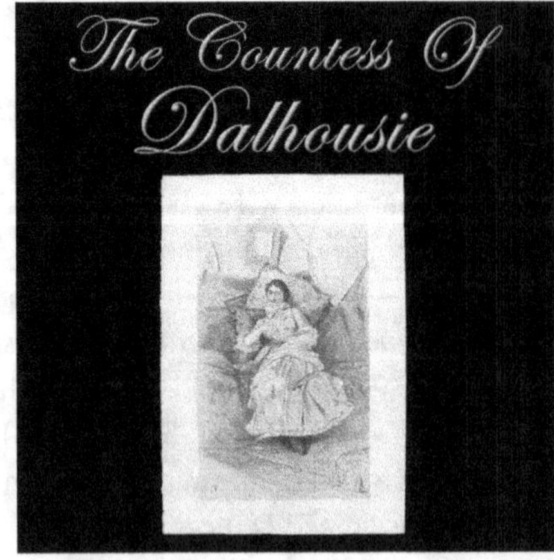
The Countess Of
Dalhousie

Scottish Dance Masters, Vol. 5 (1991, 2002)
  With George MacIlwham (Flute)
The Whisky Collection—Heather Mixture (1991, 2007)
Ron Gonnella's Fiddle Magic (1992)
  With Bill Hendry (Digital Piano)
FolkMusic From Scotland (1993 Compilation)
Scotland Forever (1984, 2007)
A Beginner's Guide to Traditional Scottish Music (1994, 2007 Compilations)
Bill McCue Visits the Heart of Scotland (1995, 2003)
  With Bill McCue (vocals), Francesca Wood (vocals), Kinlochard Ceilidh Band
Scottish Collection: A Scottish Evening II (1996 Compilation)
Hawks & Eagles (1996 Compilation)
The Bagpipes & Drums of Scotland (1996 Compilation)
The Folklore of Scotland (1999)
The Tartan Top Twenty Greatest Fiddle Hits (2002 Compilation)
Platinum—70 Years of Dancing in St. Andrews (2007)
  With David Cunningham Trio
Folksongs From Scotland (2007 Compilation)
Ceilidh in the National Park (2008 Compilation)
Legendary Melodies (2014 & 2016 Compilations)
The Countess of Dalhousie (2012)
Scotland's Top Tunes, Vol. 9 (2014 Compilation)
Great Folk Medleys (2014 & 2016 Compilations)
Great Scottish Songs (2014 Compilation)
Flowers of Edinburgh (2014 & 2016 Compilations)
Scotland . . . At Its Best! (2014 Compilation)
Ariel Yoga (2016 Compilation)
Dancing in the Kyle (2016 Compilation)
The Music of Historic Scotland (1994?)
Highlights from the 1st National Festival of Popular Music (no date - compilation)
Ron Gonnella Plays the Fiddle (no date)
Ron Gonnella's Fiddle & Pipe Favourites (no date)
  With John Carmichael (Accordion), John (Piano), Billy Thom (Drums), John Crawford (Piano), John Strachan (Double Bass)
A Fife Fairing (no date)
  The Ron Gonnella Quartet (members not specified)

APPENDIX E
Judging Soliloquy

Gonnella's tongue-in-cheek description of the complexity of the competition setting from an adjudicator's perspective.

"FESTIVALS ARE FUN"

Festivals are fun, or are they? Have you ever given the poor adjudicator a thought? Oh, well, your name looks good on the bills, the fees are first class, and the prestige tremendous, but then so is the strain. I try to arrive early, not because I'm all that punctual by nature, but being early helps me to miss the mothers of budding fiddle players and all those who on festival days who suddenly find my company stimulating. An excellent bunch of other ancillary services provided by a thoughtful committee usually see me through the first competition safely.

It's amazing how a feeling of well-being increases one's tolerance of wayward rhythm, a vague sense of pitch, and some excruciating tone, born of a bowing action reminiscent of cross-cut sawing. Not that all strathspey and reel players come into these categories. Many are very good players indeed. But how can one do justice to player X when players N, B, G and sundry others have assailed one's ears with a cacophony of sound which has to be heard to be believed. Take Willie Sharp for instance. Apart from playing just a shade flat most of the time, Willie has a fiddle which tonally lives up to its trade description of soap-box. Yet to see Willie in action plowing his way courageously through the most intricate reels in the repertoire, one might think from his facial expression that his performance was God's gift to adjudicators.

Another frequent visitor to festivals is the gimmick expert. Invariably he has just had the very latest gadget fitted to his fiddle—a new type of sound post, a bridge guaranteed to improve tone and resonance by at least 100%, or the last word in super flexible strings imported at enormous expense from either Vienna or from somewhere north of the Mason-Dixon line. Unfortunately, from the distance of some forty feet, I can't see the finer points of his fiddle.

Equally to be feared, for want of a better expression, might be called the non-playing competitors. One corner is the Scott Skinner contingent. For them, no other composer exists, and woe betide the adjudicator who dares to award a first prize for a performance of airs by say Gow or Marshall. If only they knew the overdose of Skinner which the average festival throws up is enough to sicken even the strongest of adjudicators and causes us to refer scathingly to that celebrated figure as Scott Skinner-ed. In the opposite corner are most of the pundits. They have seen and heard it all before. During the renditions they nod knowingly to each other and go into states of ecstasy whenever a competitor plays a tune exactly as Niel Gow played it in 1785. At the crucial moment when the adjudications are being delivered, they sit tense yet confident that their predictions are about to come true. And the glaring misjudgments of yours truly only seem to reinforce their collective faith in themselves.

Somewhere near the back of the hall and usually too close to the adjudicator for comfort, can be found those competitors, who having played, are now waiting with varying degrees of apparent indifference for the end of the proceedings, so that once the results are announced they can with all possible speed remove themselves to the nearest hostelry, there to celebrate or drown their sorrows as the case may be. Now what they do outside the hall is not my concern, but I could see them far enough when before they debauch dramwards they show the sportsmanship by applauding each and every succeeding player vociferously just when I am desperately trying to (A), decipher my scribbled notes on the last performance and (B), remember just how good competitors 1–5 were, when it has been at least an hour since I heard them. Then, just as my thoughts are beginning to attain some semblance of order, the minute differences between player 2 and player 32 disappear in a clatter of cups as the secretary's wife firmly plants the refreshment tray right on top of my adjudication sheets.

However, bearing in mind St. Paul's famous epistle to adjudicators which ends with the words, 'And now abideth faith, hope, and charity, these three, and the greatest of these. . . . ' Most of us weather the storms of a festival day and live to re-live the competitions over a convivial glass in the company of the Willie Sharps, the pundits, and Scott Skinner-ites, most of whom, if truth be told, are crack golfers who can and do beat me hollow when I compete in golfing festivals. (Smith Collection n.d.)

APPENDIX F

Transcripts of *On The Fiddle*

ON THE FIDDLE

PRESENTER: Ron Gonnella

GUESTS: Angus Fitchett and Jimmy Shand

<MUSIC PLAYING: 'CRIEFF HYDRO MARCH'—PLAYED BY GONNELLA AND FITCHETT>

RON GONNELLA: Hello, glad you could join us this Sunday evening. Tonight, I'm going to be talking to a very old friend of mine in the world of fiddle music, from Dundee, Angus Fitchett.

ANGUS FITCHETT: Good evening.

GONNELLA: Welcome Angus, nice to have you here.

FITCHETT: Well, it's nice to be here, really a pleasure for me.

GONNELLA: Angus, you've been connected with Dundee all your days, did the music start there?

FITCHETT: Yes, my father of course played the fiddle and this is where I learned eventually. In fact, the whole family had played something and we had a band of our own. My father had a wee dance hall and we all played in this place, so I was always thinking it's a cheap, cheap band.

GONNELLA: Well, it's maybe a cheap band but it's experience that you couldn't buy, Angus.

FITCHETT: Oh, yes.

GONNELLA: And you got it at the right age, didn't you?

FITCHETT: Yes, this is the experience you get right enough, play with other people and learn tempos, etc.

GONNELLA: That's right. And playing in public too, which is something which everybody has to acquire.

FITCHETT: Yes.

GONNELLA: What other public playing did you do apart from playing in the family dance band?

FITCHETT: Oh, when you couldn't get jobs playing at dances you reverted to the cinemas. There was always a job in the cinema and I got associated with two or three of them, which is another great experience, really good.

GONNELLA: That was before the . . .

FITCHETT: Before the talkies.

GONNELLA: Before the talkies came in.

FITCHETT: And I remember clearly, I played with this organist. She was an organist as well as a good pianist, and I learned an awful lot from her. It was straight music, you see.

GONNELLA: Straight music. So you had to be a good sight-reader.

FITCHETT: Yes. And if you couldn't play it you had to learn it all for the next day or so on.

GONNELLA: And you had to be adaptable too.

FITCHETT: Yes, very adaptable.

GONNELLA: What sort of situations did you have to adapt to, Angus?

FITCHETT: You had to adapt, alright. I remember playing certain nights in the week where it was full of kids and you were battered with whelks.

GONNELLA: Was that because they didn't like the music?

FITCHETT: It was the music, not the film

GONNELLA: Not the film. Well, let's hope sometimes it was the film and not the music.

FITCHETT: Yes.

GONNELLA: Well, you're not going to get battered with whelks tonight, but would you like to play a strathspey and reel for us to open the program?

FITCHETT: I would. Because once again, I was awful fond of Skinner and his music, and this is two of his numbers I'm going to play. The first one's called Little John's Hame. And the second one is Donald Stewart the Piper.

GONNELLA: Fine, off you go then.

<MUSIC PLAYING>

GONNELLA: That's fine, Angus. Played with all the typical Fitchett flair.

FITCHETT: Thank you.

GONNELLA: What other composers do you enjoy playing, apart from Scott Skinner?

FITCHETT: Oh, I love Peter Milne, Marshall was another great man. There's various others, Gow was another marvelous man. And all the sons as well. But they left us a legacy of music, good music.

GONNELLA: And it's still here because they've put it down.

FITCHETT: Yes, yes.

GONNELLA: You put music down on paper too, because not only can you play other people's music but you're adept at writing your own.

FITCHETT: Yes, I've wrote quite a few now. I would say over a hundred.

GONNELLA: Over a hundred, well it's a lot more than I have, Angus. Which tunes of yours have proved the most popular? Because hardly a week goes by that they're heard on the air.

FITCHETT: Well, I would think the strathspey John Steven of Chance Inn is the most popular one now. A. M. Shinnie, maybe J. B. Milne. They were all very, very popular.

GONNELLA: Angus, I'm sure a lot of folk would be interested to know if you have any set plan when you write a tune.

FITCHETT: No, no, you just get the paper and a pencil and the fiddle beside you, right enough. And once they reach in here you start writing it. And I'm one of these lucky chaps that never stop until I'm finished.

GONNELLA: Do you write from in your head or do you write with the fiddle or the piano?

FITCHETT: It's in the head, what you're singing to yourself inside.

GONNELLA: And do you have to do much polishing and changing?

FITCHETT: No, no. But I do have to do that now and again. You've got to polish them up and see where you've maybe made a wrong phrase. It's really a funny business, but it's a fruitful one, isn't it?

GONNELLA: Oh, indeed. Well, I'm sure all the tunes you write, they're very adapted for the fiddle because the fiddle sounds well when you play them. Have you anything you'd like to play for us just now?

FITCHETT: Well, as I mentioned Skinner, Scott Skinner died 1927, and when it came to 1977 I wrote this, this march. And I call it Salute to Scott Skinner.

GONNELLA: Well, I'm sure if it's like your other compositions it would be a very worthy tribute to him.

FITCHETT: Oh, thank you. I'll play this.

<MUSIC PLAYING>

GONNELLA: First class, Angus.

FITCHETT: Thank you.

GONNELLA: I'm sure many Scottish dance bands will be playing that before too long.

FITCHETT: Well, I hope so.

GONNELLA: But talking of Scottish dance bands, you've had a long association with the Scottish dance music world, haven't you?

FITCHETT: Oh, yes, I would think so. Since its infancy I was there and thereabouts.

GONNELLA: You had your own band for quite a while.

FITCHETT: Yes, I played for Jimmy Shand for a while and I started my own band, and then I went back to Jimmy. That was the highlight of my career.

GONNELLA: Well, you enjoy playing with Jimmy obviously.

FITCHETT: Oh, yes, very much so.

GONNELLA: Would you like to have a tune with him now?

FITCHETT: Yes, we're just going to do that.

GONNELLA: Well, fine.

<ENTER JIMMY SHAND>

FITCHETT: Come in, Jimmy, please. Got him all here ready for you.

JIMMY SHAND: Well, it's a bit hot in here.

GONNELLA: Yes. It's a good fire, Jimmy. We're enjoying the tune and we're about to enjoy it even more. Jimmy, you of all people in Scotland need no introduction to Scottish audiences, indeed audiences all over the world. You must be the only Scottish musician who has a racehorse named after him, and a pub. How far have you travelled playing the accordion, Jimmy?

SHAND: Well, Canada and the States, New Zealand, Australia. And the continent, Germany.

GONNELLA: Where were you last?

SHAND: Australia.

GONNELLA: And who was that with?

SHAND: Peter Morrison.

GONNELLA: How long have you been playing the box, Jimmy?

SHAND: Since I was a wee lad.

GONNELLA: You're not giving anything away, is he?

FITCHETT: No.

GONNELLA: You've played all over the place, and there must be one tune maybe which has stood out over the years as being a public favorite.

SHAND: Well, the Bluebell Polka.

GONNELLA: Well, what about having that now then?

<MUSIC PLAYING>

GONNELLA: Fine, fine. Jimmy. What radio or television programs have you enjoyed doing most over the years?

SHAND: Oh, we did some of the early Kilt Is My Delight programs, and White Heather Club.

GONNELLA: And the Bluebell Polka, that was on Housewife's Choice.

SHAND: Aye, that's what made it popular.

GONNELLA: Absolutely, yes. Well, tonight brings back memories for me because when I was a young laddie I used to come and watch you, and occasionally play with you, in kids' rooms in Dundee. And the Shand and the Fitchet magic is still with us. Angus, you've been in this business a long time, are there any funny stories you'd like to tell us?

FITCHETT: When you talk about early days, I remember sitting ready to play, and this youth came over the dancehall with a fiddle under his arm, and it was Ron Gonnella, because I knew you at that time, and you sat in with us and you really enjoyed yourself that night. In fact, we let you play yourself with Jimmy, and the second accordion, George McKelvey and the pianist, Norman Whitelaw, we decided we'd go down and have a dance, and I turned my jacket outside in, and it was a hilarious dance because we knew nothing about it. We could play it but not dance it.

GONNELLA: Well, I'm sure folk round about enjoyed it because your terrific personality is a big factor in your success over the years, Angus. Jimmy, is there any one thing that you might like to pass on to young budding accordionists who are watching us tonight?

SHAND: Well, if a youngster is very keen to be a musician I'd advise him to learn music, and I hope he has a good ear for tuning. He'll get all the experience he needs nowadays on a plate from all the various dance bands. Mind you, there's some good bands today.

GONNELLA: There are indeed. Well, talking of good bands, let's turn the clock back again, Jimmy. Because one of the earliest tunes I remember you playing was the Dundee City Police Pipe Band. Would you like to finish off with that?

<MUSIC PLAYING>

<CUT>

ON THE FIDDLE

PRESENTER: Ron Gonnella

GUEST: Tom Anderson

<MUSIC PLAYING: CRIEFF HYDRO MARCH PLAYED BY GONNELLA AND ANDERSON>

RON GONNELLA: Tonight my guest is a kenspeckled figure in the world of Scottish fiddle music in general, and in Shetland fiddle music in particular. It's my pleasure to welcome from Lerwick, Tom Anderson. Nice to have you on the program, Tom.

TOM ANDERSON: Thank you, Ron.

GONNELLA: Have you come down from Shetland?

ANDERSON: No, I've been down a fortnight, I've been at Pitlochrie.

GONNELLA: Pitlochrie.

ANDERSON: I had to write some music for a play that's going to go on in Shetland, the music for the songs. So I had to be down to rehearse with the cast, it's taken a fortnight, and I think it's okay. It's interesting that the fiddle is for the linking up the things there, and also playing the accompaniments, which I think is quite nice.

GONNELLA: Well, it's apt because Shetland fiddle music has a great vogue these days. How long has this vogue been on the go in Shetland, Tom?

ANDERSON: Well, the earliest composition we know the date of is 1759 for a read out. And as far as I can reckon the fiddle came in about 1700. So it's been around quite a time, you know.

GONNELLA: Well, you've been around a wee bit. Maybe not as long as that, Tom.

ANDERSON: Oh, no, no, I wouldn't have said as long as that.

GONNELLA: When did you actually start? What age did you begin playing fiddle music?

ANDERSON: Well, really eighteen, the time when I started to play for my grandfather and my uncle.

GONNELLA: And in the course of your daily work, was that any help to you in building up the collection of tunes that you have?

ANDERSON: Well, in the early days we were in the croft, but later on when I grew up and got the job as an insurance agent, then that was a great thing because I could go around and listen to the tunes and meet all these other people, because I was meeting a lot of fiddlers early on when I first started to go to dances, meet the early fiddlers.

GONNELLA: Have you any tune from these early days that you'd like to play for us?

ANDERSON: I'd like to play an old tune from the west side of Shetland called New Rigged Ship, this is a very old tune which uses rather ringing strings and other sort of things. But it is a tune where the fiddler is buying a boat, which he fondly christens his ship and puts on new sails and everything and calls it Da New Rigged Ship.

<MUSIC PLAYING>

GONNELLA: Tom, living in Shetland for as long as you have done you must have seen many changes, and none more dramatic than the oil boom, which came to Shetland a few years ago.

ANDERSON: That's very true, yes. The oil boom has been a mixed blessing. We got a lot money, a lot of jobs and everything else. In some ways it's not helped the indigenous industries. But music-wise it hasn't had very much effect because, you see, we, our own authority, started getting meetings to teach traditional music in '71, just about the time the thing was starting. And we build up a tremendous amount of pupils, so that music is being kept up, augmented by the people who were coming in. Fortunately we get a lot of them coming in too and integrating.

GONNELLA: And you found that they took kindly to the Shetland fiddle music?

ANDERSON: Oh, very much so. They come to the folk festivals and everything else. There's no question about that.

GONNELLA: You talked about passing on your knowledge way back as far as 1971, how many pupils did you have at the peak of this, Tom?

ANDERSON: At the peak when I was doing six days a week and nine schools, I had 162.

GONNELLA: My goodness. And where else do you pass on your great fund of knowledge about Shetland music?

ANDERSON: Well, because there is this summer school in Stirling University, the Heritage of Scotland Summer School, which is fiddle music, ballads, you name it, but I go down there as a tutor along with other people to teach my style and the northeast style. We get students there from literally all over the world, although I don't think we've had them from Russia so far.

GONNELLA: When you get such an international audience what do you try to pass onto them, Tom?

ANDERSON: Well, mainly about the history of the tune, the history of the islands, and why the tunes have come along. Mainly another thing too, our connection with Scandinavia, because a lot of our older music comes from the music of the [inaudible].

GONNELLA: And that attractive accent you've got, that's partly Scandinavian too, isn't it?

ANDERSON: Well, I suppose it is because we have our own dialect, you know. Well, they say in the old days 150 years ago Norn was spoken, which was a mixture of dialect and Norwegian.

GONNELLA: Well, that comes through in the accent and in the fiddle music. Have you got a tune especially connected with the course at Stirling?

ANDERSON: Yes, with the course at Stirling, probably I should play you the signature tune which I wrote the first year there called Airdrie Castle, it's a march. We teach in Airdrie Castle so it's very appropriate.

<MUSIC PLAYING>

GONNELLA: Fine, Tom. If you are going about Stirling and still teaching up home, and I know you go across to America with Aly Bain now and again, and does the converse work? Are there any people who have come up from the mainland and other parts to Shetland who have given you something which you feel is of value?

ANDERSON: Oh, yes. Very early on, you see, this is personally true because at the age of fourteen when I first went into Lerwick a man that I heard playing there was the late George Stark from Dundee, who was fondly known as the Blind Fiddler, he was blind, I believe you met him.

GONNELLA: That's right, I met him just in his last few years, yes.

ANDERSON: Well, I met him first when I was fourteen. And all my life I had chased a tune called The Soo's Lament for the Tatties, which is a description of an old sow looking for potatoes in the spring when there's none. And the old guys used to say to me "oh, you're not bad but what about The Soo's Lament for the Tatties?" And I thought it was a con until I happened to ask George Stark in the very last appearance that he was there. I said "did you ever hear of a tune called . . ." "Oh, aye, I got it from <INAUDIBLE 23.09> 1902." I said "hold everything until I get a tape recorder." So I recorded it. Would you like to hear it? It's a sort of novelty thing, you know.

<MUSIC PLAYING>

GONNELLA: Fabulous. Tom, I won't ask you how you do it because that may well be a trade secret, but can you tell me what the two parts of the tune mean?

ANDERSON: Well, the first one when you're down low on the D and G string is when the old sow is finding tatties, potatoes, she's quite happy, you see. Then suddenly she comes up against a stone or something so she squeals. That's the idea.

GONNELLA: That's a real catchy tune. You've written many catchy tunes yourself, Tom. Mainly reels?

ANDERSON: No, I've written many things, slow airs, all kind of things like that.

GONNELLA: Have you got a favorite slow air that we might have then?

ANDERSON: I've got one that is a favorite, It's called Da Slockit Light, or The Light That's Gone Out. I wrote it when I went back on a visit to where I was born and came out of the little village at midnight, looked back and nearly all the lights were going out, all the people had gone. Also at that time I had lost my late wife, so Da Slockit Light.

<MUSIC PLAYING>

GONNELLA: Well, I'm sure that tune brings back memories not only for yourself, Tom, but for all the people who lived in your little village of . . . ?

ANDERSON: Eshaness.

GONNELLA: Eshaness. Where is that in Shetland?

ANDERSON: Up right northwest, the furthest northwest on the mainland. Next up <INAUDIBLE 27.05>.

GONNELLA: Tom, have you another tune of your own composing that we might have next? I know that you wrote Willie Pottinger's Reel, didn't you?

ANDERSON: I did, yes.

GONNELLA: And any other well-known characters featured?

ANDERSON: Well, I wrote a tune once for a boy who was playing the piano in the dance band, I used to have a dance band. And actually did one or two broadcasts for Scottish Dance Piece, and I wrote a tune for him when he was always on a boat that he's acquired, a peerie boat, small boat, so I wrote a tune called Peter's Peerie Boat.

And it was taken up, you see, by the dance people, and it was for Hooper's Jig, do you remember it?

GONNELLA: I do. When you had your dance band going, did you do purely Scottish country dancing?

ANDERSON: Yes, we had an audition and these were the times when to get on the air with Scottish dance music was a big achievement. And these were all young people. And I came home in '46, '47 from the war and took up these young people to see if we could do something. We were playing for dancing <INAUDIBLE 28.06>.

GONNELLA: Well, I'm sure I know this tune that you're going to play.

ANDERSON: You should do.

GONNELLA: What's the dance?

ANDERSON: Hooper's Jig. Jimmy Shand knew the lot.

GONNELLA: A peerie for me, Tom, was a top that went round and round.

ANDERSON: Oh, peerie for us means small.

GONNELLA: A small boat. Well, let's have a small rendering of Peter's Peerie Boat.

ANDERSON: Come on, join me then.

GONNELLA: Okay.

<MUSIC PLAYING>

<CUT>

ON THE FIDDLE

PRESENTER: Ron Gonnella

GUEST: Douglas Lawrence

<MUSIC PLAYING: CRIEFF HYDRO MARCH PLAYED BY GONNELLA AND LAWRENCE>

GONNELLA: My guest this week is a Scottish fiddle player who is unique in as much as he also is a professional violinist with the Scottish National Orchestra. It's a very warm welcome to Douglas Lawrence from Buckie, and I'm not talking about the fire, Douglas, I'm delighted to have you here. I first met you at the festivals at Banchory, Elgin, and Kirriemuir. How do you feel now about these sort of festivals? Would you go back again if you had the time over again and go in for them?

LAWRENCE: Oh, certainly. I think these festivals are very important from the aspect of performing, getting up to play in front of people. You must get over the nervous thing and get out and perform to people. You also firstly have the opportunity of meeting other fiddle players, and this is what was most beneficial to me in the beginning, going to such places as Kirriemuir, which I incidentally thought was the best competition. And you can develop your playing quite a lot by listening to other fiddle players.

GONNELLA: It's an imitative art, isn't it?

LAWRENCE: It exactly is.

GONNELLA: And then there's the social side because there's a lot of camaraderie as well, isn't there?

LAWRENCE: Oh, very much so.

GONNELLA: Especially after the festival's finished.

LAWRENCE: Yes, and sometimes during as well.

GONNELLA: What sort of tunes did you play at these festivals, Douglas?

LAWRENCE: Well, a typical strathspey and reel would have been Lady Mary Ramsay, Nathaniel Gow, and Sir David Davidson of Cantray.

GONNELLA: By John Low. Well, we're not at the festival but we might have them now, can we?

LAWRENCE: Yes.

GONNELLA: Grand.

<MUSIC PLAYING>

GONNELLA: That's a fine strathspey and reel. Who taught you to play the fiddle just in that particular style?

LAWRENCE: Well, at that time I was going to the fiddle festivals, the greatest influence was my late teacher Hector MacAndrew.

GONNELLA: Who at that time was undoubtedly the greatest living exponent of fiddle music.

LAWRENCE: Oh, yes. Definitely. Well, in my own opinion, the last of the real old style players.

GONNELLA: And what did you get from Hector that you feel was priceless and you couldn't have had from anyone else?

LAWRENCE: Well, the two things that I remember most about him were his tremendous musicianship, covering all sorts of music, not just Scottish music, but the main point which impressed me most of all was his use of the bow. Never would you see him playing away at the point of the bow, six inches.

LAWRENCE: As you could do with reels if you wanted to.

LAWRENCE: You could do. But when the music starts, once you get down to this lower half of the bow, that was his great forte, use of the bow.

GONNELLA: He knew exactly where he had to be at any given time.

LAWRENCE: Exactly. And it was in keeping with the mood, rhythm, and feeling of the music.

GONNELLA: He must also have given you a great love of the great classics of Scottish fiddling.

LAWRENCE: Oh, yes. Well, I think William Marshall's collection, I wouldn't have known half of the tunes in it if it hadn't been for Hector.

GONNELLA: Indeed. He was a great exponent of Marshall's music. And Gow, of course. Can you give us a tune from somewhere near your native heath, not necessarily Marshall.

LAWRENCE: Well, I'll play a pipe march. Because of course Hector was a very keen piper in those days.

GONNELLA: Indeed.

LAWRENCE: And a fine performer of pipe music on the violin. Play the pipe march, The Braes of Castle Grant.

<MUSIC PLAYING>

GONNELLA: Now, that sort of playing is the sort of playing which makes me put you and Willie Hunter right at the top of Scottish fiddle players, Douglas. After you went to the festivals and got experience there and went to Hector you then moved on to the Royal Scottish Academy of Music and Drama, and then you followed Willie MacPherson's footsteps into the Scottish National Orchestra. How do you feel about playing all the classics, Brahms, Mozart, Mendelssohn and so on, what effect has that had on your thinking and performance of fiddle music?

LAWRENCE: I think many people are surprised to hear this, but many of my views have been strengthened, cemented, so to speak, by having worked with other conductors, soloists, and musicians. Many points apply to Scottish music as they do to baroque music, for example, the partitas.

GONNELLA: Because it's the same period, isn't it?

LAWRENCE: Exactly, and it's also dance music. And Mozart as well, there's none of this jumping down the first and third beat of the bar in Mozart and it shouldn't be done in Scottish music.

GONNELLA: What fiddle do you use for your fiddle music? Do you have a different instrument for that as against your Scottish National Orchestra playing?

LAWRENCE: Well, then again many people think that you must play on a different fiddle for Scottish music and a violin for playing in the orchestra, this is exactly the same instrument. It must be comfortable to play because many of these tunes are extremely difficult to get around, and there's no point in giving yourself a handicap by having to jump all over the strings to find the notes.

GONNELLA: No. And to change fiddles too frequently, because that upsets your technique.

LAWRENCE: Yes, it does, unless you've got a violin which is exactly the same position.

GONNELLA: And you don't get them like that. Would you like to play something to show off your classical technique? What about a slow air?

LAWRENCE: Well, I know you like slow airs, so we'll play one by a famous Aberdeen composer, and it's called Robert Cormack.

GONNELLA: Wonderful.

<MUSIC PLAYING>

GONNELLA: A bonny tune, Douglas. Do you ever get the chance to play anything which is Scottish oriented with the Scottish National?

LAWRENCE: Well, from one extreme you've got the Hebrides Overture by Mendelssohn. Then you've got Land of Mountain and The Flood by Hamish McCann, Tam O'Shanter, all by classical composers. Nowadays we've had Ian White, Eightsome Reel, and Ian Hamilton, Scottish dances. As far as I know there isn't a concerto for solo fiddle and orchestra yet.

GONNELLA: Except the Max Bruch Scottish Fantasy.

LAWRENCE: That's as close to the . . .

GONNELLA: You play that one?

LAWRENCE: We've played it in the orchestra, yah.

GONNELLA: Well, you're only twenty-five, Douglas, and you've been playing fiddle music and classical music for a long time, where do you see yourself going in fiddle music now?

LAWRENCE: Well, I'd like just to keep along the lines I have been, maybe get to some places that I haven't played in before. I'd like to go up the west and play some of the places up there, maybe eventually have a few recordings later on in life.

GONNELLA: Yes, well I hope so. What about going up to Shetland, have you been up to Shetland at all?

LAWRENCE: Yes, I had a great experience up in Shetland many years ago when I met Willie Hunter, Tom Anderson. And I hope to be going back sometime soon.

GONNELLA: Good, good. Well, I don't know about you, I went to Shetland, I found the folk great but the weather was terrible.

LAWRENCE: Well, this is true.

GONNELLA: Have you a piece that we can close on, Douglas?

LAWRENCE: I'll close with a type of tune that isn't played much, but I think should be played much more, and that's a slow strathspey. We don't hear many slow strathspeys. This one's called The Beauty of the North, and it's followed by the reel Geordie Affleck.

GONNELLA: Fine.

<MUSIC PLAYING>

<CUT>

ON THE FIDDLE

PRESENTER: Ron Gonnella

GUEST: Willie Hunter

<MUSIC PLAYING: CRIEFF HYDRO MARCH PLAYED BY GONNELLA AND HUNTER>

RON GONNELLA: Hello, glad you can join us for tonight's program. I'm delighted to welcome a man who would never be out of the top two of anyone's list of foremost fiddle players in Scotland, including mine. It's my great pleasure to welcome Willie Hunter from Lerwick. Did you have a nice flight down, Willie?

WILLIE HUNTER: Yes, no bother at all.

GONNELLA: Not any fog?

HUNTER: Very enjoyable. No, easy.

GONNELLA: And you weren't airsick.

HUNTER: No, never airsick. I enjoyed it very much.

GONNELLA: You know, Willie, apart from your reputation as one of our finest fiddle players, you've got a very enviable one, Young Willie Hunter you're known as up in Shetland.

HUNTER: Yes, Young Willie Hunter indeed.

GONNELLA: Despite the grey locks. How did that happen, Willie?

HUNTER: Well, my father played, you see, since he was eight years old and has played all his life, he's over eighty and still playing, playing well. And I suppose he was Willie Hunter, and when I came along I was just Young Willie, and the name is sticking so far.

GONNELLA: Is there another Willie Hunter coming up?

HUNTER: Well, we have a son, yeah. He's Billy.

GONNELLA: You see, once you have elder and younger you can't go any further, can you? And your father still plays?

HUNTER: He still plays, yes.

GONNELLA: Anybody else in the family?

HUNTER: Well, I was fortunate indeed to have my mother played, didn't play a lot, she didn't play a lot, she didn't play reels or horn pipes, but she played slow airs and slow bonny kinds of things. And she would take a lovely tone. So I was really lucky to have music from both sides.

GONNELLA: Two great models to look to.

HUNTER: Oh, yeah. I was the luckiest bloke in the world because it was music every day, all the time. Very happy house when I was a boy.

GONNELLA: Did your father write any tunes as well as play?

HUNTER: Yes. He didn't write a lot, but he's written a few. Yes, he's done one or two that are quite good.

GONNELLA: Any one that you'd like to play for us now?

HUNTER: He did one a number of years ago called the Nort Rodd, or the North Road. There's a handful, but this is one that he did, the North Road, it's quite a good tune, I think. We speak about the difference between the Shetland style of playing and the Scottish style of playing. I think this resembles more the kind of Skinner sound. But this is in D.

<MUSIC PLAYING>

GONNELLA: Aye, you're right, it's a wee bit Skinner-ish, isn't it?

HUNTER: Yeah, well, I always think he always leans more towards the Scottish tunes than the Shetland ones.

GONNELLA: How many other Scottish composers do you play a lot of, Willie?

HUNTER: Well, mostly Skinner, I would say. I've been asked lots of times 'who's your favorite composer?' And I have to say right away Scott Skinner.

GONNELLA: Which of Skinner's tunes in particular do you like?

HUNTER: Well, it's difficult to say, isn't it? There's things like Arthur's Seat, Eugene Stratton, Madame Neruda, things like that. The Fiddler's Cramp, Carnie's Canter.

GONNELLA: All pretty difficult, Willie.

HUNTER: Yeah. Kind of difficult. I mean, Mathematician, King Robert the Bruce, tunes like that are difficult tunes, but they have something kind of special, I think.

GONNELLA: Indeed they do. What about a traditional Lerwick and Shetland tune, Willie? We've just heard one which is very mainland-ish, would you like to play a wee tune that would illustrate the Shetland native style for us?

HUNTER: Yeah. Well, if we take something like The Bonnie Isle O' Walsay, or something like that which is . . .

<MUSIC PLAYING>

HUNTER: Kind of get the idea? It's a different kind of lilting style. And that's tradition. But the thing that sometimes a lot of folk on the mainland seem to think, if you're a Shetland fiddler, if you're a Shetland bloke and you play the fiddle then you play Shetland traditional tunes all the time.

GONNELLA: But that's not the case.

HUNTER: That's not really the case. And don't misunderstand me, I appreciate our Shetland tradition and our Shetland traditional tunes, but as a general rule if I handed this fiddle to the average Shetland player and said "try a tune on my fiddle" the chances are he's going to play a Scottish tune rather than a Shetland traditional tune.

GONNELLA: Now, is there anyone today writing the mainland type tunes?

HUNTER: Oh, yeah, there are a lot of composers. The present-day composers, some of the boys passed on, unfortunately, the noteables; the Ronnie Coopers and the Frank Jamiesons. But there are a lot of tunes written in Shetland. I went to music lessons first when I was eleven, twelve, and thirteen. I went to a lovely old man Gideon Stove.

GONNELLA: I've heard the name.

HUNTER: Well, his tunes hopefully will be published by his son, I believe, in the near future. And he had some fantastic stuff, absolutely marvelous tunes that were different.

GONNELLA: What do you feel you learned from Gideon Stove?

HUNTER: Well, I learned to read, first and foremost. But he was such a marvelous musician that he would have enjoyed a session with

Ritchie or somebody. And he was a wonderful teacher, he was always very calm and everything.

GONNELLA: What about one of his tunes then?

HUNTER: Yeah, well, he did so many. There's one in four sharps, Da Bonxie, he called it.

<MUSIC PLAYING>

GONNELLA: That's a bright tune, Willie.

HUNTER: Different, isn't it?

GONNELLA: Well, it is different. You don't get much in the key of E major, do you?

HUNTER: No.

GONNELLA: Nice to get that harmonic at the end.

HUNTER: Isn't it?

GONNELLA: What's the state of fiddle making in Shetland, Willie? Is there much?

HUNTER: Oh, yeah, there's a lot of fiddle-making going on. There's always been somewhat of an interest in making fiddles as well as playing them. And there's a number of fairly young fellows still making them and keeping it going. A couple of lads, in fact, were away on a course just last year somewhere down in England, I think.

GONNELLA: Do you have a Shetland fiddle yourself?

HUNTER: Yes, I have an Alec Leask, 1966. But that's not in fact this particular fiddle I'm playing tonight. I played on that for years and years.

GONNELLA: Where did you get this one?

HUNTER: Well, this is Joseph Guarneri, 1730. And this fiddle belongs to a good friend of mine, a Shetland man new living in Newcastle-on-Tyne.

GONNELLA: Hugh Houston, I think.

HUNTER: Hugh Houston.

GONNELLA: And how do you come to have it at the minute?

HUNTER: Well, he said for a number of years that when he died he would leave the fiddle to me in his will. And we always have a laugh every time we meet, well, we used to, about who was going to live longest, whether I'd ever see the fiddle or get the fiddle.

GONNELLA: Well, we hope you're going to live a long time to play on this beautiful fiddle. Have you got a slow air that would show off the tone?

HUNTER: Well, we'll try The Flower of The Quern. This is asked for a lot by a lot of people at home, and one bloke in particular.

<MUSIC PLAYING>

GONNELLA: A beautiful fiddle, Willie.

HUNTER: Absolutely marvelous fiddle.

GONNELLA: And living in Shetland you must have plenty time to play. Are there any disadvantages at being so far away from the mainland?

HUNTER: Well, there's disadvantages in lots of ways living in Shetland. You can't jump in the car and come and have a tune with you, for instance. Or go and look up Angus Fitchett or a hundred other people.

GONNELLA: There must be many tunes that you can play with all your friends in Shetland.

HUNTER: That's what I was going to say, I think there must be more advantages living there, as far as I'm concerned.

GONNELLA: Well, what about one of these tunes that you have an evening with your friends?

HUNTER: Well, as we were saying earlier there's a lot of modern composers, fellows that are putting tunes together. And a good pal of mine, John Pottinger, affectionately known as Pottsy, he did one for the late Ronnie Cooper, this is a number of years ago. And he called it John Pottinger's Compliments to Ronnie Cooper. I think it's a super tune, it's in F.

<MUSIC PLAYING>

GONNELLA: Well, I think we have to move on to the very latest events in Shetland, Willie. The Cape Breton boys were up there, weren't they?

HUNTER: Yes, indeed. They had a marvelous tour.

GONNELLA: And everybody enjoyed them.

HUNTER: Oh, they were absolutely first class in Lerwick. Yes, just marvelous.

GONNELLA: You didn't by any chance write a tune to celebrate their visit?

HUNTER: I did indeed, yes. I put a few notes together and called it Cape Breton Visit to Shetland.

GONNELLA: Good work, can you finish off with that for us now?

HUNTER: Yes, yes. In A.

<MUSIC PLAYING>

<CUT>

ON THE FIDDLE

PRESENTER: Ron Gonnella

GUEST: Jimmy Moir

<MUSIC PLAYING: CRIEFF HYDRO MARCH PLAYED BY GONNELLA>

RON GONNELLA: Well, if you haven't guessed already my guest tonight is the conductor of the Glasgow Strathspey and Reel Society, and of other great mast ensembles. It's my pleasure to welcome, from Montrose and lately Glasgow, Jimmy Moir. Jimmy, nice to have you with us tonight.

JIMMY MOIR: Thanks very much.

GONNELLA: Where did you start your involvement with fiddle music, Jimmy?

MOIR: As a boy at home, on the farm at home near Montrose, where there was a number of fiddle players all round about. <audio drops> I had to sit in along with him and start playing.

GONNELLA: And of course you do play the fiddle, although nowadays you're . . .

MOIR: Oh, yes, I'm afraid I've had to give it up through rheumatics in my arms and my fingers.

GONNELLA: Well, these things happen. I hope it doesn't impair you conducting.

MOIR: No, oh, no. I'm still at it in a smaller way.

GONNELLA: Where did you go after you left Montrose?

MOIR: Oh, I went to Glasgow. Went to Glasgow 1925 and joined the police.

GONNELLA: Well, if you stood up then everybody would realize that you're a pretty tall chap. In fact, an ideal physique for a conductor.

MOIR: Well, it appears so.

GONNELLA: And you continued your fiddle-playing in Glasgow.

MOIR: Oh, yes. Very much so.

GONNELLA: Who with?

MOIR: Well, I had a dance band of my own for quite a number of years, and I used to go and play solo at the Highland Gatherings and ceilidhs and things that went on in Highland circles.

GONNELLA: And of course you're in trousers tonight but I usually see you in the kilt.

MOIR: Well, you know, I was almost going to bring my kilt with me because I feel that a lot of the fiddlers that will probably be watching this program say "no, that's not Jimmy Moir, he hasn't got a kilt on."

GONNELLA: Well, we can assure you it is Jimmy Moir. And you were connected, of course, for a long time with the Glasgow Strathspey and Reel Society.

MOIR: Yes. I was a player from 1926 until 1954, and I was elected to conductor in 1954 and I retired last year,

GONNELLA: Right. And why did you elect to become the conductor? Why did you accept?

MOIR: Well, it was just a piece of fun. Bravado, maybe you'd like to call it. One likes to advance in life and to think you're going to do something big. And I was asked if I would do it and I said 'I'll take it on for a year and see how I get on.'

GONNELLA: And how many years did you in fact do it?

MOIR: Twenty seven. So it was a long year.

GONNELLA: How do you feel looking back on all your experience with mass fiddles, how do you look back and think about your early days conducting?

MOIR: It was marvellous, great feeling.

<MUSIC PLAYING>

GONNELLA: Jimmy, there must have been a great many problems, because to conduct such a huge crowd of fiddle players, even a man as tall as you and with all the authority of the Glasgow police behind you, you must have had problems on many occasions.

MOIR: Oh, many of them.

GONNELLA: What were your main problems?

MOIR: Well, the main problem was getting them all to play as near as one as humanly possible. Tempo was your biggest worry, to keep them all in tempo. Because you had fiddle players all over Scotland, right from Shetland down to the Borders, and from south of the border. And all those various groups coming from the various parts of the country all had their own interpretation of the music, they all had their own tempo they played at, and this is where the difficulties come in.

GONNELLA: And of course fiddle players tend to like to play the things their own way.

MOIR: Oh, absolutely. You don't need to tell me that, by Jove, I know.

GONNELLA: And you had one group and they said 'Jimmy Moir wants it this way but we've played it that way for thirty years and we're not going to change now.'

MOIR: You're right. I've been told that many times.

GONNELLA: And laughs that you had over this problem of control, Jimmy?

MOIR: Well, the only laughs that I've had that I remember once at rehearsal, thank goodness it wasn't at the actual performance, we were playing a selection of tunes, and I think it was the Atholl Highlanders' Farewell to Loch Katrine we were playing, and one side of the orchestra forgot to repeat the part, and the other side did repeat it. And here we had just a . . . one could call it a complete jar of marmalade, if you'd like to call it.

GONNELLA: Well, that's a good word. It's a big word, isn't it?

MOIR: Oh, it's a big word. Oh, it used to be laughable, you know. Of course you just had to stop and lay the heavy hand down and tell them.

GONNELLA: And what happens if that happens during a public performance, Jimmy?

MOIR: Oh, don't mention it. It never happened, and I hope it never does.

GONNELLA: Well, I can see you're sitting with all your fingers crossed.

MOIR: Aye, sometimes I had more than my fingers crossed.

GONNELLA: Jimmy, what's your favorite hall for conducting mass fiddles?

MOIR: Oh, now . . . well, I would say if I was going to look at it from an audience point of view I would say the Kelvin Hall. The Kelvin Hall Arena in Glasgow. Because the Glasgow audience are terrific. They're just beyond. But I must say the Usher Hall is a lovely hall to play.

GONNELLA: It is indeed. And what about the Caird Hall in Dundee?

MOIR: Yes, yes. The Caird Hall is good. They're all good. Don't forget, they're all very good.

GONNELLA: And of course being in Beech Grove tonight we simply have to mention the Music Hall in Aberdeen.

MOIR: The Music Hall is very good too. One golden fiddle concert was played in the Music Hall in Aberdeen, and it was quite good.

GONNELLA: Good. At this point we can have a look at you actually in action in the Music Hall in Aberdeen playing, very appropriately, Scott Skinner's Duke Of Fife Welcome to Deeside.

<MUSIC/VIDEO PLAYING>

GONNELLA: Well, Jimmy, I enjoyed the Duke Of Fife. What was the second tune?

MOIR: The Iron Man.

GONNELLA: The Iron Man. And who was the Iron Man?

MOIR: You're asking me a question, I don't know if I could just tell you who the Iron Man was, actually who he was.

GONNELLA: I think he was one of Skinner's friends, wasn't he?

MOIR: Oh, he was.

GONNELLA: We'll just maybe leave it at that.

MOIR: If I'd thought that was the answer you were looking for I could have given you that one. Because he was a great man to compose tunes about his friends. Even Angus Campbell was a great friend of his.

GONNELLA: Did you know any of the people that Skinner wrote tunes for?

MOIR: No. No, I can't say. Not personally. But I'll tell you a man who was a great friend of Skinner's and he was a very personal friend of mine was Murdoch Henderson.

GONNELLA: Now, Murdoch collected lots of tunes, and I asked you if you knew any of the people that Skinner wrote his tunes for, so you couldn't have picked Skinner's tunes because of that. How did you pick Skinner's tunes, and all the other composers that you used? What were the yardsticks you were looking for in a tune, Jimmy?

MOIR: Well, I looked for a tune with great embodiment in it. And one that a huge orchestra could play. One that I knew that throughout the country was played by the various societies. And I knew if I put that forward they could play it.

GONNELLA: In other words we needed not just a small clique of tunes which suited Jimmy Moir and the Glasgow Strathspey or the Aberdeen Strathspey or some of the others, it had to be things that were common and loved all over the country.

MOIR: Yes. And during my life I've travelled about a lot and played with the various societies. I've played with Elgin a few times, I've played up in Inverness, and Dunkeld and all round about the country. And I knew the tunes that they played. And I knew that if I was choosing the like of the Iron Man, The Well, I've heard so-and-so playing that, and I knew that I was safe in putting it there.

GONNELLA: Yes, because so many folk would recognise it.

MOIR: Yes. Well, it's a popular tune, Iron Man.

GONNELLA: Not only have the audience recognised the tune, what other things do you hope to do with the massed fiddles? Because it's a most unique sound, Jimmy, isn't it?

MOIR: Oh, yes. Oh, dear me, aye, it is a most unique sound. Well, you can't do anything more than I've been doing, but just to try, keep giving them new stuff to play, new tunes that we haven't played before, and hope that they will be able to fit in and play them.

GONNELLA: And then the audience, you want them to be entertained, of course.

MOIR: Oh, yes. Well, what you do here to entertain them is you introduce a dance selection. Something that the Gay Gordons can dance to, and you invite the audience to get up and dance in their little spare spaces in the hall, and they do it.

GONNELLA: And of course they do it. Well, Jimmy, thanks very much for coming in and talking to me tonight. I'm sure that we all wish you health and happiness to go on wagging your stick in front of these huge orchestras for many years to come.

MOIR: Thanks very much. It's been a pleasure, I can assure you.

GONNELLA: Grand.

<MUSIC PLAYING>

<CUT>

ON THE FIDDLE

PRESENTER: Ron Gonnella

<MUSIC PLAYING: CRIEFF HYDRO MARCH BY GONNELLA>

GONNELLA: Tonight I've left the cosy confines of Beech Grove and have come on a pilgrimage. One fiddle player I'd have loved to talk to was Niel Gow, the father of Scottish fiddle music. But since he died in eighteen-hundred and seven, this would've been quite a problem. But I've done the next best thing and come to the lovely Vale of Atholl to the Gow country to see the places Gow lived and worked with his very musical family.

Born in Perthshire near the ancient cathedral town of Dunkeld, Niel Gow was destined to become the leading fiddle player of his generation with a reputation that spread the breadth and length of the country. His tunes which are as popular today as they were two-hundred years ago were often linked to his surroundings—to the towns and villages which he knew—and to the features of architecture that particularly appealed to him.

<GONNELLA PLAYING> 'DUNKELD BRIDGE'

One of the finest examples was a reel called 'Dunkeld Bridge' which was composed in honor of the new Telford Bridge over the River Tay. The bridge, which he did not live to see completed.

<GONNELLA PLAYING: DUNKELD BRIDGE (CONT.) >

Before the bridge was opened in eighteen-hundred and nine, the Wester ferry crossed at this point connecting Dunkeld and Inver on the main road north. Although comprising a mere handful of houses, Inver was once a thriving community with an inn at its center which has changed little since Gow's day—the inn now a private house, serving as a reminder of its past importance.

Overlooking the village is the Gow cottage. It was here that Niel Gow was brought up and lived his long life. His father was a weaver and Niel was expected to follow in his footsteps, but that was not to be. At an early age he showed an aptitude for playing the fiddle and was often found sitting beside the house on this large flat stone with his fiddle to hand playing and composing and was saved from reduction to road metal some years ago and so was preserved.

And above it is the plaque erected to mark the spot for future generations and to commemorate the Inver fiddler.

"Nae fabled wizard's wand I trow,
Had e'er the magic airt o' Gow,
When wi' a wave he draws his bow,
Across his wondrous fiddle-o!"

[Some praise – said by some to be penned by Robert Burns]

Round about Inver Niel Gow had several favorite spots where he would come to play the fiddle. Just downstream on the other side of the River Tay, was Dunkeld House. Here under this Oak tree, is possibly the very spot where he wrote the tune of that name.

<GONNELLA PLAYS DUNKELD HOUSE (REEL)>

<GONNELLA PLAYS DUNKELD HERMITAGE BRIDGE (AIR)>

A favorite haunt was the nearby Hermitage—a beautiful wooded area on the banks of the river Braan. Beside a stretch of tumbling water the third Duke of Atholl constructed Ossian's Hall, a folly which overlooks the spectacular falls as they plunge through a narrow gorge. Visitors to the Hermitage folly didn't always enjoy the spectacle, especially when the sound and visual impact was exaggerated by the once metal-lined viewing chambers, but Gow was clearly very fond of the place and not surprisingly transferred his impressions into fiddle music.

But Niel's interest didn't stop with the local beauty spots in and around Inver. He was a keen student of current affairs and he was reputed to have travelled as far as Sterling with the Jacobite army in 1745. Whether his feet or his enthusiasm gave out first, we can't quite tell at this point.

Another interesting event which gave rise to Gow's lament 'Farewell to Whisky' was the disastrous barley harvest of 1799 following a very wet summer and the crop was all diverted to human consumption; and by law, distillation of whisky from malt was prohibited. The tune was a Highlander's natural sorrow at being deprived of his favorite beverage.

<GONNELLA PLAYING 'FAREWELL TO WHISKY' (AIR)>

When the ban was lifted the following year, it was a more cheerful tune, 'Whisky Welcome Back Again.'

<GONNELLA PLAYING WELCOME WHISKY BACK AGAIN (STRATHSPEY)>

For a man of such lowly origins, Gow enjoyed the unique relationship with all the local gentry. He was treated as an equal. Indeed, his presence at any gathering was considered essential to its success. Probably his first contact with a local landowner came about when he received fiddle lessons from John Cameron, a retainer for the Laird of Grantley.

Dr. Stewart of Bonskeid was a particularly close friend. Known affectionately as the "fiddling doctor," he was a local landowner and a general practitioner in Dunkeld. His family no longer occupied Bonskeid house though his descendants still live in the area. Alec Barbour, the factor of Atholl Estates is a descendant and he took me to look at the portrait of his great, great, great Grandfather, which still hangs in the house.

ALEC BARBOUR: I don't think there's any place else in the house that is big enough to take it. When we were kids we used to be told the kilt was thought to be immodestly short in Victorian times and they got an artist in to lengthen it so it would cover his knees a bit more effectively.

GONNELLA: Would I be right in saying that the good doctor here was instrumental is bringing Robert Burns and Niel Gow together?

BARBOUR: Yes, that's quite correct. Burns did a Highland tour in 1787 and stayed in Dunkeld and his diary records that on Friday he had breakfast with Dr. Stewart, Gow played and that Gow was a small steadily built man with an honest Highland face.

GONNELLA: Yes, a lovely description, isn't it?

BARBOUR: Yes, it's nice.

GONNELLA: It's also recorded somewhere that he was supposed to have played 'Major Graham of Inchbraikie' for Burns.

BARBOUR: I imagine they played a lot of tunes because Burns, of course, was a fiddler as well and the interesting things about that tune is that Burns originally wrote the words of 'My Love is Like a Red, Red Rose' to that tune and not to the modern tune which is better known now.

GONNELLA: Gow had great scope in his social contacts, didn't he?

BARBOUR: He was on very good terms with everybody in the community and particularly the local gentry and successive Dukes of Atholl were his patrons and he played at Blair Castle a great deal and was always a very welcome guest there.

GONNELLA: Is there any tangible evidence of this at Blair Castle today?

BARBOUR: Yes, his picture is there, painted by Sir Henry Raeburn, a leading artist of his day, and it's interesting that he was held in such esteem that Raeburn should paint his portrait, whereas Dr. Stewart is painted by some unknown artist whom we know nothing about.

GONNELLA: Blair Castle, the home of the Dukes of Atholl, has been the focal point for mementos of Gow. The Raeburn portrait hangs in a prominent position in the Castle ballroom. Three other copies are known to have existed and one could be seen in the National Portrait Gallery in Edinburgh.

In contrast, there's a charming little sketch of Gow in a book of music belonging to Jane Cathcart, wife of the fourth Duke. It depicts Gow playing for her two children, Lady Charlotte and Lord James.

The item I most wanted to see and handle was shown to me by the man who had been castle administrator for many years, Alistair Munro.

MUNRO: That is his fiddle and that is probably the best known, the one which most people who visit the castle look at and identify with.

GONNELLA: Where was it made Alastair?

MUNRO: Well, it's a locally made fiddle and there's a date, 1786, made about the same time as that portrait.

GONNELLA: How old do you thing Niel Gow was at the time the portrait was being made?

MUNRO: 60, probably.

GONNELLA: How long did he live after that?

MUNRO: He lived for another 20 years.

GONNELLA: That was a long life in those days wasn't it?

MUNRO: Yes, it was. He was fiddler of course to the 2nd, the 3rd Duke, and the 4th Duke

GONNELLA: I've got the fiddle in my hands. May I have a wee tune on it?

MUNRO: I hoped you'd say that.

GONNELLA: Anything in particular?

MUNRO: Oh I think 'Niel Gow's Fiddle' would be the appropriate tune to play.

GONNELLA: Okay, here we go.

<GONNELLA PLAYING 'NIEL GOW'S FIDDLE'>

GONNELLA: You know Alastair, it's wonderful to be able to play on Niel Gow's fiddle. Would Gow have actually played this fiddle in here?

MUNRO: No. The ballroom here is only about one-hundred years old, but it's almost certain that he would have played up in the large drawing room.

<GONNELLA PLAYING IN LARGE DRAWING ROOM> 'MISS SALLY HUNTER OF THURSTON' (JIG) AND 'LARGO'S FAIRY DANCE' (REEL)

GONNELLA: These tunes were by Niel's son, Nathaniel, and they were the jig, Miss Sally Hunter of Thurston, and Largo's Fairy Dance. It's a real privilege to play Niel Gow's fiddle in the drawing room of Blair Castle—a place where Gow must have played on many occasions for the Dukes of Atholl and his circle. The Gows were much indebted to the Murrays of Atholl for many social and musical connections and they showed their gratitude by naming tunes after members of the family.

John, the fourth Duke, still looks down from the wall, as does his second wife Marjory from above the fireplace. On a more personal note, Niel Gow must have had a great sadness in his life. He was predeceased by both his wives, and by all but two of his family. When his second wife died, he wrote this poignant lament.

<GONNELLA PLAYING 'NIEL GOW'S LAMENT FOR THE DEATH OF HIS SECOND WIFE'>

GONNELLA: This is the last resting place of Niel Gow's family, in the churchyard of Little Dunkeld. Although the man is gone, his music and memory live on, not only here but all over Scotland and beyond. Here in the Vale of Atholl, the fiddle tradition is still with us—even in Gow's cottage itself.

<YOUTHS PLAYING 'HIELAND WHISKY' (STRATHSPEY)>

<CUT>

APPENDIX G:

Transcript of *Take the Floor*

BROADCAST IN HONOR OF GONNELLA

TAKE THE FLOOR

PRESENTER: Robbie Shepherd
GUESTS: James Hunter and George MacIlwham
ROBBIE SHEPHERD . . . from the Scottish dance music world, all to pay respect to the one whose name is synonymous with the excellence of fiddle playing. In our Glasgow studio I'm joined now by two of his closest friends and musical associates. First, James Hunter, author of *The Fiddle Music of Scotland*, producer at one time of our Saturday night dance music program, and before he retired, head of BBC Scotland television. And with James, George MacIlwham, celebrated flute player and someone who has joined Ron at numerous recordings. He has a long and distinguished career as an orchestral player too, first with the Scottish National Orchestra, until recently as principal flute and piccolo with the BBC Scottish Symphony Orchestra. So by way of introduction then, let's listen to Ron and George combining with Yla Steven, also on fiddle, Bill Henley on the piano and John Strachan on string bass. From the Scottish Dance Masters Volume 3, here's Ron's own jig, Duncan MacDonald's Fancy.

<MUSIC PLAYING>

SHEPHERD: Duncan MacDonald's fiddle, used by Ron Gonnella on many an occasion, is that signature tune, and in fact for his radio series of Dancing Fiddles. And in Glasgow Jim Hunter and George MacIlwham, welcome to the program gentlemen. Thanks for coming in.

RESPONSE: Thank you Robbie.

RESPONSE: Thank you Robbie.

SHEPHERD: Start with you, Jim, when did you first become aware of the talents of Ron Gonnella?

JIM HUNTER: Well, I was, as you know, producer of the various Scottish dance music shows in the '60s, but we also used to know not just Scottish dance music but every second program as it were, had a singer or a fiddle player. So we had quite a lot of solo fiddle players, and Ron was one of the big names at that time who came in. Now, he was a producer's delight, I have to say, because his programs were always meticulously prepared. He gave you the tune, the publisher, the length, and came in and played it immaculately. The playing was of a beautiful, smooth, lyrical tone which actually came across on the radio very well. So he was a delight to work with.

SHEPHERD: Yes, of course, and an individual touch there that everybody would just say "ah, that's Gonnella this evening."

HUNTER: Well, I think that's important, Robbie, you see . . . traditional music, you can't say . . . some people seem to think "this is the way it goes." It doesn't, there's no set way of going. Everybody has a different style. You can tell a record immediately of Jimmy Shand. I could always tell John Ellis' band. And you could always tell Ron Gonnella. And that's a great tribute to him, that he had his own style, it was a lovely style, and it was him.

SHEPHERD: George, your early connection with Ron Gonnella, was it through the music?

GEORGE MACILWHAM: Yes, indeed, Robbie. I first remember meeting Ron away back more years than I care to admit, and it was at Morrison's Academy. Some professional musicians had been asked to go up and help out with the orchestra there, and of course Ron was in the orchestra, that's where I met Ron. And I must say, ever since I've been very privileged, as have many, many people, to know Ron Gonnella, and to have had the opportunity of working with him.

SHEPHERD: How easy was it to blend in flute and this distinctive fiddle of Gonnella?

MACILWHAM: When Ron and I started to play together, Scottish Strathspeys particularly, we found that we had the same approach and that we didn't need to spend hours trying to figure out how we were going to play all the short notes. We just automatically fell into this same style, even if it wasn't in the music we managed to do it together. And this is what encouraged us so much. And Robbie, if you can remember, one of the most important things about Ron was that he was endeavouring to get back to what the old style of Niel Gow and Nathaniel Gow perhaps would have been if it had been developed to the full before the accordion came onto the scene. Because remember, when I worked with Ron it was fiddle, flute, keyboard, double bass, and, if we had the money, harp was added, and another fiddle player. Angus Cameron used to play with us many times too.

SHEPHERD: Well, that takes us onto the Gow family and the first choice, I'm going to give you the first choice, Jim, Ron, as well as playing, had a great knowledge of the history of the great fiddle masters.

HUNTER: Well, I think he did a lot of work which will be brought to the fore in the future on that, and we should all be very grateful for that. He had a special affection for the music of Gow and did a lot of research into the work. And I remember sitting with him one night, and he says, "have you been to Gow's grave at Dunkeld recently?" I said no, he said "it's in a shocking state. The stone is falling to bits, we must do something about it." So he was really instrumental in setting up the Niel Gow Memorial Trust, which replaced that headstone and got the old one put in the cathedral, and a magnificent new replica stone above that grave which will stand for another two hundred years. So I think it's appropriate. And also, he's the only person that I know that's recorded on all the famous fiddlers' fiddles, as it were, you know, of Gow, of Marshall, and the stroh fiddle of Skinner. So I think it's appropriate to start with one of Niel Gow's great airs, and one with which Ron had a special affinity, and that he plays on Niel Gow's fiddle, it speaks to us over these two hundred years of history, Niel Gow's Lamentation for James Murray of Abercairny.

<MUSIC PLAYING>

SHEPHERD: Niel Gow's Lamentation for James Murray of Abercairny played on Gow's own fiddle. Back to you, James, the quality of that fiddle, how do you rate that now it has been recorded?

HUNTER: Well, it's a very interesting sound, isn't it? It's a very sweet sound, and I think the important thing to notice about it is on the G string, the bottom string, it's not as rich as fiddles would be nowadays, but it's a sweet mellow sound and would have blended in, I'm sure, with a lot of other fiddles in the Gow band. Yes, a very interesting sound, and it's fascinating to hear it two hundred years later, isn't it?

SHEPHERD: Indeed. And on the same album to hear Marshall's own fiddle and Scott Skinner's fiddle too.

HUNTER: Indeed.

SHEPHERD: That's a stroh fiddle, was it?

HUNTER: It was a stroh fiddle, aye.

SHEPHERD: Well, I've seen Ron playing the stroh fiddle, and so have you many a time, it's a very difficult instrument to handle, let alone record.

HUNTER: Oh, my goodness, you think you ought to pour whisky into the top of it and drink it, rather than play it, but Ron would never waste good whisky.

SHEPHERD: George, you spoke about the way that Ron tried to get back into the style and the lineup in Gow's days, and you can imagine that being played in the gallery of Blair Castle. Was Ron's idea to compensate for the absence of recordings in these days? Was that his idea on it?

MACILWHAM: No, I think Ron's idea was really to further the classical element of Scottish folk fiddle music. And of course in Niel Gow's day, and Nathaniel Gow's day, they didn't have accordions, they didn't use accordions and drums. And Ron, with all due respect, he loved the accordion, loved the drums, but with all due respect to them, Ron wanted to get away from that and create something new. He was a great creator, was Ron. And I was the lucky flute player that he chose to work along with him. So it was fiddle, flute, a bass instrument, and a keyboard, and that was exactly what was used in the 18th century in Edinburgh when all this wonderful Scottish music was really being published. And of course Niel Gow was instrumental in publishing at least three collections of all the tunes that we now take for granted practically. So this is what Ron was trying to create, and we were using it at Blair Castle. And this ties in with what Jim was saying there about Niel Gow, and Ron's great interest with Niel Gow.

SHEPHERD: He also had a great interest in Burns because of Niel Gow's connection with Robbie Burns, I presume.

HUNTER: That's true. And he did a number of broadcasts, in actual fact, on Radio Scotland. I remember some on Radio Three linking Burns and fiddle music. In fact, I think he was working on another project, which he discussed with me, until his sad death.

MACILWHAM: In fact, the project which perhaps Jim's referring to was the album, or the volume, the book, that Ron produced commemorating Robert Burns 1787 Highland tour, which of course took him to Blair Castle. And of course Burns met Niel Gow and had a lot to say about Niel Gow. And when Ron produced his book he wrote the actual text for the book, which contains about twenty of Ron's own tunes, and it was a collaboration with Evelyn Murray who was of course the Royal Scottish Country Dance Society's President to North America at that time. And they collaborated together to produce this wonderful book which is called the New Atholl Collection of Scottish Fiddle Music and Dances. Evelyn Murray devised the dances, Ron wrote the music, and the Duke of Atholl, his grace The Duke was kind enough to write a nice foreword to the book, and I'm glad to say I've got at least a couple of copies of the book, and you can imagine, Robbie, they're my treasured possession. Because Ron all through it with photographs, and quotations from Burns lets us realise just how much he loved The Bard, Rabbie.

SHEPHERD: Let's go onto the band sound now, Jim, and over to you in that because of your work with BBC on the band scene. Was he fussy in which band he played with? I know he played with more than one. Had they to be kindred sort of players?

HUNTER: Oh, very much so, because we've heard airs, and you hear marches, but Ron I think was actually preeminent in jigs and Scots measures, which are not played a lot nowadays. He had a very, very lifting, lilting style on that. And people like, say, Andrew Rankin or especially Lyndsey Ross, Lyndsey had a very sharp attack on the keys and that suited Ron's style very well, and it made an ideal partnership.

SHEPHERD: And I always spoke about the velvet touch coming through. And Roger Crook, I read a letter from Roger last week, he mentioned this particular album. And you can fill us in on it, because there's no Gonnella, it's Gonnella's fiddle, though you wouldn't know that on this Lyndsey Ross recording, but it's under the name of Davie Duncan.

HUNTER: Well, now you're raising a lot of things about pseudonyms and everything else like that.

SHEPHERD: The reason I raised it, because you write under the name of Ian Monroe.

HUNTER: Ah, you're giving lots of stories away here, Robbie. I think in those days when I was recording there were very few really, really top-class fiddle players around. And there were a lot of good accordion bands, a lot of good accordionists, and well, you didn't want to be seen appearing with too many bands at any given time.

SHEPHERD: Well, Davie Duncan was in fact his grandfather's name. But let's listen to Lyndsey Ross' band now with Donald Ian Rankin, and a tune written by one Ian Monroe called Tam's Hunting Horn and The Wind That Shakes the Piggery.

<MUSIC PLAYING>

SHEPHERD: Lyndsey Ross' Scottish dance band with Donald Ian Rankin, Tam's Hunting Horn and The Wind That Shakes the Piggery—that track has played on my programs more than any other. And back to my two guests, Jim Hunter and George MacIlwham on tribute to Ron Gonnella. The Reverend Richard Bell at the crematorium gave a marvelous tribute in Perth, and he spoke about the singing fiddle as being Ron's voice. Jim, where did Ron get this voice, this fiddle sound?

HUNTER: Well, I think in a sense we've mentioned Italian descent and I think there's a little bit in that because if you look back in history at the time of Gow, Marshall, and others, there were Italians coming across, playing Scottish music. For example, Stabilini comes immediately to mind. And they brought this Italian fluid style, that equal tone to it. And I'm sure that imbued some of Ron's music. But the minister at the funeral said something very, very important about Ron, and that was intonation. Ron had faultless intonation, as well as a smooth style, and I think that marked him out. It wasn't over-ornate playing, it was individual playing.

<MUSIC PLAYING>

SHEPHERD: Do you go along with that, George, the Italian influence?

MACILWHAM: Oh, I certainly do, Robbie. And it is quite obvious, anybody reading the history of music in Edinburgh about the time, say, of Nathaniel Gow would realize only too well. And just listening to music that was written at that time, it's very, very influenced by the Italians. But the interesting thing, as Jim was saying there, not only Italians, but Yehudi Menuhin in his foreword to Jim's own book, *Fiddle Music of Scotland*, he makes the point that Scottish fiddlers, and especially if they're of the stamp of Ron Gonnella, did play in tune naturally. But if I could just add a wee point to this, although

Ron's tone was unmistakably Italian, the vibrato, everything about it seemed to be so different, and that was the Italian influence. It was in the blood there. But the real strong influence was the Scottish blood of his mother, Lizzie Duncan, she really seemed to have given him his real Scottish attitude to music, to poetry, and everything like that.

SHEPHERD: And I think it was being brought up in that dance atmosphere that his reels and jigs were quite special.

MACILWHAM: Oh, they were indeed. Ron's idiom, the way he used Scottish music, especially Strathspeys, reels, jigs, were absolutely unmistakable. And fortunately he's left quite a number of these for posterity to enjoy.

SHEPHERD: Yes. James, just briefly, he had a lovely voice for radio and for stage as well, a lovely way of putting his music or the story of his music out, and also as an adjudicator—can you take these two together?

HUNTER: Yes. I think the thing that marked him out there, both as a presenter and an adjudicator, and I think you need that for both, is enthusiasm. He communicated his enthusiasm for the music. He was in it for the love of the music, he wanted others to feel that. And so when he was presenting radio programs he got that across.

SHEPHERD: From those various comments about Scott Skinner the man, let's pick up his career again. For many years he operated as much as a dancing master as a fiddle player, and apart from beating the celebrated dancer John McNeil in competition, he taught dancing to the children on Balmoral Estate. The first of his many collections of Scottish fiddle music was published in 1865, and from 1871 when he married Jean Stewart, the couple took dancing assemblies working from their home in Aberlour and then Elgin.

HUNTER: On the adjudication front I never heard him say a bad word about playing. There was always a good side to somebody's playing, something they could work on, and he'd give some time, some practical demonstration of how that should be done, but it was always an encouraging word, and I think that's very important.

SHEPHERD: Yeah. The next choice of music, I'm going to go to you this time, George. A piece of music that you would like to highlight the playing of Ron.

MACILWHAM: If I could revert back to the days when Ron was a form master at Morrison's Academy, his pupils must have loved him because as Jim was saying there, what a wonderful voice, his voice was like his violin, it was a beautiful voice. He was a very erudite man, well-read, and really a joy to be with all the time. Anyway, his pupils had to learn a little nonsense rhyme by A. A. Milne, of Winnie-the-Pooh fame, and of course it went like this, if I could quote a line from it. It was entitled 'Disobedience,' and you can just imagine he had a class and he had to get them to learn this. And it was:

James, James,
Morrison, Morrison,
Weatherby, George Dupree
Took great
Care of his Mother,
Though he was only three.
James James Said to his Mother,
'Mother,' he said, said he;
'You must never go down
to the end of the town,
if you don't go down with me.

Now, to get the students to memorize this, Ron set it to music, and the jig James James Morrison Morrison was born. And of course we included it in Volume 5, believe it or not, of the *Scottish Dance Masters*. Another tune that went with it in that particular selection was Janie Duncan's 92nd Birthday. Well, Janie Duncan must have been his auntie, his mother's sister, of course. But James James Morrison Morrison was the tune that helped the children to understand and learn the poem.

SHEPHERD: I'm nearly convinced this is going to be double tracking.

<MUSIC PLAYING>

SHEPHERD: From the album of the *Scottish Dance Masters, Volume 5*, Murdoch, I knew that it was a jig but we played the James James Morrison Morrison and Janie Duncan's 92nd Birthday, and to complete our tribute to Ron Gonnella, I go back to my guests in our Glasgow studio, Jim Hunter and George MacIlwham. Starting with you, Jim, had you been writing the book, I think it was 1978, '79, *The Fiddle Music of Scotland*, had you sat down to write this book at the start of the next century where would you place Ron Gonnella in the history side of your book?

HUNTER: Well, I think the history is the important side, and I would place him right at the top of the tree in his own brand of playing. Because I think there are many brands of playing, and all brands should be accepted. And as a smooth, faultless player who taught us new tunes and through our research advanced our knowledge, we owe him a great debt. We owe him a great debt also for communicating his love for the music and above all for holding to tradition and being an inspiration for those who follow on.

SHEPHERD: George, what legacy left behind as far as you're concerned?

MACILWHAM: Well, a very important legacy, Robbie, of course is the fact that he left numerous compositions, and his friends are remembered in these compositions. And it's lovely to think that Ron at the end there actually was married. Now, this was a thing we used to joke, many a time we used to joke with Ron because as you know he was a bachelor.

SHEPHERD: I used to joke about it as well.

MACILWHAM: Of course, we all did. And we used to say 'Ron, what a wonderful institution marriage is,' and he would say 'aye, but who wants to live in an institution?' Well, believe it or not he kept knocking at the door of that institution for years and along came Elizabeth, and she had the key that opened that door. And at least he had the happiness of being married for the last few years. There's another thing, Robbie, I'd like to say, I feel in many ways we have been robbed because Ron had so much more to give, and we looked forward to collaborating in so many ways. I know Jim would look forward to collaborating with him too. And alas, it has been cut short. But we must go on, and Ron is one of the indispensable links in the fiddle history of Scotland, a very important one. And Ron himself, he said at the end of his little book, *The New Atholl Collection*, he quoted from Burns, and it was Burns's Epistle of Mrs Scott, and you could just imagine Ron saying this himself:

E'en then, a wish, (I mind its pow'r),
A wish that to my latest hour
Shall strongly heave my breast,
That I for poor auld Scotland's sake

Some usefu' plan or book could make,
Or sing a sang at least.

MACILWHAM: Well Ron certainly made his fiddle sing for Scotland.

SHEPHERD: He made his fiddle sing to the very end, and Jim, a final, we're privileged to have a tape of the *Music of Historic Scotland*, which is due out in April, and Ron had been working on this just very shortly before he died. It isn't the fiddle-playing you would think of a sick man, Jim?

HUNTER: No, I don't think so. I think it's a legacy of which he can be proud. It will remind us of the best of Ron Gonnella, and through that the best of Scottish fiddle music playing.

SHEPHERD: Gentlemen, thanks for coming in this morning. 'The Honours of Scotland' is the selection that we've chosen. In this set can identify is in honour of the Scottish crown jewels, and especially written for the purpose. The Crown of Scotland, Sceptres of Spey, and The Sword of Scotland.

<MUSIC PLAYING>

SHEPHERD: The last recording of the late Ron Gonnella with that track from a cassette compact disc due to be released around April, the Honours of Scotland, with The Crown of Scotland, The Sceptres of Spey, and The Sword of Scotland. And that set indeed played at Ron's funeral service. And thanks to David Cunningham for sending up the tape, David did the recording, and to Historic Scotland for the use of the tape before it comes out. The Music of Historic Scotland celebrating some of the 330 historic properties which Historic Scotland cares for and opens to the public on behalf of the nation. Thanks, of course, to Jim Hunter and George MacIlwham as well.

<MUSIC PLAYING>

SHEPHERD: William Hannah there and the old 78th Regal MR 1091, and a Canadian Three Step, a wee bit later, but I said we would have our phone in . . .

LILY-ANNE GRANTWICH: . . . and that it was a Simon Fraser tune from, I think, 1815.

<MUSIC PLAYING>

SHEPHERD: Lily-Anne, I wonder if you would recite that poem for us. And I see in the frontispiece before the poem you have given Ron credit.

LILY-ANNE: Yes, just briefly, I have a few lines under the title I've said. Lines upon re-reading after twenty-five years, letters written to me during World War Two from a prisoner of war camp in Germany, and it's to be sung to the old Jacobite air, Hard Is My Fate, from the 1815 Simon Fraser collection. This beautiful melody was first played to me by the Dundee violinist Ronald Gonnella, whom I always think of as the Yehudi Menuhin of Scottish fiddle music. And now the poem:

Oh my love, I dreamed of your yellow hair,
Scaling o'er your breests indeed o nicht,
But when I cam to my wakening hour
There was neither love nor lecht.
Hard is my fate in this dark gloom,
So deep within my dungeon tomb.
But the gentle memory of your love
Breaks through to fill my heard.
We twa may never meet again,
But love like oors is an air in vein,
So let me ever captive bide,
In the prison of your heart.
Oh my love, I dreamed of your yellow hair
Scaling o'er your breests indeed o nicht.
But when I cam to my wakening hour
There was neither love nor lecht.

<MUSIC PLAYING>

SHEPHERD: Lily-Anne Grantwich with her poem Hard Is My Fate, and that tune from a Simon Fraser collection played by Ron Gonnella. And we're coming rapidly to the end of the program. I've no time this morning to play the Brian McNeil and Tom McDonagh vocal track but I'll keep that one back for next week.

We're going to finish with Judith Linton again, amongst friends, and it's another band track, it's reels, J. B. Milne, Welcome the Time Aside <UNSURE 38.31> Helgen Esther Gray, and Dr. Robertson. I'll make that a request for Ken and Morag Campbell of Norvell Place, Longforgan in Dundee. I played Bobby Crode to finish off the program last week folks, and meant it for you but the request got lost somewhere. It's for brother-in-law Rab Souttar of Duff, who's been in hospital recently, all the best to you.

And for our competition, once again, our write-in competition, Radio Scotland, Beechgrove Terrace, Aberdeen, AB9 2ZT. Here's the questions again, if you were to sail due east from Dornoch past Tarbetness, what would be the first country you arrived at? Number two, which covered shopping complex in Glasgow, which was totally recreated in 1988 was singled out for praise by the Prince of Wales?

<END OF TRANSCRIPTION>

APPENDIX H

Gonnella Memorial Concert Program

DUNKELD CATHEDRAL

PROGRAMME

Part I

READING:	The Daft Days
ORCHESTRA:	Set of Reels
CHOIR:	Old Scottish Psalm Tunes
READING:	A Cotter's Saturday Night
READING:	Dunkeld
FIDDLE:	Air, March, Strathspey, Reel
READING:	A Song of the Road
FLUTE:	O'er the Hills and Far Away
READING:	Burns' Letter of 1793
CHOIR:	Ye Banks and Braes
READING:	She's Fair and Fause
SONG:	Cradle Song
READING:	To a Mouse
FLUTE:	Airs and Jigs
READING:	Tullochgorum
FIDDLE:	Strathspeys and Reels
READING:	Women Folk
SONG:	O Whistle and I'll Come Tae Ye
READING:	Willie Wastle
FIDDLE/FLUTE:	Soldier's Joy; Corn Riggs
READING:	Thee Caledonia
ALL:	Scots Wha Hae

Part II

BAND:	Selection
REEL:	Dancing in the Ramparts
MEDLEY:	Inverugie Castle
JIG:	The Earl of Errol
ORCHESTRA:	Hills of Perth; Sidlaw Hills; St Johnstone Reel
PIPES/DANCE:	Highland Solo Dance
BAND:	Selection
REEL:	Rob Roy
JIG:	Up in the Morning Early
MEDLEY:	Tribute to Ron Gonnella
BAND:	Selection

RON GONNELLA
(1931 – 1994)

Ron Gonnella was one of Scotland's best known traditional fiddlers. He was of Italian descent, his grandfather having emigrated to Dundee, where he set up business as a restorer of musical instruments and paintings. His mother was a well-known teacher of country dancing, who nurtured her son's keen interest in traditional music.

Ron trained as a teacher, and latterly taught at Morrison's Academy, Crieff.

Ron had a very personal style of fiddle playing, specially noted for its neat bowing, faultless intonation and a smooth, lyrical, melodic flow. In the 1950's and 1960's he played with many of the leading Scottish country dance bands, such as Andrew Rankine and Lindsay Ross. In the 1970's he formed his own string group, re-creating the melodic sound of Scottish dance music as it was played in the golden era of the Gows, Marshall and MacIntosh. Latterly he was also the conductor of the Dundee Strathspey and Reel Society.

Ron was a frequent broadcaster, both on radio and television, and also a prolific recording artist. He was a splendid ambassador for fiddle music, and was a regular visitor to Canada and the United States, where he gave concerts and master classes to expatriates and aspiring young fiddle players.

Ron Gonnella had a great love of the poetry of Robert Burns. He had a special affection for the music of the Gow family, and he was instrumental in the formation of the Niel Gow Memorial Trust, which raised funds to replace the ageing headstone on Niel Gow's grave at Little Dunkeld. The original now lies in safe keeping in the Chapter House of this Cathedral.

Tonight, as we perform and listen to some of the music, poetry and dances that Ron Gonnella so dearly loved, we honour his memory as a friend, fiddler, teacher and above all, as a dedicated champion of Scottish Traditional Music.

Fiona Brownsmith

Fiona was taught singing by Edna Auld and Donald Maxwell. A former member of Southern Light Opera Company, she is currently a member of Tayside Opera, where she has played a variety of roles over the past five years. In 1990 she won the gold medal for singing at the Perth Music Festival.

Walter Blair

Walter Blair is one of Scotland's best known accompanists. An all-round musician and teacher, he was Head of the Music School for gifted children in Strathclyde before taking up his present position as Director of the Junior School at the Royal Scottish Academy.

James Hunter

James Hunter has worked most of his career in broadcasting and was until recently the Head of Television for BBC Scotland, before relinquishing the position to concentrate on his freelance career.

As a television producer and concert promoter, James Hunter has worked with all the leading figures in Scottish music and entertainment. The traditional music of Scotland has been a lifelong interest, and he has collected and arranged many traditional airs. In 1972 he directed for TV the famous film *Mr. Menuhin's Welcome to Blair* in which the world famous violinist explored the art of traditional fiddling. In 1979 Mr. Hunter published *The Fiddle Music of Scotland* the most authoritative and all-embracing collection of Scotland's national violin heritage undertaken this century.

He is one of the best known choral conductors in Scotland and is currently Music Director of the Bearsden Burgh Choir and the Male Voice Choir of Scotland.

Part III

ORCHESTRA:	Selection of Marches
READING:	Epistle to Major William Logan
FIDDLE:	Hornpipes
ORCHESTRA:	The Flowers of Edinburgh
CHOIR:	Up Wi' the Carles
READING:	The Country Fiddlers
ORCHESTRA:	Shetland Reels
FIDDLE/FLUTE:	Air and Reels
READING:	Fair Grow the Flowers
ORCHESTRA:	The Flower of the Quern
CHOIR:	Afton Water
READING:	Orthodox! Orthodox!
ORCHESTRA:	Favourite Scottish Psalms
READING:	Holy Willie's Prayer
ORCHESTRA:	Andrew Rankine Jigs
SONG:	Rowan Tree
ORCHESTRA:	Dundee Medley
READING:	Burns' Address to Niel Gow
FIDDLE:	Niel Gow Selection
READING:	A Man's a Man For A' That
ALL:	Auld Lang Syne

* *

The Dunkeld and Birnam Arts Festival Society wishes to express its thanks to His Grace the Duke of Atholl for the loan of the Niel Gow fiddle for tonight's Concert.

Tom Fleming

Tom Fleming has had a long and illustrious career in radio, television and the theatre. Renowned for the timbre of his voice, and his impressive descriptive powers, he became famous throughout the world for his commentaries on Royal and State occasions.

He co-founded the Edinburgh Gateway Company in 1953, and in the mid-sixties was a leading member of the Royal Shakespeare Company. The founder and first director of the Royal Lyceum Company, he subsequently became director of the Scottish Theatre Company.

Tom Fleming has played many famous roles on television, including Robert Burns, William Wallace, Jesus of Nazareth, Henry IV, and Sir John Reith. The recipient of many awards and honours, he was made an O.B.E. in 1980.

Maureen Turnbull

Maureen started to play the violin at the age of seven, with classical lessons in Dundee, and then at the Junior Department of the Royal Scottish Academy of Music. She was the leader of the Dundee Schools' Symphony Orchestra and a member of the National Youth Orchestra of Scotland.
Maureen has always taken an interest in Scottish Fiddle Music, and played with both the Dundee and Angus Strathspey and Reel Societies. She has won many fiddle competitions – The Golden Fiddle, Young Fiddler of the Year, and in successive years the prestigious Glenfiddich Fiddle Championship held annually at Blair Castle.

George McIlwham

George McIlwham, the Scottish flautist and composer, has had a distinguished career as a soloist and an orchestral player with both the Royal Scottish National Orchestra and the BBC Scottish Symphony Orchestra. He also is a highly respected performer on the Highland Bagpipe.
George is also a founder member of several chamber music ensembles, and is a regular performer for the Council for Music in Hospitals.

APPENDIX I

F.I.R.E. Competition Judging Form

(*following page*)

Scottish F.I.R.E. Alternative Competition Form

Competition Name : ______________________ **Date:** __________

Name: ______________________ **Category** ______________________ **Air:** ______________________

Address: ______________________ **Order of Play:** ______________________ **March:** ______________________

______________________ **Final Rank:** ______________________ **Strathspey:** ______________________

Email: ______________________ **Special Award:** ______________________ **Reel:** ______________________

Directions: Choose the appropriate descriptor and score. Unlisted values may be indicated as needed.

	Interpretation/Expression (40)					Time (30)			Execution (30)			Totals
Tune Type	**Ornamentation**	**Dynamics/Color**	**Phrases**	**Interpretation**	**Encing/Trans.**	**Tempo**	**Rhythm**	**Pulse**	**Intonation**	**Tone**	**Bowing**	
Air	0 none 1 evident 3 non-stylistic 6 well done 9 superior	0 no contrast 3 some 6 tasteful effect 9 approp/superior	0 none 3 evident 6 well done 9 superior	0 none 1 safe 3 non-stylistic 6 well done 9 superior	0 none 2 too abrupt 4 tasteful	2 extreme (fast/slow) 6 approx. 10 superior	1 erratic 4 inexact 7 approp 10 superior	0 inapprop. erratic 5 inapprop. variable 10 appropriate	1 frequent errors 4 occasional 7 isolated 10 accurate	2 unfocused 6 acceptable 10 superior	0 non-stylistic 5 semi-stylistic 10 stylistic	
Comments												/100
March	0 none 1 evident 3 non-stylistic 6 well done 9 superior	0 no contrast 3 some 6 tasteful effect 9 approp/superior	0 none 3 evident 6 well done 9 superior	0 none 1 safe 3 non-stylistic 6 well done 9 superior	0 none 2 too abrupt 4 tasteful	2 extreme (fast/slow) 6 approx. 10 superior	1 erratic 4 inexact 7 approp 10 superior	0 extremely variable 5 variable 10 steady	1 frequent errors 4 occasional 7 isolated 10 accurate	2 unfocused 6 acceptable 10 superior	0 non-stylistic 5 semi-stylistic 10 stylistic	
Comments												/100
Strathspey	0 none 1 evident 3 non-stylistic 6 well done 9 superior	0 no contrast 3 some 6 tasteful effect 9 approp/superior	0 none 3 evident 6 well done 9 superior	0 none 1 safe 3 non-stylistic 6 well done 9 superior	0 none 2 too abrupt 4 tasteful	2 extreme (fast/slow) 6 approx. 10 superior	1 erratic 4 inexact 7 approp 10 superior	0 extremely variable 5 variable 10 steady	1 frequent errors 4 occasional 7 isolated 10 accurate	2 unfocused 6 acceptable 10 superior	0 non-stylistic 5 semi-stylistic 10 stylistic	
Comments												/100
Reel	0 none 3 evident 5 non-stylistic 7 well done 10 superior	0 no contrast 3 some 6 tasteful effect 9 approp/superior	0 none 3 evident 6 well done 9 superior	0 none 1 safe 3 non-stylistic 6 well done 9 superior	0 none 2 too abrupt 4 tasteful	2 extreme (fast/slow) 6 approx. 10 superior	1 erratic 4 inexact 7 approp 10 superior	0 extremely variable 5 variable 10 steady	1 frequent errors 4 occasional 7 isolated 10 accurate	2 unfocused 6 acceptable 10 superior	0 non-stylistic 5 semi-stylistic 10 stylistic	
Comments												/100

Performance Comments:

Grand Total: /400

Judge's Signature ______________________ rev. 10/5/15

APPENDIX J

Retirement Announcement

Morrison's Academy
Written by Mollie MacCallum

Mr R. D. Gonnella, Dip.C.E., F.S.A. Scot.
September 1973 saw a new face in the then Morrison's Academy boys' School Primary Department—that of Ron Gonnella. Previously employed in industry, Mr Gonnella had done what has now become quite fashionable—changed stream in mid-life: he deserted the Export and Shipping Department of Briggs of Dundee for a career in teaching (perhaps a different kind of exporting?), and trained to become one of that increasingly rare breed, a male Primary teacher.

Mr Gonnella has taught mainly in the middle and upper stages of the Primary Department, bringing his own individual style of humour to the classroom, balancing a relaxed manner with firm discipline. However, he has also had the unusual distinction (for a man) of teaching preps. Some of the long-standing Morrisonians in the current Sixth Form were taught during P2 and P3 by Mr Gonnella, an experience which I think he rather enjoyed.

But Mr Gonnella has given so much more to Morrison's. He has been a resident House Tutor in Glenearn; he valiantly tried to revive the Morrison's Cub Pack; he has run record and drama clubs; he has shared his lively interest in soccer; he has taken school parties on holidays to Austria and France.

Far greater than that, however, has been his contribution through music. An internationally renowned musician, Mr Gonnella has both enriched the musical life of, and brought honour to, the School. Within the Primary Department he has worked with recorder groups, taught class music for several years, and for very many years played at morning Assembly. Recognising the benefits of colour television, he gave a most interesting lecture-recital based on the life and music of Scott Skinner and generously donated the proceeds to up-grade the Department's black-and-white set to colour. Within the wider life of the School, he has lent his expertise to the Ceilidh Band and added weight—his own description—to the School Orchestra.

1985, with the Queen's visit in honour of the 125th Anniversary celebrations, was a particularly felicitous year for the School, and was marked musically by Mr Gonnella. For the Pipe Band he composed the "Morrison's Academy Anniversary March," and both composed and played, for our royal visitors, the fiddle air, "The Queen's Visit to Morrison's Academy."

Is he even now composing "Ron's Retiral from Morrison's Academy"? Whether you are or not, we wish you, Ron, many years of—not rest, but globe-trotting with your fiddle, and golf with your friends.
M.L.M. (1985)

APPENDIX K

Gonnella Obituary

Ron Gonnella
The Herald
Saturday 18 February 1994
One of Scotland's best-known fiddlers and authorities on the history of Scottish traditional music, Mr Ron Gonnella has died at his home in Crieff at the age of 63.

The grandson of an Italian immigrant to Dundee who restored musical instruments and paintings, Mr Gonnella learned to play the great Scottish tunes at the knee of Jimmy Shand.

His mother took country dancing classes in Dundee and at the age of nine Ron would climb up on the platform carrying his fiddle and join in with Jimmy Shand and his band.

He trained as a teacher and taught latterly at Morrison's Academy, Crieff. He also taught the violin privately.

Mr Gonnella emigrated briefly to Canada but soon decided to return to Scotland, although he made frequent visits to Canada and the United States to give concerts and workshops to "ex-pat" Scots and lovers of Scottish fiddle music.

Mr Gonnella made a number of radio and television programs, most recently a television tribute to the Scottish composer James Scott Skinner.

He also recorded music for local tourist boards to promote their areas.

His playing career was probably at its height in the halcyon days of Scottish music in the 1950s and 1960s, when he played with Andrew Rankine and his band, Lindsay Ross, and many others.

When touring in Canada Mr Gonnella often played with Stan Hamilton and his country dance band.

Fellow musician Ian Powrie yesterday paid tribute to Mr Gonnella's research into the history of music, particularly into the old Scottish airs.

Mr Robbie Shepherd, broadcaster and traditional music enthusiast, said: "He was the most prolific performer in the recording studio of solo Scottish fiddle music."

Mr Gonnella is survived by his wife Elizabeth.

Herald, The (1994). "Ron Gonnella Obituary" [online]. Available from http://www.heraldscotland.com/news/12683947.Ron_Gonnella/.

Discography of Scottish Fiddling Recordings Referenced in This Work

Anderson, T. (1963) *Scottish Violin Music*—Vol. 2. [LP] Edinburgh: Waverly

Cunningham, D. and Gonnella, R. (1987) *Saint Andrews Branch Golden Jubilee.* [LP] Edinburgh: Royal Scottish Country Dance Society

Dickie, J. F. (1976) *James F. Dickie's Delights: Scottish Fiddling in the Style of Scott Skinner.* [LP] Uppingham: Topic Records

Gonnella, R. (1966) *Scottish Violin Music.* [LP] Glasgow: Scotdisc

———. (1973) Scottish Violin Music From the Gow Collections. [LP] Glasgow: Scottish Records

———. (1975) *Fiddler's Fancy.* [LP] Glasgow: Lismor

———. (1975) *Fiddle Gems* [LP] Glasgow: Lismor

———. (1977) *Ron Gonnella's Burns Night.* [LP] Glasgow: Lismor

———. (1980) Ron Gonnella: Scottish Fiddle Master. [LP] Glasgow: Lismor

———. (n.d.) Ron Gonnella's Fiddle & Pipe Favourites. [Cassette] Glasgow: Scotdisc

———. (1981) Ron Gonnella and Friends Live From the Crieff Hydro. [LP] Crieff: Crieff Hydro

———. (1982) Ron Gonnella Plays the Fiddles of Gow, Marshall and Skinner. [LP] Turriff: Ross Records

———. (1982) *Scottish Fireside Fiddle Chats.* [Cassettes] Crieff: Barga

———. (1983) *Music for Eight Scottish Country Dances* [Cassette] Edinburgh: RSCDS

———. (1984) The Scottish Sound of Ron Gonnella Playing a Stradivarius. [LP] Cambridge, Massachusetts: Atholl Brose

———. (1987) *A Tribute to Niel Gow.* [LP] Glasgow: Lismor

———. (1988) Ron Gonnella's International Friendship of the Fiddle. [Cassette] Glasgow: Scotdisc

———. (1986) *The Lad of Kyle.* [LP] Cambridge, Massachusetts: Atholl Brose

———. (1992) *Ron Gonnella's Scottish Fiddle Magic.* [LP] Crieff: Barga Music

———. (2012) *The Countess of Dalhousie.* [Digital download] Unknown: Vantage Music

———. (2007) *Platinum—70 Years of Dancing in St. Andrews.* [LP] Edinburgh: Royal Scottish Country Dance Society

Gonnella, R. and Cunningham, D. (1987) *Saint Andrews Branch Golden Jubilee.* [LP] Edinburgh: Royal Scottish Country Dance Society

———. (2007) *Platinum—70 Years of Dancing in St. Andrews. [CD]* Edinburgh: Royal Scottish Country Dance Society

Gonnella, R. and Crowe, B. *A Fife Fairing.* [LP] Edinburgh: RSCDS

Gonnella, R. and Hamilton, S. (1988) *Scottish Dance Masters,* Vol. 4. [LP] Edinburgh: Royal Scottish Country Dance Society

Gonnella, R. and MacIlwham, G. (c. 1985) *Scottish Dance Masters,* Vol. 3. [LP] Edinburgh: Royal Scottish Country Dance Society

———. (1991) *Scottish Dance Masters,* Vol. 5. [LP] Edinburgh: Royal Scottish Country Dance Society

Gonnella, R. and MacPhail, I. (1984) *Scottish Dance Masters,* Vol. 2. [LP] Edinburgh: Royal Scottish Country Dance Society

Gonnella, R. and Rankine, A. (1982) *Scottish Dance Masters,* Vol. 1. [LP] Edinburgh: Royal Scottish Country Dance Society

Grant, A. (1978) *Angus Grant—Highland Fiddle.* [LP] Uppingham: Topic Records

Hardie, A. (1981) *The Caledonian Companion.* [CD] London: EMI Music Publishing

Hardie, W. (1956) *Scottish Country Fiddle.* [LP] London: Beltona

———. (1986) *Beauties of the North*. Edinburgh: The Hardie Press

Hardie, W. and Skinner, J.S. (1975) *The Music of Scott Skinner.* [LP] Uppingham: Topic Records

Lorne Scottish Dance Band (1973) *Ecossaises,* Vol. 2. [LP] Paris: Arfolk

MacAndrew, H. (1963) *Scottish Violin Music,* Vol. 1. [LP] Middlesex: EMI

———. (1975) *Hector MacAndrew—Scots Fiddle.* [LP] Glasgow: Scottish Records

Robertson, A. S. (1975) *Scotland's Champion Fiddler.* [LP] Unknown: Spectrum

———. (c. 1972) *Champion's Choice.* [LP] Unknown: Spectrum

———. (1991) *Champion's Choice.* [CD] East Lothian: Greentrax

Steven, Y. (1976) *Back to the Hills.* [LP] Glasgow: Scottish Records

Various Artists (1964) *An Edinburgh Fancy.* [LP] Glasgow: Scottish Records

Various Artists (1980) *The Fiddler's Companion.* [LP] London: EMI

Various Artists (1970) *Scottish Fiddlers to the Fore.* [LP] London: BBC Records

Various Artists (1977) *The National Fiddle Championship*. [LP] London: EMI

Bibliography

Abrams, L. and Brown, C. G. (2010) *A History of Everyday Life in Twentieth Century Scotland*. Edinburgh: Edinburgh University Press

Alexander, J. (2014) *Scottish Fiddler and Teacher* [interview by MacMorran, J.] Fochabers, 18 May 2014

Alburger, M. A. (1996) Scottish Fiddlers and Their Music. Edinburgh: The Hardie Press

———. (2001) *Making the Fiddle Sing: Captain Simon Fraser of Knockie and his Airs and Melodies Peculiar to the Highlands of Scotland and the Isles.* [PhD Thesis] [online] University of Aberdeen. Available from <http://ethos.bl.uk/OrderDetails.do?uin=uk.bl.ethos.395253> [18 February 2014]

Allen, B. and Montell, W. L. (1981) *From Memory to History: Using Oral Sources in Local Historical Research.* Nashville: American Association for State and Local History

Anderson, K. and Jack, D. C. (1998) "Learning to listen: interview techniques and analyses." In *The Oral History Reader*. ed. by Perks, R. and Thomson, A. London: Routledge, 172–182

Anderson, T. (1970) *Da Mirrie Dancers: A Book of Shetland Fiddle Tunes*. Lerwick: Shetland Folk Society

———. (1963) *Scottish Violin Music*—Vol. 2. [LP] Edinburgh: Waverly

Anon. (2014) *Taxi Driver* [conversation with MacMorran, J.] Aberdeen, 16 May 2014

———. (1953) "Frae a the Airts They Came to Fiddle at Alyth." *Dundee Courier* 19 October, n.p. Available from <https://www.britishnewspaperarchive.co.uk/search/results?basicsearch=frae%20a%20the%20airts%20they%20came%20to%20fiddle%20at%20alyth'&retrievecountrycounts=false> [10 September 2017]

———. (1994) "Ron Gonnella Obituary." *The Herald.* [online] Available from <http://www.heraldscotland.com/news/12683947.Ron_Gonnella/> [22 September 2013]

——. (1960) "The Cameron Kerr Began in the Boys' Brigade." *Dundee Courier* 26 December, 6

——. (1942) "Pupils' Recital Helps Children's Fund." *Dundee Courier*. Available from <http://www.britishnewspaperarchive.co.uk> [22 September 2017]

——. (1947) "Young Violinists Excel." *Dundee Courier* 12 June. Available from <https://www.britishnewspaperarchive.co.uk/viewer/bl/0000564/19470612/013/0002> [22 September 2013]

——. (1975) "More Scots Folk Music Going Around." *The Aberdeen Press and Journal*. 26 March 1975. Available from <https://www.britishnewspaperarchive.co.uk/viewer/bl/0000578/19750326/062/0006> [21 November 2017]

——. (1809) *The Scots Magazine*. Vol. 71, 3. Edinburgh: Archibald Constable and Company. Available from <https://archive.org/stream/sim_edinburgh-magazine-and-literary-miscellany1809–0171/simedinburgh-magazine-and-literary-miscellany1809–0171djvu.txt> [22 December 2023]

Bakhtin, M. M. (1981) *The Dialogic Imagination: Four Essays*. (ed. by Holquist, M. trans. By Emerson, C. and Holquist, M.) Austin: University of Texas Press

——. (1986) *Speech Genres and Other Late Essays*. (ed. by Emerson, C. and Holquist, M. trans. by McGee, V. W.) Austin: University of Texas Press

Barnard, S. (1989) *On the Radio: music radio in Britain*. Milton Keynes: Open University Press

Barthes, R. (1977) *Image-Music-Text*. London: Fontana

Bauer, M. W. and Gaskell, G. (eds) (2000) *Qualitative Researching With Text, Image and Sound: A Practical Handbook for Social Research*. London: Sage

Baumann, M. P. (1996) "Folk Music Revival: Concepts Between Regression and Emancipation." *The World of Music* 38 (3), 71–86

Bell, E. (2008) *Theories of Performance*. London: Sage

——. (2004) *Questioning Scotland: Literature, Nationalism, Postmodernism*. Hampshire: Palgrave Macmillan

Bennett, R. (2006) *Willie Macpherson: The Elgin Fiddler*. Essex: Fraser Macpherson

Bithell, C. (2006) "The Past in Music: Introduction." *Ethnomusicology Forum* 15 (1), 3–16

Bithell, C. and Hill, J. (eds) (2014) *The Oxford Handbook of Music Revival*. Oxford: Oxford University Press

Blank, T. J, and Howard, R. G. (eds) (2013) *Tradition in the Twenty-first Century: Locating the Role of the Past in the Present*. Boulder: University of Colorado Press

Blatz, P. K. (1990) "Craftsmanship and Flexibility in Oral History: A Pluralistic Approach to Methodology and Theory." *The Public Historian* [online] 12 (4), 7–22. Available from <http://www.jstor.org/stable/3378782> [1 January 2014]

Blaustein, R. (2003) *The Thistle and the Brier: Historical Links and Cultural Parallels Between Scotland and Appalachia*. Jefferson: McFarland

——. (1993) "Folk Music Revivals in Comparative Perspective." *Tennessee Folklore Society Bulletin* 56 (2), 54–63

——. (2014) "Grassroots Revitalization of North American and Western European Instrumental Music Traditions From Fiddlers Associations to Cyberspace." In *Oxford Handbook of Music Revival.* ed by Hill, J. and Bithell, C. Oxford: Oxford University Press, 551–572

Bohlman, P. V. (2008) "Returning to the Ethnomusicological Past." In *Shadows in the Field: New Perspectives for Fieldwork in Ethnomusicology.* 2nd ed. Edited by Barz, G. and Cooley, T. J. Available from <http://web.a.ebscohost.com.iris.etsu.edu:2048/ehost/ebookviewer/ebookbbacf9a9a742b@sessionmgr4010&vid=0&format=EB&rid=1> [26 August 2017]

Boorman, S. (1999) "The Musical Text." In *Rethinking Music,* ed. by Cook, N. and Everist, M. Oxford: Oxford University Press, 403–423

Bort, E. (ed.) (2011) *Tis Sixty Years Since: The 1951 Edinburgh People's Festival Ceilidh and the Scottish Folk Revival.* Ochtertyre: Grace Note Publications

Bowman, W. D. (1998) *Philosophical Perspectives on Music.* New York: Oxford University Press

Box and Fiddle Magazine (2016) "Box and Fiddle Archive." [online] Available from <http://boxandfiddlearchive.weebly.com/mar-1994.html> [17 May 2015]

British Broadcasting Company Archives (2016) "Audition Letters." Hard copies through correspondence.

British Broadcasting Company Genome (2015) *Radio Times: 1923–2009 – Dancing Fiddles.* [online] Available from <https://genome.ch.bbc.co.uk/search/0/20?q=ron+gonnella#search> [24 May 2016]

British Broadcasting Company Radio Scotland (2015) *Take the Floor.* [online] Available from <http://www.bbc.co.uk/programmes/b04mgwd9> [23 May 2015]

British Broadcasting Company (1982) *On The Fiddle.* [Transcribed from broadcast recordings]

Bruce, D. A. (1996) *The Mark of the Scots.* Secaucus: Citadel Press

Burnim, M. (1985) "Culture Bearer: An Ethnomusicologist's Research on Gospel Music." *Ethnomusicology* [online] 29 (3), 432–447. Available from <http://www.jstor.org/stable/851798> [18 February 2014]

Burman-Hall, L. (1984) "American Traditional Fiddling: Performance Contexts and Techniques." In *Performance Practice: Ethnomusicological Perspectives,* ed. by Behague, G. Westport: Greenwood Press, 149–221.

Campbell, K. (2013) "Traditional Music" in *Scottish Life and Society: An Introduction to Scottish Ethnology.* ed. by Fenton, A. and Mackay, M. A. Edinburgh: John Donald, 217–235

——. (2007) *The Fiddle in Scottish Culture.* Edinburgh: John Donald

Campbell, P. S. (2001) "Heritage: The Survival of Cultural Traditions in a Changing World." *International Journal of Music Education* [online] 37, 59–63. Available from <http://ijm.sagepub.com/content/os-37/1/59> [4 January 2015]

Cameron, I. and Shepherd, R. (2001) *The Jimmy Shand Story*. Dalkeith: Scottish Cultural Press

Casciani, E. (1994) *Oh, How We Danced: The History of Ballroom Dancing in Scotland*. Edinburgh: Mercat Press

Chandler, D. (1994) *Semiotics for Beginners.* [online] Available from <http://www.aber.ac.uk/media/Documents/S4B/> [5 January 2017]

———. (2002) *Semiotics: The Basics.* 2nd ed. London: Routledge

Chenier. C. (2002) "Experience and Fieldwork: A Native Researcher's View." *Ethnomusicology* [online] 46 (3), 456–486. Available from <http://www.jstor.org.iris.etsu.edu:2048/stable/852719> [25 August 2017]

Clark, K. and Holquist, M. (1984) *Mikhail Bakhtin*. Cambridge: Harvard University Press

Clarke, D. (1996) "Language Games." *The Musical Times* [online] 137 (1835), 5–10. Available from <http://www.jstor.org/stable/1003378> [2 April 2014]

Clayton, M., Herbert, T. and Middleton, R. (2003) *The Cultural Study of Music: a critical introduction*. New York: Routledge

Clifford, J. and Marcus, G. E. (eds) (1986) *Writing Culture: The Poetics and Politics of Ethnography.* Berkeley: University of California Press

Colpi, T. (2013) "Made by Italo-Scots. The Italian Factor in Scotland Today." [online] Available from <http://www.ed.ac.uk/files/imports/fileManager/16th%20April%20Scottish%20Parliament%20paper.pdf> [19 February 2016]

Collinson, F. (1966) *The Traditional and National Music of Scotland*. London: Routledge and Kegan Paul

Cook, N. (1998) *Analysing Musical Multimedia*. Oxford: Oxford University Press

Cook, N. and Everist, M. (1999) *Rethinking Music*. Oxford: Oxford University Press

Cooke, P. (1986) *The Fiddle Tradition of the Shetland Isles*. Cambridge: Cambridge University Press

———. *Ron Gonnella Research* [email] to MacMorran, J. [24 April 2014]

———. (1985) "*The Fiddle Music of Scotland* by James Hunter; *The Caledonian Companion* by Alastair J. Hardie; *Scottish Fiddle Music of the 18th Century* by David Johnson; *Scottish Fiddlers and Their Music* by Mary Anne Alburger." *Popular Music* [online] 5, 273–275. Available from <www.jstor.org/stable/853302> [2 July 2016]

Covach, J. (1999) "Popular Music, Unpopular Musicology." In *Rethinking Music*. ed. by Cook, N. and Everist, M. Oxford: Oxford University Press, 452–470

Cowrie, M. (1999) *The Life and Times of William Marshall*. Self-published, 59

Dallas, K. (1997) "Fit as a Fiddle." *Melody Maker*, 11 June 1997, 36

Davie, C. T. (1980) *Scotland's Music*. Edinburgh: William Blackwood

Davies, S. (1994) *Musical Meaning and Expression*. Ithaca: Cornell University Press

Davis, C., Black, K. and MacLean, K. (1977) *Oral History: From Tape to Type*. Chicago: American Library Association

DeBlasio, D., Ganzert, C., Mould, D., Paschen, S., and Sacks, H. (2009) *Catching*

Stories: A Practical Guide to Oral History. Athens: Swallow Press/Ohio University Press

Dickie, J. F. (1976) *James F. Dickie's Delights: Scottish Fiddling in the Style of Scott Skinner.* [LP] Uppingham: Topic Records

Dinwiddie, M. (1948) *The Scot and His Radio: Twenty-five Years of Scottish Broadcasting.* Edinburgh: The British Broadcasting Corporation

Donaldson, E. A. (1986) *The Scottish Highland Games in America.* Gretna: Pelican Publishing Company

Dorson, R. M. (1976) *Folklore and Fakelore: Essays toward a Discipline of Folk Studies*. Cambridge: Harvard University Press

Downie, B. L. (1997) *William McGibbon and Niel Gow: Reflections of Traditions and Taste in Eighteenth-Century Lowland Scotland.* [online] Masters dissertation. Rice University. Available from <https://scholarship.rice.edu/bitstream/handle/1911/17081/1384358.PDF?sequence=1&isAllowed=y> [18 February 2014]

Duesenberry, M. P. (2000) *Fiddle Tunes On Air: A Study of Gatekeeping and Traditional Music at the BBC in Scotland, 1923–1957*. [PhD Thesis] University of California, Berkley [online] Available from <http://search.proquest.com.iris.etsu.edu:2048/docview/304584043/B85969A74B324CC5PQ/1?accountid=10771> [13 October 2013]

Dunaway, D. and Baum, W. (1996) *Oral History: An Interdisciplinary Anthology.* 2nd edn. London: AltaMira Press

Dundee City Archives (2016) *Registrar of Births, Deaths and Marriages.* [online] Available from <http://www.dundeecity.gov.uk/supportservs/registrar/> [8 June 2014]

———. (2016) *Photopolis.* [online] Available from <http://photopolis.dundeecity.gov.uk/wc0461.htm> [Accessed 25/6/2017]

Dundee Strathspey and Reel Society (2016) *Facebook Page.* [online] Available from <https://www.facebook.com/groups/dundeesrs/> [14 February 2016]

Dunkeld and Birnam Arts Festival Society (1994) "Airs and Graces: A Celebration of Scottish Music, Dance and Song to Honour the Memory of the Fiddler Ron Gonnella." Concert Program

Dwyer, S. C. and Buckle, J. L. (2009) "The Space Between: On Being an Insider-Outsider in Qualitative Research." *International Journal of Qualitative Methods* 8 (1), 56–63

Emmerson, G. S. (1971) *Rantin' Pipe and Tremblin' String: A History of Scottish Dance Music.* Montreal: McGill-Queens University Press

Eydmann, S. (2014) *Traditional Artist in Residence, Celtic and Scottish Studies University of Edinburgh.* [interview by MacMorran, J.] Edinburgh, 20 May 2014

———. (2017) *The Fiddle in the Scottish Folk Music Revival.* [online] Available from <http://www.blogs.hss.ed.ac.uk/revival-fiddle/> [6 June 2014]

———. (2017) *Ron Gonnella Research* [email] to MacMorran, J. [19 July 2017]

Farmer, H. G. (1947) *A History of Music in Scotland.* New York: Da Capo Press

Farmer, H. G. (1970) *A History of Music in Scotland*. 2nd ed. New York: Da Capo Press

Feintuch, B. (2006) "Revivals on the Edge: Northumberland and Cape Breton: A Keynote." *Yearbook for Traditional Music* [online] 38, 1–17. Available from <http://www.jstor.org/stable/20464969> [16 February 2014]

———. (ed.) (2003) *Eight Words for the Study of Expressive Culture*. Urbana: University of Illinois Press

Fenton, A. and Mackay, M. A. (eds) (2013) *Scottish Life and Society: An Introduction to Scottish Ethnology*. Edinburgh: John Donald

Fish, S. (2011) *How to Write a Sentence and How to Read One*. New York: HarperCollins

———. (1994) *There's No Such Thing as Free Speech*. Oxford: Oxford University Press

———. (1980) *Is There a Text in This Class? The Authority of Interpretive Communities*. Cambridge: Harvard University Press

Fraser, S. (1982) *The Airs and Melodies Peculiar to the Highlands of Scotland and the Isles*. [Originally published in 1815. The 1982 edition contains all of revised 1874 edition.] Sydney, Nova Scotia: Paul Cranford

Fiske, J. (1990) *Introduction to Communication Studies*. 2nd ed. [online] London: Routledge. Available from <https://ymerleksi.wikispaces.com/file/view/Introduction_to_Communication_Studies.pdf> [Accessed 1 October 2017]

Friedlander, P. (1998) "Theory, Method and Oral History." In *The Oral History Reader*. ed. by Perks, R. and Thomson, A. London: Routledge, 311–19

Gatherer, N. (2013) *Nigel Gatherer's Traditional Music*. [online] Available from <http://www.nigelgatherer.com/perf/fiddlers/gonel.html> [16 February 2014]

———. (2013) *The Music Gatherer*. [online] Available from <http://themusicgatherer.blogspot.de/2014/> [29 September 2017]

Geertz, C. (1973) *The Interpretation of Cultures*. New York: Basic Books

Georgii-Hemming, E., Burnard, P. and Holgersen, S. (eds.) (2013) *Professional Knowledge in Music Teacher Education*. Farnham: Ashgate

Gibson, R. (2014) *The 'Invention' of a Scottish Fiddle Tradition*. [online] Available from <http://scottishfiddlemusic.com/2014/01/17/the-invention-of-a-scottish-fiddle-tradition-c-1850/> [28 June 2015]

———. (2016) *Continuity, Change, and Revival in the History of Scottish Fiddle Music*. [unsubmitted PhD thesis, University of Aberdeen], [page unknown].

———. (2016) *Scottish Violin Competitions* [email] to MacMorran, J. [22 June 2016]

———. (2019) "The status of the master fiddler in eighteenth-century Scotland." In *From Dancing to Listening: Fiddle and Dance Studies from around the North Atlantic 5*. ed by Doherty, L. and Vallely, F. Aberdeen: The Elfinstone Institute, University of Aberdeen

Gibson, W. L "Review of 'Four Samples of Oral Biography." *The Oral History Review* [online] 24 (2), 101–106. Available from <http://www.jstor.org/stable/3675555> [1 January 2014]

Glassie, J. (2003) "Tradition." *In Eight Words for the Study of Expressive Culture*. ed. by Feintuch, B. Urbana: University of Illinois Press, 176–197

Glen, J. (1891) *The Glen Collection of Scottish Dance Music*, vol. 1. Edinburgh: J & R Glen [Out of Print]

Glen, J. (1895) *The Glen Collection of Scottish Dance Music, vol 2*. Edinburgh: J & R Glen Note: This long out-of-print collection was re-printed in Inverness by Highland Music Trust in 2001.

Goertzen, C. (1985) "American Fiddle Tunes and the Historic-Geographic Method." *Ethnomusicology* [online] 29, 448–473. Available from <http://www.jstor.org/stable/851799> [6 April 2014]

——. (1997) *Fiddling For Norway: Revival and Identity*. Chicago: University of Chicago Press

Gonnella, R. (n.d.) *Visit to Mary Ogilvie*. William L. and Gowan Merson Smith Collection: 1957–1976. Archives of Appalachia at East Tennessee State University, Johnson City, Tennessee [Tape WGS-41bD1]

——. (1977) *The Ron Gonnella Collection of Fiddle Music*, Vol. 1. Glasgow: Mozart Allan

——. (1979) *The Ron Gonnella Collection of Fiddle Music*, Vol. 2. Glasgow: Mozart Allan

——. (1982) *The Ron Gonnella Collection of Fiddle Music*, Vol, 3. Crieff: Self-published

Gonnella, R. and Murray, E.M.E. (1986) *The New Atholl Collection*. West Virginia: ScotPress

Goodheart, E. (1983, 2003) "The Text and the Interpretive Community." *Daedalus* [online] 112 (1), 215–231. Available from <http://www.jstor.org/stable/20024844> [15 May 2014]

Gordon, R. (1970) *Rob Gordon's Book of Scottish Music*. Glasgow: James S. Kerr

Gore, C. (1998) *A Fiddlers Book of Scottish Jigs From the 18th & 19th Century*. ed. by Hardie, A. Edinburgh: The Hardie Press

——. (2008) *Echoes of a Golden Age: Rediscovering Scotland's Original Fiddle Music*. Inverness: Highland Music Trust

——. (1994) *The Scottish Fiddle Music Index*. Musselburgh: The Amaising Publishing House, Ltd.

——. (2014) *Scottish Fiddler* [phone conversation with MacMorran, J.] [18 May 2014]

Gow, N. (1986) [ed. by Carlin, R.] *The Gow Collection of Scottish Dance Music*. Pacific: Mel Bay

——. (1983) *The Beauties of Gow*. [First published in three volumes 1870] London: Jefferys

Grele, R. J. (1991) *Envelopes of Sound: The Art of Oral History*. New York: Praeger

Grey, H. (1994) *Ron Gonnella Research* [phone conversation with MacMorran, J.] [18 May 2014]

Hajkowski, T. (2010) *The BBC and National Identity in Britain, 1922–53* [online]. Manchester: Manchester University Press. Available from <http://web.b.ebscohost.com.iris.etsu.edu:2048/ehost/ebookviewer/ebook/bmxlYmtfXzUxNTEzMF9fQU41?sid=343ccf63-b45c-42a0–9a1db3171644e3d5@sessionmgr107&vid=0&format=EB&rid=1> [28 December 2015]

Hall, S. (1980) "Encoding/Decoding in Television Discourse." [Conference Presentation at Council of Europe Colloquy. September 1973. University of Leichester] Available from <https://spstudentenhancement.files.wordpress.com/2015/03/stuart-hall-1980.pdf> [6 October 2017]

Hamilton, P. (2005) "The Oral Historian as Memorist." *The Oral History Review* [online] 32 (1), 11–18. Available from <http://www.jstor.org/stable/3675447> [1 January 2014]

Hammersley, M. (2000) *Social Research: Essays on Partisanship and Bias.* London: Routledge

Hardie, A. and Hardie, W. (1992) *The Caledonian Companion.* 2nd edn. Edinburgh: The Hardie Press

Harrison, F., Hood, M. and Palisca, C. (eds.) (1963) *Musicology.* Englewood Cliffs: Prentice-Hall, Inc.

Harvie, C. (1981) *No Gods and Precious Few Heroes: Scotland 1914–1980.* Toronto: University of Toronto Press

Have, P. ten (2007) *Doing Conversation Analysis: A Practical Guide.* 2nd edn. Thousand Oaks: Sage Publication

Hirschkop, K., and Shepherd, D. (eds.) (2001) *Bakhtin and Cultural Theory*. Manchester: Manchester University Press

———. (1992) "Is Dialogism for Real?" *Social Text* [online] 30, 102–113. Available from <http://www.jstor.org/stable/466470> [20 April 2014]

Hobsbawm, E. and Ranger, T. (eds) (1983) *The Invention of Tradition.* Cambridge: Cambridge University Press

Holgersen, S. and Holst, F. (2013) "Knowledge and Professionalism in Music Teacher Education." In *Professional Knowledge in Music Teacher Education.* ed. by Georgii-Hemming, E., Burnard, P. and Holgersen, S. Farnham: Ashgate, 51–71

Honeyman, W. C. (1984) *Strathspey Players Past and Present.* 2nd ed. Edinburgh: The Hardie Press

Hooper, G. (2006) *The Discourse of Musicology*. Burlington: Ashgate

Horner, B. (1998) "On the Study of Music as Material Social Practice." *The Journal of Musicology* [online] 16 (2), 159–199. Available from <http://www.jstor.org/stable/764139> [16 February 2014]

Hunter, A. (2014) *Former Morrison Academy Faculty Member* [interview by MacMorran, J.] Crieff, 23 May 2014

Hunter, J. (2009) "Remembering The BBC National Fiddle Competition." *The Scottish Fiddlers Calendar* (September 2009) Available from <http://www.thescottishfiddlesociety.ork.uk> [12 July 2017]

——. (1988) (eds. Hardie, A. and Hardie, W.) *The Fiddle Music of Scotland*. Edinburgh: The Hardie Press

——. (ed.) (1972) *Kerr's Thistle Collection*. Glasgow: James S. Kerr

Irving, G. (1994) "Ron Gonnella Obituary." *The Stage and Television Today* [online] [14 April 1994] Available from <https://www.britishnewspaperarchive.co.uk/viewer/bl/0001180/19940414/153/0033> [21 December 2016]

Jackson, A. (1987) *Anthropology at Home*. New York: Tavistock Publications

Jackson, H. (2000) *Niel Gow's Inver*. Perth: Perth & Kinross Libraries

Jeansonne, G. (1983) "Oral History, Biography, and Political Demagoguery." *Oral History Review* 11, 87–102.

Jewitt, C. (2012) *Glossary of multimodal terms*. [online] Available from <https://multimodalityglossary.wordpress.com> [29 September 2017)

Johnson, D. (1997) *Scottish Fiddle Music in the 18th Century*. 2nd edn. Edinburgh: Mercat Press

——. (1972) *Music and Society in Lowland Scotland in the Eighteenth Century*. Oxford: Oxford University

Johnson, J. (c. 1797) *The Scots Musical Museum*. Edinburgh: James Johnson & Co. Note: The referenced phrase comes from Robert Burns' comments in Robert Riddell's interleaved copy of *The Scots Musical Museum*. The collection was eventually published in six volumes between 1787–1803.

Jones, M. O. (2000) "Tradition" in Identity Discourses and an Individual's Symbolic Construction of Self." *Western Folklore* [online] 59 (2), 115–141. Available from <http://www.jstor.org/stable/1500156> [2 October 2014]

Karpeles, M. (1951) "Some Reflections on Authenticity in Folk Music." *Journal of the International Folk Music Council* [online] (3), 10–16. Available from <http://www.jstor.org/stable/835763> [11 January 2016]

Kaul, A. (2009) *Turning the Tune: Traditional Music, Tourism, and Social Change in an Irish Village*. New York: Berghahn Books

Keegan-Phipps, S. (2008) *Teaching Folk: The Educational Institutionalization of Folk Music in Contemporary England*. [PhD Thesis] University of Newcastle, Newcastle. Available from <http://ethos.bl.uk/OrderDetails.do?uin=uk.bl.ethos.445593> [22 August 2017]

Kerr, J. (c. 1880) *Kerr's Collection of Merry Melodies for the Violin, Books 1–4*. Glasgow: James S. Kerr

Kisliuk, M. (2008) *"(Un)*doing Fieldwork: Sharing Songs, Sharing Lives." In *Shadows in the Field: New Perspectives for Fieldwork in Ethnomusicology*. ed. by Barz, G. and Cooley, T. J. Oxford: Oxford University Press.

Kivy, P. (1998) *Authenticities: Philosophical Reflections on Musical Performance*. Oxford: Oxford University Press

——. (2007) *Music, Language, and Cognition*. Oxford: Clarendon Press

Korsyn, K. (1999) "Beyond Privileged Contexts: Intertextuality, Influence, and Dialogue." In *Rethinking Music*. ed. by Cook, N. and Everist, M. Oxford: Oxford University Press, 55–72

Lawrence, D. (2014) *Scottish Fiddler and Teacher* [interview with MacMorran, J.] Glasgow, 15 May 2014

Leishman, M. (2006) *My Father–Reith of the BBC.* Edinburgh: Saint Andrew Press

Levy, A. and Tischler, B. (1990s) "Into the Cultural Mainstream: The Growth of American Music Scholarship." *American Quarterly* [online] 42 (1), 57–73. Available from <http://www.jstor.org.iris.etsu.edu:2048/stable/2713225> [1 October 2013]

Livingston, T. E. (1999) "Music Revivals: Towards a General Theory." *Ethnomusicology* [online] 43 (1), 66–85. Available from <http://www.jstor.org/stable/852694> [16 February 2014]

———. (2014) 'An Expanded Theory for Revivals as Cosmopolitan Participatory Music Making'. In *Oxford Handbook of Music Revival.* ed. by Hill, J. and Bithell, C. Oxford: Oxford University Press

Lockhart, G. W. (1998) *Fiddles and Folk: A celebration of the re-emergence of Scotland's musical heritage.* Edinburgh: Luath Press

Lockhart, J. G. (1828) *Life of Robert Burns.* Edinburgh: Constable, 158

MacCallum, M. (2014) *Former Morrison Academy Faculty Member.* [interview with MacMorran, J.] Crieff, 23 May 2014

MacDonald, K. N. (1980) (ed by Cranford, P.) *The Skye Collection of Best Reels and Strathspeys Extant.* Sydney, N.S.: Paul Cranford [first published in 1887 Edinburgh: Paterson & Sons]

MacDonald, P. (2000) "Jean Carignan: A Folk Violinist." *Fiddler Magazine,* March 2000.

MacGregor, A. (2021) *Historical Music of Scotland.* <https://hms.scot> [13 December 2023]

Machin, D. (2002) *Ethnographic Research for Media Studies.* London: Arnold

———. (2007) *Introduction to Multimodal Analysis.* London: Bloomsbury

MacKay, H. (1975) "Pop Talk" *The Dundee Courier* 9, July 1975, n.p.

Maguire, J. S. and Matthews, J. (2012) "Are We All Cultural Intermediaries now? An Introduction to Cultural Intermediaries in Context." *European Journal of Cultural Studies* [online] 15 (5), 551–562. Available from <http://ecs.sagepub.com.iris.etsu.edu:2048/content/15/5/551> [8 August 2016]

Manuel, P. (2013) "Front Matter." *Ethnomusicology* 57, (1), 124–9 Champaign: University of Illinois Press

Marshall, W. (1978) *William Marshall's Scottish Melodies.* Alstead, NH: Fiddlecase Books

Martin, C. (2017) *Ron Gonnella Research* [email] to MacMorran, J. [14 July 2017]

Maxwell, L. (2016) *Glenfiddich Fiddle Championship.* [email to MacMorran, J.] [31 July 2016]

McDowell, W. H. (1992) *The History of BBC Broadcasting in Scotland, 1923–1983.* Edinburgh: Edinburgh University Press

McGann, J. C. (2003) *Dan. R. MacDonald: Individual Creativity in the Cape Breton Fiddle Tradition.* [Master's Thesis] [online], Memorial University of Newfoundland. Available from <http://search.proquest.com.iris.etsu.edu:2048/pqdtglobal/docview/305471802/D27486D4D1464108PQ/1?accountid=10771> [16 February 2014]

McKay, A. (1975) "Fiddler Has Other Strings To His Bow." *Aberdeen Press and Journal*, 5 November 1975. Available from <https://www.britishnewspaperarchive.co.uk/viewer/bl/0000578/19751105/160/00 05> [16 November 2017]

McKean, T. (1998) "Celtic Music and the Growth of the Féis Movement in the Scottish Highlands." *Western Folklore* 57 (4), 245–259

McKerrell, S. (2016) *Focus: Scottish Traditional Music.* New York: Routledge

McNeill, L. S. (2013) "And the Greatest of These Is Tradition: The Folklorist's Toolbox in the Twenty-First Century." In *Tradition in the Twenty-First Century* [online]. ed. by Blank, T. J. and Howard, G. H. Boulder: University Press of Colorado. Available from <http://www.jstor.org/stable/j.ctt4cgpg0> [29 June 2015]

Merriam, A. P. (1977) "Definitions of 'Comparative Musicology' and 'Ethnomusicology': An Historical-Theoretical Perspective." *Ethnomusicology* 21 (2), 189–204

Miller, J. (2017) *Ron Gonnella Research* [email] to MacMorran, J. [13 July 2017]

Moore, A. (2002) "Authenticity as Authentication." *Popular Music* [online] 21 (2), 209–223. Available from <http://www.jstor.org.iris.etsu.edu:2048/stable/853683?seq=1#page_scan_tab_contents> [24 May 2016]

Monaco, J. (1981) *How to Read a Film*. New York: Oxford University Press

Muise, J. and Muise, M. (2015) *Muise Family Collection: Traditional Irish and Cape Breton Music in Boston.* Available from <https://johnjburnslibrary.wordpress.com/2015/10/14/traditional-cape-breton-and-irish-music-in-boston-the-muise-family-collection/> [November 2015]

Munro, A. (2001) *The Democratic Muse: Folk Music Revival in Scotland.* 2nd edn. Aberdeen: Scottish Cultural Press

Murray, E. (2016) *Ron Gonnella Research.* [email] to MacMorran, J. [19 September 2017]

——. (2017) *Fireside Fiddle Chats.* [email] to MacMorran, J. [22 September 2017]

——. (2017) *Fireside Fiddle Chats.* [email] to MacMorran, J. [24 November 2017]

Mustrad.org (2016) *Doug MacPhee.* Available from <www.mustrad.org.uk/articles/mclellan.htm> [12 December 2015]

Narayan, K. (1993) "How Native Is a "Native" Anthropologist?" *American Anthropologist* [online] 95 (3), 671–686. Available from <http://www.jstor.org/stable/679656> [24 August 2017]

Nebel, D. *Reviving Scottish Fiddling: An Ethnographic Study of Scottish Fiddling Competitions in the United States.* [online] Masters dissertation. Available from <http://digitalcommons.kent.edu/epar/vol1/iss1/3> [18 February 2015]

Neil, J. M. (1991) *The Scots Fiddle: Tunes, Tales & Traditions.* Northampton: Interlink Publishing Group Inc.

Nettl, B. and Bohlman, P. (1991) *Comparative Musicology and Anthropology of Music.* Chicago: The University of Chicago Press

Nettl, B. (1999) "The Institutionalization of Musicology: Perspectives of a North

American Ethnomusicologist." In *Rethinking Music.* ed. by Cook, N. and Everist, M. Oxford: Oxford University Press, 287–310

——. (2014) *A Life of Learning.* [American Council of Learned Societies Occasional Paper, No. 71] New York: ACLS

Noyes, D. (2009) "Traditions: Three Traditions." *Journal of Folklore Research* 46 (3), 233–249 O'Halloran, K. (ed.) (2004) *Multimodal Discourse Analysis: Systemic-functional Perspectives.* London: Continuum

Paddison, M. (1996) *Adorno, Modernism and Mass Culture: Essays on Critical Theory and Music.* London: Kahn and Averill

Pekacz, J. T. (2006) *Musical Biography: Towards New Paradigms.* Burlington: Ashgate Publishing

——. (2006) "The Nation's Property: Chopin's Biography as a Cultural Discourse." In *Musical Biography: Towards New Paradigms.* ed. by Pekacz, J. Burlington: Ashgate Publishing, 43–68

Perks, R. and Thompson, A. (1998) *The Oral History Reader.* London: Routledge

Perlis, V. (1994) "Oral History and Music." *The Journal of American History* [online] 81 (2), 610–619. Available from <http://www.jstor.org/stable/2081176> [1 January 2014]

Perlman, K. (2015) *Couldn't Have a Wedding Without the Fiddler.* Knoxville: University of Tennessee Press

Pittock, M. G. H. (1999) *Celtic Identity and the British Image.* Manchester: Manchester University Press

Portelli, A. (1998) "What makes oral history different." In *The Oral History Reader.* ed by Perks, R. and Thomson, A. London: Routledge, 172–182

Posen, S. "On Folk Festivals and Kitchens: Questions of Authenticity in the Folksong Revival." In *Transforming Tradition: Folk Music Revivals Examined.* Urbana: University of Illinois Press, 1993.

Pratt, M. L. (1988) "Fieldwork in Common Places." *In Writing Culture: The Poetics and Politics of Ethnography.* ed. by Clifford, J. and Marcus, G. E. Berkeley: University of California Press

Purser, J. (1992) *Scotland's Music: A History of the Traditional and Classical Music of Scotland from Early Times to the Present Day.* Edinburgh: Mainstream Publishing

Quigley, C. (1995) *Music From the Heart: Compositions of a Folk Fiddler.* Athens: University of Georgia Press

Rahkonen, C. and Goertzen, C. (1999) *"Fiddling for Norway: Revival and Identity." Yearbook for Traditional Music* 31, 170

Randell, J. (2015) "The Boston States: a Presentation of Familial Cape Breton Musical History." *North Atlantic Fiddle Convention,* "Trans-Atlantic Transactions." Held 9–17 October 2015 at Cape Breton Island, Nova Scotia

Rapport, N. (2000) "Best of British"? "The New Anthropology of Britain." In *Anthropology Today,* 16 (2), 20–22. Available from <http://www.jstor.org/stable/2678237> [4 September 2017]

Rattray, I. *Dundee Strathspey and Reel Society*. [email] to MacMorran, J. [17 December 2015]

Ray, C. (2001) *Highland Heritage: Scottish Americans in the American South*. Chapel Hill: University of North Carolina Press

Reith, J. C. W. (1924) *Broadcast Over Britain*. London: Hodder and Stoughton

Rice, T. (1987) "Toward the Remodeling of Ethnomusicology." In *Ethnomusicology* 31 (3), 469–488. Available from <http://www.jstor.org/stable/851667> [2 September 2017]

Ritchie, D. A. (2003) *Doing Oral History: A Practical Guide*. Oxford: Oxford University Press

Ronstrom, O. (1996) "Revival Reconsidered." *The World of Music*, 38 (3), 5–20

———. (2014) "Traditional Music, Heritage Music." In *Oxford Handbook of Music Revival*. ed by Hill, J. and Bithell, C. Oxford: Oxford University Press, 43–59

Rosenberg, N. V. (ed.) (1993) *Transforming Tradition: Folk Revivals Examined*. Chicago: University of Chicago Press

Ross, B. M. (1993) *Writings About Scotland's Music: An Annotated Bibliography*. [online] [PhD Thesis] Claremont Graduate School. Available from UMI Dissertations Publishing, 9238872. [24 April 2014]

Royal Conservatoire of Scotland (2016) *Programme Handbook*. [online] Available from <http://inspire.rcs.ac.uk/pluginfile.php?file=%2F3546%2Fmod_resource%2Fcontent%2F1%2FBMus%20Traditional%20Music%20Handbook%202015-16%20v2.pdf> [6 March 2016]

Russell, I. (2006) "Working with Tradition: Towards a Partnership Model of Fieldwork." *Folklore* [online] 117 (1), 15–32. Available from <http://www.jstor.org/stable/30035319> [February 2014]

Sabbe, H. (2004) "A Philosophy of Totality." In *Contemporary Music: Theoretical and Philosophical Perspectives*. ed. by Paddison, M. and Deliege, I. London: Routledge, 175–182

Severin, W. J. and Tankard, J. W. (2001) *Communication Theories: Origins, Methods, and Uses in the Mass Media*. New York: Longman

Scottish Country Dance Database (n.d.) [online] Available from <https://my.strathspey.org/dd/index/> [7 September 2014]

Scottish Fiddling Revival Ltd. (2016) *F.I.R.E. Sanctioned Competitions and Judges*. [online] Available from <http://www.scottishfiddlingrevival> [7 September 2014]

Scottish Post Office Directory. (1878–9) [online] Available from <http://digital.nls.uk/directories/browse/pageturner.cfm?id=85008420> <http://digital.nls.uk/directories/browse/archive/85906328?mode=transcription> [12 July 2014]

Shelemay, K. K. (2011) "Musical Communities: Rethinking the Collective in Music." *Journal of the American Musicological Society* 64 (2) (Summer), 349–390

Sims, M. and Stephens, M. (eds.) (2011) *An Introduction to the Study of People and Their Traditions*. 2nd edn. Boulder: University of Colorado

Shoemaker, P. J. and Vos, T. P. (2009) *Gatekeeping Theory*. New York: Routledge

Skinner, J. S. (1984) *A Guide to Bowing: Strathspeys, Reels, Pastoral Melodies, Hornpipes, etc.* Edinburgh: The Hardie Press [Originally Published 1900 by Bayley & Ferguson]

——. (1979) *A Scottish Violinist.* Glasgow: Bayley & Ferguson

——. (1994) *My Life and Adventures.* Aberdeen: Wallace Music

——. (1904) *The Harp and Claymore.* London [Reprinted in 1984. Morgantown: Scotpress]

Slobin, M. (1983) "Rethinking 'Revival' of American Ethnic Music." *New York Folklore Quarterly* 9 (3–4), 37–44

Smith, W. L. and Smith, G. M. (1957–1976) *William L. and Gowan Merson Smith Collection.* Archives of Appalachia at East Tennessee State University, Johnson City, Tennessee

Stephens, J. (2013) "Artistic Knowledge in Practice." In *Professional Knowledge in Music Teacher Education.* ed. by Georgii-Hemming, E., Burnard, P. and Holgersen, S. Farnham: Ashgate, 73–97

Small, C. (1998) *Musicking: The Meanings of Performing and Listening.* Middletown: Wesleyan University Press

Stewart-Robertson, J. (1884) *The Athole Collection of the Dance Music of Scotland.* Reprinted Edinburgh: 1961

Stock, C. (2000) "The Reflective Practitioner: Choreography as Research in an Intercultural Context." *World Dance 2000* [online], 209–225. Available from <http://www.researchgate.net/publication/27463075_Reflective_Practitioner_choreography_as_research_in_an_intercultural_context/file/72e7e52bd3f4a4165a.pdf 209–225> [11 March 2014]

Stock, J. P. J. (2010) "Toward an Ethnomusicology of the Individual, or Biographical Writing in Ethnomusicology." In *The World of Music* [online] 52 (1/3), 332–346. Available from <http://www.jstor.org/stable/41700038> [22 August 2017]

Strathern, M. (1987) 'An Awkward Relationship: The Case of Feminism and Anthropology'. *Signs,* 12 (2) 276–294. Available from <http://www.jstor.org/stable/3173986> [27 June 2017]

Note: Broadly speaking, "at home" signifies that the researcher and research subject share cultural experiences and the findings of the research express the emic perspective of the author. The general assumption is that this type of research increases reflexivity.

Taylor, D. (2003) *The Archive and the Repertoire: Performing Cultural Memory in the Americas.* Durham: Duke University Press

——. (2006) "Performance and/as History." *Qualitative Sociology Review* [online] II (1), 67–86. Available from <http://www.jstor.org/stable/4492659> [16 February 2014]

Thompson, P. (1978) *The Voice of the Past: Oral History.* Oxford: Oxford University Press

Thwaites, T., Davis, L. and Mules, W. (2002) *Introducing Cultural and Media Studies: A Semiotic Approach.* New York: Palgrave

Titon, J. T. (2012). "Authenticity and Authentication: Mike Seeger, The New Lost City Ramblers, and the Old-time Music Revival." *Journal of Folklore Research* [online] 49 (2), 227–245. Available from <http://search.proquest.com/docview/1285228817?accountid=10771> [10 January 2016]

——. (2003) 'Text'. In *Eight Words for the Study of Expressive Culture.* ed. by Feintuch, B. Urbana: University of Illinois Press, 69–98

Tobin, E. and Kielty, M. (2010) *Are Ye Dancin'?: The Story of Scotland's Dance Halls – And How Yer Dad Met Yer Ma!* Glasgow: Waverly Books

Todd, C. (2016) "Box and Fiddle Archive." [online] Available from <http://boxandfiddlearchive.weebly.com/mar-1994.html> [17 May 2005]

Toelken, B. (1996) *The Dynamics of Folklore.* Logan: Utah State University Press

Tompkins, J. P. (1980) "Introduction." In *Reader-Response Criticism: From Formalism to Post-Structuralism.* ed. by Tompkins, J. P. Baltimore: Johns Hopkins University Press, ix-xxvi

Turner, J. W. (2014) *Former United States National Fiddling Champion and Scottish F.I.R.E. Board Member.* [interview by MacMorran, J.] Valle Crucis, North Carolina [18 August, 2014]

Van Leeuwen, T. and Jewitt, C. (2005) *Introducing Social Semiotics.* New York: Routledge

Van Maanen, J. (1988) *Tales of the Field: On Writing Ethnography.* Chicago: University of Chicago Press

Vansina, J. (1961) *Oral Tradition: A Study in Historical Methodology.* Chicago: Aldine Publishing Company

Veeser, H. A. (ed.) (1999) *The Stanley Fish Reader.* Malden: Blackwell Publishers

Vice, S. (1997) *Introducing Bakhtin.* Manchester: Manchester University Press

Way, L. C. S. and McKerrell, S. (eds) (2017) "Understanding Music as Multimodal Discourse." In *Music as Multimodal Discourse: Semiotics, Power and Protest.* London: Bloomsbury. Available from <http://bloomsburycp3cp3.codemantra.com/Marketing.aspx?ID=MusicAsMultimod&ISBN=9781474264426&sta=b#25> [Accessed 1 October 2017]

Weber, W. (1999) "The History of Musical Canon." In *Rethinking Music.* ed. by Cook, N. and Everist, M. Oxford: Oxford University Press, 336–355

West, G. (2012) *Voicing Scotland: Folk, Culture, Nation.* Edinburgh: Luath Press

Winter, T. and Keegan-Phipps, S. (2014) "Contemporary English Folk Music and the Folk Industry." In Oxford *Handbook of Music Revival.* ed by Hill, J. and Bithell, C. Oxford: Oxford University Press, 489–509

——. (2013) *Performing Englishness: Identity and Politics in a Contemporary Folk Resurgence.* Manchester: Manchester University Press

Wood, D. (2015) "Fiddles and Fiddlers: A Fiddler's Notes." *North East Folklore Archive.* Available from <http://www.nefa.net/archive/songmusicdance/fiddles/notes.htm> [14 February 2014]

Index

Entries in **boldface** refer to images.

www.ingramcontent.com/pod-product-compliance
Lightning Source LLC
Chambersburg PA
CBHW070133080526
44586CB00015B/1680

* 9 7 8 1 6 2 1 9 0 9 8 0 4 *